SMART BY NATURE
Schooling for Sustainability

By Michael K. Stone
Center for Ecoliteracy

CONTEMPORARY ISSUES SERIES

Watershed Media

Published by Watershed Media
513 Brown Street
Healdsburg, California 95448
www.watershedmedia.org
707.431.2936

Produced by the Center for Ecoliteracy
The David Brower Center
2150 Allston Way, Suite 270
Berkeley, CA 94704-1377
www.ecoliteracy.org
510.845.4595

Distributed by University of California Press
Berkeley and Los Angeles, California
University of California Press, Ltd.
London, England
www.ucpress.edu

Library of Congress Cataloging-in-Publication Data available upon request from the publisher.

Cover Design: Roberto Carra

Printed on Gladfelter Nature 30% post-consumer waste (PCW), 70% Forest Stewardship Council (FSC) certified fiber.

Cover Stock: Mohawk Via Cool 100% post-consumer waste (PCW) with wind-power energy offset.

Mixed Sources
Product group from well-managed
forests, controlled sources and
recycled wood or fibre
www.fsc.org Cert no. SW-COC-000952
© 1996 Forest Stewardship Council
FSC

ISBN 10: 0-9709500-4-7   ISBN 13: 978-0-9709500-4-8
First Edition
12 11 10 09

10 9 8 7 6 5 4 3 2 1

CREDITS

Dan Bodette: 117

Borrego Solar Systems, Inc: 69

Robin Catalano/Darrow School: 60, 91

Center for Ecoliteracy/Zenobia Barlow: 7, 18, 55, 129, 132, 153, 180

Center for Ecoliteracy/Karen Brown: 11, 20, 22, 24, 26, 29, 62, 86, 87, 94, 98, 154, 178

Center for Ecoliteracy/Michael K. Stone: 65, 74, 80, 95, 118, 123

Center for Ecoliteracy/James Tyler: Front cover (boy at right), 2, 4, 12, 25

Bruce Cook: 131

Courtesy Davis Farm to School Connection: 135

Courtesy Davis Farmers Market: 136

Dick Drew: 106

Andy Dubak Photography: 114

The Edible Schoolyard: Front cover (girl third from left)

Sarah Emerson: 171

Alan Good: 11, 24, 62

Robert Harrison: 47, 48, 50

Courtesy Head-Royce School: 150, 175, 176

Quincey Imhoff: Front cover (girl at left)

Michael Mathers: 169

Judy Meighan/Willow School: 155

Glenn Minshall: 97

Courtesy New North Florida Cooperative: 39, 40

Paul Parker/Willow School: 76

Courtesy Princeton Day School: 144

Victoria Rydberg: 152, 161, 162, 165

Courtesy Santa Monica/Riverside School Districts: 27, 43

© James Steinkamp Photography/courtesy OWP/P: 79, 82

Shelburne Farms: 126

Courtesy Steve Tanguay/Jon Thurston: Front cover (girl second from left), 21, 33, 34, 35, 113, 156, 158

Taylor Photographics: 73

Paloma Torres/The Lawrenceville School: 108, 109, 141, 142

Courtesy Troy Howard Middle School: 36

Courtesy Marshall Webb/Shelburne Farms: 124

© 2008 www.Shields-MarleyPhoto.com: 85

DEDICATION

To Peter K. Buckley,

a steadfast and passionate champion of schooling for sustainability.

CONTENTS

FOREWORD

By Daniel Goleman

Schooling for sustainability, as described in *Smart by Nature,* has never been more important. We need to cultivate thinking that comprehends complex systems, perspectives that widen empathy and nurture mindfulness, better techniques for gathering and sharing information, and new modes of cooperation. The only long-term strategy that makes sense in our changing world is education.

Knowing how things and nature work includes recognizing and understanding the countless ways man-made systems interact with natural ones, what I call "ecological intelligence." Ways of thinking that in the ancient past guided our innate ecological intelligence were well suited to the harsh realities of prehistory. But ensuing centuries have blunted the survival skills of the billions who live with modern technologies, a globalized economy, and complex webs of relationship.

Our brains are finely tuned for hypervigilance against the dangers of a world we no longer inhabit, while today's world presents us with abundant dangers we do not see, hear, taste, or smell—from such hazards as toxins in toys, to threats including global warming, to the impacts of the stuff we manufacture, grow, distribute, consume, and discard.

We need to get beyond the thinking that puts humankind outside nature. We live enmeshed in ecological systems. We need to discover and share among ourselves all the ways this intimate interconnectedness operates, to see the hidden patterns that connect human activity to the larger flow of nature, to understand our true impact on it, and to learn how to do better.

Ecological intelligence melds cognitive skills with empathy for all of life. Just as social and emotional intelligence build on the abilities to see from another's perspective, feel with them, and show our concern, ecological intelligence extends this capacity to all natural systems.

Sensory clutter and cognitive fog challenge anyone trying to get shoppers to notice the impacts of their purchases or organizations or governments to recognize the consequences of their decisions. Mindfulness marks the mental shift from running on automatic, reflexively going through long-practiced routines, to an active awareness that allows new learning–and so new choice.

The challenges we face are too varied, too subtle, and too complicated for a single person to understand and overcome. A collective, distributed intelligence spreads awareness, whether among friends or family, within schools or companies, or through an entire culture. Such shared intelligence grows through the contributions of individuals who advance and spread that understanding. And so we need to educate scouts, explorers who alert us to ecological truths.

Reducing unsustainability, finally, is just the first step. We need to inspire our students to go beyond merely lessening harmful impacts to pursuing true sustainability–flourishing levels of health, vitality, and resilience that allow both humans and earth's ecosystems to thrive. When we do, educating students in the competencies of sustainable living will change the world.

PREFACE

By Zenobia Barlow

This book presents a radical vision for education—radical in the sense of being essential, fundamental, and deeply rooted. It is founded on a conviction that the best hope for learning to live sustainably lies in schooling that returns to the *real* basics: experiencing the natural world; understanding how nature sustains life; nurturing healthy communities; recognizing the consequences of how we feed ourselves and provision our institutions; knowing well the places where we live, work, and learn.

During my nearly twenty years as executive director of the Center for Ecoliteracy, I have seen schooling for sustainability transform students and schools. Children's sense of wonder awakens as they find life teeming in a handful of soil or nurture a seed into a healthy plant to be harvested and enjoyed in a delicious meal with their classmates. Fourth-graders restoring the habitat of an endangered species learn that they can make a tangible difference in the world. A dozen years later, those students graduate from college as professionals informed by an ecological understanding and conscience. Students learn how to ask what is upstream and who is downstream, to care about and feel responsible for their actions. Test scores rise. Student health improves. "Problem" schools mired in low achievement and diminished morale become nationally recognized success stories.

K–12 education in the United States represents an immense investment in young people and our collective future: 55 million students at 120,000 schools; more than seven million teachers, administrators, and support staff; annual expenditures over $500 billion. Add the uncounted hours contributed by millions of parents, school board members, volunteers, and informal educators. Imagine applying those resources, talents, and commitments to addressing the imperatives of our time while honoring the capacities and limits of nature.

Schooling for sustainability can begin anywhere. This book features efforts that were initiated top down, bottom up, outside in, and inside out. Virtually every decision taken in this half-a-trillion-dollar enterprise presents an opportunity to use common sense and innovation to remake education into a movement that is vital, hopeful, and essentially smart by nature.

ACKNOWLEDGMENTS

This book is the product of a widespread network of friends, supporters, and change agents. Thanks to all in the schooling for sustainability movement for their vital work, and for the help of so many with this book. My apologies to anyone whom I have inadvertently omitted.

My thanks to the writers who generously contributed portions of the book: Daniel Goleman, Zenobia Barlow, and Lisa Bennett. Thanks to Dan Imhoff, president and cofounder of Watershed Media for conceiving of this book and entrusting the Center for Ecoliteracy to collaborate on it, and to his Watershed Media colleagues for their skill, helpfulness, and good spirits through rounds of design, editing, and production: Janet Blake, Roberto Carra, Emmett Hopkins, Sofie Landner, and Timothy Rice.

I am profoundly grateful to the many people who have taught me about schooling for sustainability, and for their taking time to share their experiences and wisdom in thoughtful discussions. In particular: Richard Abernathy, Claire Barnett, Mark Biedron, Dan Bodette, Marilyn Briggs, Bunny Brown, Debbie Bruick, Wynn Calder, Megan Camp, Paul Chapman, Andrew Chase, Wendy Church, Jennifer Cirillo, Jaimie Cloud, Jennifer Coté, Liz Cutler, Matt Dubel, Ann M. Evans, Michele Heller, Vincent Iturralde, Sam Kosoff, Crystal Land, Becca Leslie, Gary Luepke, Deborah Moore, Jeri Ohmart, Dorothy Peterson, Stephen Rutherford, Victoria Rydberg, Rod Shroufe, David Sobel, Mark Stefanski, Toni Stein, Steve Tanguay, Rodney Taylor, Tiffany Tillman, Kate Walsh, Craig Westcott, and Margo Wootan.

This book was made possible by innumerable contributions of Center for Ecoliteracy staff and consultants, whose creativity, competence, and dedication inspire and motivate me to do more and do better. I bow to Zenobia Barlow, Karen Brown, Nan Budinger, Leslie Comnes, Kate Cheney Davidson, Carol Denney, Alan Good, Jim Koulias, Wendy Ledger, Mark Rhynsburger, Therese Shere, Daniela Sklan, Carolie Sly, Alice Lee Tebo, James Tyler, Jacob I. Wright, and Nobuko Yamada. I honor the Center's board of directors, in addition to Zenobia, for their thoughtfulness, perseverance, and commitment to a vision of education adequate for our time: Peter K. Buckley, Fritjof Capra, David W. Orr, Nancy G. Schaub, and Wendy Williams.

Deep gratitude is owed the funders who supported this book and the Center's Smart by Nature initiative during its production, including Peter K. Buckley; Compton Foundation, Inc.; Cindy Daniel; Garfield Foundation; Green to Grow; Heller Family Foundation; J. Heller Charitable Unitrust; The Lia Fund; Linnaeus Thomson Fund, an advised fund of Silicon Valley Community Foundation; Dr. Hanmin Liu; Potrero Nuevo Fund of Tides Foundation; S. D. Bechtel, Jr. Foundation; Nancy G. Schaub; Small Planet Fund of RSF Social Finance; TomKat Charitable Trust; and Urban Village Farmers' Market Association.

I am indebted beyond words to Patricia Perry for keeping family life sustainable and for steadfast patience, support, and good humor in the face of the manifold disruptions and distractions of this project.

Michael K. Stone

CHAPTER 1

INTRODUCTION: SMART BY NATURE

What can educators do to foster real intelligence?...We can attempt to teach the things that one might imagine the earth would teach us: silence, humility, holiness, connectedness, courtesy, beauty, celebration, giving, restoration, obligation, and wildness.

—David W. Orr

There is a bold new movement under way in school systems across North America and around the world. Educators, parents, and students are remaking K–12 education to prepare students for the environmental challenges of the coming decades. They are discovering that guidance for living abundantly on a finite planet lies, literally, under their feet and all around them—in living soil, food webs and water cycles, energy from the sun, and everywhere that nature reveals her ways. Smart by Nature schooling draws on 3.8 billion years of natural research and development to find solutions to problems of sustainable living, make teaching and learning more meaningful, and create a more hopeful future for people and communities.

School gardens bloom in wintry climates and on former asphalt lots. Students learn good nutrition while eating healthy lunches of farm-fresh food. At independent schools in New Jersey, public schools in California, and charter schools in Wisconsin, education comes alive as children discover the wonders of nature while restoring rural landscapes, protecting endangered species, and creating city habitats. Classroom buildings in schools on the South Side of Chicago, in central Arkansas, and in suburban Oregon become living laboratories for energy conservation and resource stewardship.

Schools from Washington to Florida have transformed into model communities. Utilities, governments, and educators have become partners in designing energy-efficient, safe, and healthy schools that promote the welfare of students and school staff while teaching wise use of resources and care of the earth. In small towns and large cities, students practice the arts of citizenship while improving the lives of their neighbors.

This movement responds to the realization that the young people in school today will inherit a host of pressing—and escalating—environmental challenges: threats of climate change; loss of biodiversity; the end of cheap energy; depletion of resources; environmental degradation; gross inequities in standards of living; obesity, diabetes, asthma, and other environmentally linked illness.

Students appreciate the interconnectedness of human and natural systems when they experience both firsthand, as in this "Save the Bay" program.

This generation will require leaders and citizens who can think ecologically, understand the interconnectedness of human and natural systems, and have the will, ability, and courage to act.

The movement goes by many names: green schools, eco-schools, high-performance schools. We call it *schooling for sustainability* to underline its kinship with other global movements reshaping the relationships between human societies and the natural world. At the same time, we acknowledge that the term *sustainability* is problematic to some people.

"The word 'sustainability' has gotten such a workout lately that the whole concept is in danger of floating away on a sea of inoffensiveness," wrote Michael Pollan in late 2007. "Everybody, it seems, is for it—whatever 'it' means."[1] Paradoxically, many people remain unaware of the concept, while others have already concluded that it is on its way to joining *natural* and *ecological* as words that can simultaneously mean anything and nothing. "If a man characterized his relationship with his wife as sustainable," wrote architect William McDonough and chemist Michael Braungart, "you might well pity them both."[2] After reviewing the alternatives, though, writer and consultant Alan AtKisson concluded, "As a name for the future of our dreams, sustainability may be 'the worst word, except for all the others.'"[3] Thinkers and activists whose work we greatly admire use this word. It links to international movements on behalf of human and planetary well-being.

To stay useful, *sustainability* must mean more than merely surviving or trying to keep a degraded world from getting worse. Otherwise, why bother? Invoking nature's capacity for sustaining life, as Fritjof Capra suggests, is critical. A sustainable com-

Smart by Nature

munity worth imagining is *alive*, in the most exuberant sense of that word—fresh, vital, evolving, diverse, and dynamic. It cares about the quality as well as the continuation of life. It is flexible and adaptive. It draws energy from its environment, celebrates organic wholeness, and appreciates that life has more to reveal than human cleverness has yet discovered. It teaches its children to pay attention to the world around them, to respect what they cannot control, and to nurture the community with which life sustains itself.

Few question the need to prepare students for the complex world into which they will graduate, but the schooling for sustainability movement nevertheless encounters obstacles; school systems are notoriously slow to change. Responsibilities for schools' operations are often dispersed through multiple levels of authority, from the local principal to the federal government, with mandates that sometimes conflict. Virtually all schools and districts face financial challenges. Schooling for sustainability competes with other priorities, including standardized testing in public schools and pressure to focus on Advanced Placement in independent schools.

This book—the fruit of two decades of work by the Center for Ecoliteracy, a public foundation in Berkeley, California, dedicated to education for sustainable living—presents Smart by Nature, the center's framework for schooling for sustainability. It offers inspiration by documenting the accomplishments of many schools, shares the lessons they have learned, and furthers the discussion that has begun among the many parties to this movement.

We report how schools across the country are creatively overcoming barriers. In doing so, they are

also discovering that schooling for sustainability is a winning proposition with many direct and indirect benefits. What is good for the future of the environment and for communities is also good for schools and students now. Students who learn nature's principles in gardens and serve their communities through civic participation become more engaged in their studies and score better on tests of independent thinking, and in diverse subjects, including science, reading, and writing.

Designing buildings to conserve energy and water can save enough money to convince finance-minded school boards. Going green helps competitive independent schools to attract students and local communities to attract residents and businesses. Students and staff members who eat better meals and spend their days in buildings with better air quality are absent less often, report higher satisfaction, and perform better. Schools become better appreciated as assets to their communities.

One Movement, Many Routes

Schooling for sustainability is a constantly evolving process. It takes place in schools that use the woods outside their classrooms as their playgrounds and laboratories, on campuses set on inner city asphalt lots, and in schools dropped into the middle of suburban housing tracts. It takes place in schools with innovative lunch programs served in aging buildings and in schools with brand-new facilities and no lunch service at all. Our research has discovered sustainability projects initiated by superintendents and heads of school, by individual faculty members, by students, and by handfuls of parents. We have found efforts headed by paid sustainability officers and thriving projects led by informal ecology clubs with no budgets.

The schooling for sustainability movement has no central organization or structure, no membership test or entrance qualifications. It has emerged spontaneously from a longing to design and offer education adequate to today's needs. In the United States, in contrast to the many countries with national education standards and curricula, K–12 education is decentralized. The federal government, state governments, more than 14,000 local school districts, 4,000 public charter schools, and nearly 30,000 parochial and private schools share authority for education. As a result, many entry points exist for sustainability schooling; the movement's constant is its diversity.

When people think of "green schools," they often imagine solar panels, recycling programs, or school gardens. These are important, but the schooling for sustainability movement is much broader and more various, a confluence of many streams, each with its emphases, priorities, language, and pedagogies. The movement in the United States traces its lineage to H. D. Thoreau, John Muir, John Dewey, Teddy Roosevelt, Aldo Leopold, Helen and Scott Nearing, and Rachel Carson, to mention just a few of its forebears. Movements that converge here include experiential education, conservation and environmental protection, international sustainable development, systemic school reform, public health reform, and technological developments that make green design affordable.

Environmental education as a discipline that links nature study to activism is fairly young. Its goals were laid out in 1968 in the inaugural issue of *The Journal of Environmental Education*: "producing a citizenry that is knowledgeable concerning the biophysical environment and its associated problems, aware of how to help solve these problems, and motivated to act toward their solution."[4] The North American Association for Environmental Education, founded in 1971, promotes environmental literacy "in order for present and future generations to benefit from a safe and healthy environment and a better quality of life."[5]

Sustainability entered the conversation in the 1980s, especially after the publication of Lester Brown's *Building a Sustainable Society* in 1981 and the release in 1987 of "Our Common Future," the report of the U.N. World Commission on Environment and Development (the Brundtland Commission). The report offers the following, still often quoted, definition: "Sustainable development is development that meets the needs of the present generation without compromising the ability of future generations to meet their own needs." The report continues: "[Sustainable development] contains within it two key concepts: the concept of 'needs,' in particular the essential needs of the world's poor, to which overriding priority should be given; and the idea of limitations imposed by the state of technology and social organization on the environment's ability to meet present and future needs."[6]

That definition brought into the discussion the notion of intergenerational equity—a generation's responsibility to those who will follow. Arising as it did out of the movement to raise the standard of living of people around the world, this understanding of sustainability also underlined the interrelatedness of environment, economy, and social justice. Those "three pillars of sustainable

Smart by Nature

development" figure prominently today in many schools' definitions of sustainability.[7]

The 1992 U.N. Conference on Environment and Development in Rio de Janeiro added another consideration, asserting that each nation or cultural group must develop its own vision of sustainable living, a premise that guides much of today's education work. The international Eco-Schools Programme, founded in 1994 to involve young people in finding local solutions to the environmental and development challenges identified by the Rio Conference, has national programs in more than forty countries, mostly in Europe. The United States and China joined in 2009.[8]

Sustainability education has grown from its various beginnings to cover nearly everything that schools want to see sustained. The National Association of Independent Schools, the leading U.S. independent school organization, has articulated five different emphases: financial, environmental,

Teachers model practices of sustainable communities that honor, support, and cooperate with the processes and patterns by which nature sustains life.

global, programmatic, and demographic.[9] Of these five, we will focus here mostly on environmental sustainability, while noting that environmental preservation and restoration, public health, and social justice converge in education.

In the United States, lower-income and minority children suffer disproportionately from problems that schools often exacerbate. Nutrition-related diseases aggravated by poor school food, respiratory problems related to poor air quality in school buildings, and the effects of exposure to chemicals and pesticides lead to increased absenteeism, behavioral problems, and diminished learning. A sustainable school promotes the health and learning of all students, regardless of income or background, while helping them understand the relationship between environment, economy, and equity.

The School as Ecosystem

From its origin in 1991 as the Elmwood Institute Ecoliteracy Project, the Center for Ecoliteracy has understood both sustainability education and schools themselves through the scientific theory of living systems. Physicist, systems theorist, and Center cofounder Fritjof Capra observes that a definition such as the Brundtland Commission's is an important moral exhortation that reminds us of our responsibility to pass on to our children and grandchildren a world with as many opportunities as the one we inherited. However, that definition does not tell us *how* to build a sustainable community. For that, we need an operational definition.

Fortunately, says Capra, we do not need to invent human communities from scratch. We can model

GUIDING PRINCIPLES
FOR SUSTAINABLE SCHOOLING

1 Nature Is Our Teacher

2 Sustainability Is a Community Practice

3 The Real World Is the Optimal Learning Environment

4 Sustainable Living Is Rooted in a Deep Knowledge of Place

human societies after nature's ecosystems, which are sustainable communities of plants, animals, and microorganisms. As biomimicry pioneer Janine Benyus notes, "Life creates conditions conducive to life."[10] Hence, says Capra, a sustainable human community is one designed so that its ways of life, technologies, and social institutions honor, support, and cooperate with the processes and patterns by which nature sustains life.[11]

Schools resemble ecosystems. They participate in the great cycles of matter and flows of energy. They are nested within larger ecosystems. The laws of physics and thermodynamics govern them. They require resources, which they transform, incorporate, and then recycle or discharge into other systems. They follow seasonal cycles. Some members spend much of their time inside their territory, while others migrate through them. They are organized as interdependent webs of relationship. Ideas and information function as energy does in a natural ecosystem, altering the system through complex feedback loops. School "ecosystems" co-evolve with their members, while new patterns emerge through surprising nonlinear processes that their members can only partially direct.

Smart by Nature: Guiding Principles for Sustainability Schooling

The approach to schooling for sustainability that the Center for Ecoliteracy calls "Smart by Nature" can be characterized by four guiding principles:

1. *Nature Is Our Teacher*

2. *Sustainability Is a Community Practice*

3. *The Real World Is the Optimal Learning Environment*

4. *Sustainable Living Is Rooted in a Deep Knowledge of Place*

NATURE IS OUR TEACHER

To envision sustainable human communities, we look to design principles evolved since the advent of life on the planet. We can pattern human societies and institutions, including schools, after the patterns found in sustainable ecosystems. We can also learn from traditional and indigenous societies that have persisted for centuries, despite limited resources, by following these same patterns.

Inviting nature as our teacher doesn't mean turning sentimental or softheaded about the beneficence of kindly Mother Nature. She is also, says leading environmental educator and Center for Ecoliteracy board member David W. Orr, "a ruthless and unforgiving bookkeeper."[12] As Alan Weisman remarked, nature is "brutally efficient" at winnowing populations that exceed their ecosystems' capacities. This mother practices tough love, and teaches limits as well as possibilities, if we choose to learn.

Accepting nature as our teacher has several implications:

Placing ecological literacy at the center. Understanding the principles that sustain ecosystems requires basic ecological knowledge. We need, says Capra, to teach our children (and our political and corporate leaders!) the fundamental facts of life. For example:

● Matter cycles continually through the web of life.

● Most of the energy driving the ecological cycles flows from the sun.

● Diversity assures resilience.

● One species' waste is another species' food.

● Life did not take over the planet by combat but by networking.[13]

Integrating the curriculum. Focusing on ecological principles integrates teaching across disciplines and between grade levels–an antidote to the fragmentation and narrowing of subject matter that often result from standardized testing and state mandates.[14] Some teachers fear that teaching sustainability will pile yet more responsibility onto their overfull workloads. Actually, finding recurring principles that tie subjects together in ways that make sense to students can make teaching more effective.

Employing systems thinking. John Muir wrote, "When we try to pick out anything by itself, we find it hitched to everything else in the Universe." In education we often try to unhitch everything in order to study the separate parts. In fact, individual "things" (plants, people, schools, watersheds, economies) can't be fully understood apart from the larger systems in which they exist. Smart by Nature schooling includes learning to think in terms of relationships, connectedness, and context.

In systems thinking, emphases shift: from the parts to the whole, from objects to relationships, from structures to processes, from contents to patterns. Instead of asking students to copy textbook pictures of the parts of a honeybee, a teacher takes her class to the school garden to draw bees within the context of their natural settings. A nutrition lesson that tracks meals from farm to cafeteria maps the relationships between food choices, the health of local agriculture, the environmental costs of shipping food over thousands of miles, and impacts on the livelihoods of farmers halfway around the world.

Solving for pattern. Thinking systemically also changes the ways schools function. Author/farmer/philosopher Wendell Berry contrasts bad solutions, which solve for single purposes and destroy patterns, with good solutions, which are in harmony with their larger patterns and result in ramifying sets of solutions.[15] Farm-to-school programs exemplify good solutions that beget other solutions: they bring healthier foods to children, teach about nutrition, support small-scale farmers, and keep money circulating in the local economy. School districts planning new buildings discover that they can save resources, energy, and money by replacing traditional "silo thinking" with an integrated design process in which educators, architects, engineers, and contractors collaboratively create facilities whose parts work together as systems.

Becoming healthy by nature. It should not come as a surprise that nature as teacher points to solutions that fit human bodies, which evolved for millions of years before industrialization. Natural daylighting improves the health and performance of the students and adults who spend their days in classrooms and offices.[16] Students in Scandinavian "Outdoors in All Weather" programs have 80 percent fewer infectious diseases than students in conventional indoor programs.[17] Children surrounded by more nature–even if just a view out a window–experience less anxiety and depression and fewer behavioral conduct disorders.[18] Fresh, seasonal, unprocessed "whole foods for the whole body" are better choices for school meals. Many children with Attention Deficit/ Hyperactivity Disorder and other problems improve rapidly when artificial coloring and preservatives are removed from their diets.[19]

SUSTAINABILITY IS A COMMUNITY PRACTICE

Many of the central principles of ecology are variations on a single fundamental pattern of organization: nature sustains life by creating and nurturing communities. Organisms cannot exist long in isolation. Animals, plants, and microorganisms live in webs of mutual dependence.

People require each other for emotional as well as physical succor. Qualities that keep natural ecosystems vibrant and resilient, such as diversity and interdependence, shape healthier schools and other human communities as well.

A healthy network of relationships that includes all members of a community makes the community more sustainable. When teachers, students, parents, trustees, and others decide and act collaboratively, students acquire the leadership and decision-making skills they will need to become effective agents of change. Repeatedly, we have heard the same advice for would-be change agents: first identify the people who share your concerns, then build your effort by working together.

UNDERSTANDING INTERDEPENDENCE

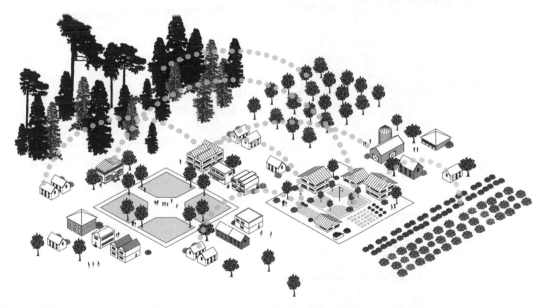

An ability to think ecologically reveals connections (colored dots) within the school and between the school and communities, farms, and natural ecosystems with which it interacts. Students and educators discover their interdependence and their place in the greater scheme of living things.

Living systems are dynamic. Understanding how change occurs in living systems informs efforts to change schools, districts, and other social systems. Large-scale transformations that have great impact begin as small, local actions, says systems change theorist Margaret Wheatley. "While they remain separate and apart, they have no influence beyond their locale. However, if they become connected, exchanging information and

learning, their separate efforts can suddenly emerge as very powerful changes, able to influence a large system."[20]

Nested systems constitute another basic ecological pattern. Schools nest within districts, local communities, economies, and ecosystems. David Orr proposes a standard for designers that could apply to any nested systems. Think upstream, he says, to the wells, mines, forests, farms, and manufacturers that supply materials. Look downstream to the effects on the climate and health of people and ecosystems. If there is ugliness at either end, you cannot claim success, regardless of the artfulness of what you make.[21]

Schools teach—whether they are conscious of it or not—by how they treat their neighbors, invest their money, and provision themselves with food, energy, materials, shelter, transport, and water. Their actions become lessons about their understanding of their relationship with the rest of the world, how they regard students and their health, and what they really believe about sustainability.

THE REAL WORLD IS THE OPTIMAL LEARNING ENVIRONMENT

Whether restoring the habitat of an endangered species, tending a school garden, or designing a neighborhood recycling program, students learn more when their actions matter and have meaning. "Give the pupils something to do, not something to learn," wrote John Dewey, "and the doing is of such a nature as to demand thinking; learning naturally results." In schooling for sustainability, students connect with the natural world and human communities through project-based learning, which inspires them to learn because they need the knowledge to accomplish something

A "habitat hat" project helps children reflect on their direct experience of the natural world through science, language, math, and the arts.

they care about. They also discover that they can make a difference, which lays a foundation for responsible, active citizenship.

Children experience, explore, and understand nature's basic patterns—the web of life, the cycles of matter, the flow of energy—through immersion in the natural world. Instead of reading about these processes or looking at simplified drawings, they encounter nature in the rich, messy ways in which it actually exists. They learn about nature's rhythms, and the time scales at which natural events occur, when they plant and harvest in the garden or watch a creekside they have restored come back to life. They appreciate safe water and healthy soil, and the importance of conserving them.

Buildings can also teach. According to "Sustainable Design for Schools," an incisive Pacific Northwest Pollution Prevention Resource Center essay, "A building, simply by the nature of its design, may be used as a concrete symbol of learning. A building designed on the premise of our link to and interdependency with natural systems is a statement of our respect for the environment and of our accepting responsibility to care for the environment through deliberate and thoughtful design decisions."[22] Some schools post signage identifying their buildings' green features. Others leave conduits, ducts, and other structural elements exposed so that students can understand how sustainable buildings work; some offer displays on energy and resource use in real time.

Finally, students learn what communities value by collaborating with people who lived there before they arrived and who will still be there long after they graduate. By working closely with community members, students learn how to recognize community resources.

SUSTAINABLE LIVING IS ROOTED IN A DEEP KNOWLEDGE OF PLACE

When people acquire a deep knowledge of a particular place, they begin to care about what happens to the landscape, creatures, and people in it. When they understand its ecology and diversity, the web of relationships it supports, and the rhythm of its cycles, they also develop an appreciation for and sense of kinship with their surroundings. Place-based education is fundamental to schooling for sustainability. Places known deeply are deeply loved, and well-loved places have the best chance to be protected and preserved, to be cherished and cared for by future generations.

The world reveals itself in its fullness in particular places. "A great deal of what passes for knowledge" in contemporary education, says David Orr, "is little more than abstraction piled on abstraction, disconnected from tangible experience, real problems, and the places where we live and work." These actual places, he continues, "are laboratories of diversity and complexity, mixing social functions and natural processes."[23] Even "common" settings yield rich experiences. City students can learn more about nature's principles by close study of the animals they see every day than by reading or watching films about more exotic species.

Studying one place in depth also creates an opportunity for bridging disciplines and for looking at the world as people experience it. A "Golden Gate" course at Marin Academy in California combines natural and human history with literature, geology, and ecology and helps students discover their identity as members of a biotic community. Ninth-graders at Lawrenceville

SCHOOLING FOR SUSTAINABILITY—
SOME MILESTONES

1970: First Earth Day

1971: North American Association for Environmental Education founded

1986: *Green Teacher* magazine in UK published (North American edition 1991)

1987: Brundtland Commission report defines sustainable development

1991: The Elmwood Institute Ecoliteracy Project, forerunner to the Center for
Ecoliteracy, founded to promote education for sustainable living

1992: David W. Orr writes *Ecological Literacy*

1994: Eco-Schools Programme in Europe initiated

1995: Center for Ecoliteracy founded

1995: The Sustainability Education Center (now Cloud Institute for Sustainability Education) founded

1995: The Edible Schoolyard breaks ground at the Martin Luther King Middle School in Berkeley, California

1995: Healthy Schools Network founded to do research, education, and
advocacy on behalf of healthy learning environments

1996: First farm-to-school programs created, to combine access to farm-fresh food with nutrition education

1997: Center for Ecoliteracy Food Systems Project funded by the U.S. Department
of Agriculture Community Food Security Program

2000: Vermont adopts state standards for sustainability education

2000: National Farm to School Program organized

2001: Collaboration for High Performance Schools creates first credentialing program
for green design and construction tailored for K–12 schools

2004: Green Schools Initiative founded to provide tools to make schools healthier and more ecologically sustainable

2005–2014: United Nations Decade for Education for Sustainable Development

2005: Environmental Charter Schools Network founded

2007: U.S. Green Building Council creates LEED for Schools certification program

School in New Jersey read letters written by Aldo Leopold when he was a student there, then trace the trails he followed.

Embracing localism can supply answers to our environmental problems, whether through buying food locally, removing invasive species, or creating decentralized energy systems. "What has served our species well in the past could serve us well in the future if we only relinquish the modern tendency to impose universal solutions upon the infinite variability of both people and the planet. Local diversity lies at the heart of humanity's biological and cultural success," write educators David Gruenewald and Gregory Smith.[24] Students practice this strategy when they become involved in finding solutions to issues on campus and in local communities.

"I'm anxiously awaiting a good explanation why it's important for second-graders to know the order of the planets from Mercury to Pluto," writes Antioch New England professor and place-based education researcher David Sobel. "Wouldn't it be more useful to develop a solid understanding of the geography of the town the second-grader lives in?"[25] A movement from close and familiar to far and strange, he adds, mirrors the development of children's minds.

The Sustainable Schools Project in Vermont helps students understand how we're connected globally, says Shelburne Farms director of professional development Jen Cirillo, "but you need to know your own place before you can make that leap."[26]

This book explores four broad topic areas of schooling for sustainability—food, the campus, community, and teaching and learning—from the perspective of the Smart by Nature guiding principles. Each chapter includes profiles of schools or districts that have creatively addressed these topics, and the strategies they have employed to overcome obstacles, create change within institutions, and incorporate schooling for sustainability into curricula.

The examples used throughout were chosen in order to present a range of experiences and approaches, applied in a variety of school types and geographical regions. Many other exemplary schools and programs could have been included. We plan to continue chronicling schooling for sustainability in future publications and on the Center for Ecoliteracy website, www.ecoliteracy.org. We invite readers to become part of our ongoing collaboration and to share their experiences in furthering this movement.

WHAT YOU

Five Steps toward Becoming Smart by Nature

No two schools' circumstances are the same; there is no one-size-fits-all plan for schooling for sustainability. These suggested steps, based on the work of the Center for Ecoliteracy and incorporating the collective wisdom of several other organizations and agencies working in the field,[27] can be adapted for your circumstances. If you're just getting started, remember that large changes to whole systems often begin with small steps. What's most important is to find like-minded others, take some action that gets you started, remind yourself regularly why you're doing this, persevere, and learn from your experiences.

1. ORGANIZE. Identify the people who share your concerns and interests, and build your efforts around them.

Sustainability is a community practice. Expect to be surprised by who is (and by who isn't) interested. Your allies could include students, PTA and PTO members, parents, teachers, the school nurse, board members, or local businesses. The wider the representation within your school community, the better your chances for success, but you need not use all your valuable time trying to bring everyone on board. The support of principals, heads of school, and school boards can be crucial. Include administrators, custodians, food service staff, and others whose work your efforts will affect. If your school seems ready, establish a green team, eco-council, or similar committee. If possible, work to free a key person from some other responsibilities to coordinate the process.

2. ENVISION. Keep the end in mind by developing a vision statement or a working definition of what sustainability means to your school.

The process of collaborating to create a vision that fits your school can be as important as the vision itself. Visualize the Smart by Nature graduate. What should he or she know, value, and be able to do? Take the time to ensure that key people on campus understand and support the vision. Presenting it to the rest of the community creates opportunities for students to produce art, writing, music, and drama. Gaining support from faculty councils, parent associations, school boards, or boards of trustees strengthens the community's commitment.

3. TAKE STOCK. Conduct sustainability and curriculum audits to set priorities.

Sustainability is rooted in a deep knowledge of place. Begin by knowing your own place. Review the environmental impact of the school's policies and practices in order to set priorities and establish baselines to measure your success.

CAN DO

Audits can cover almost anything: energy and water use; "food miles" in the cafeteria; chemicals used in science labs, for cleaning, or for pest control; purchasing policies; or recycling and waste management. They may focus on one issue or provide an extensive look at a whole range of issues.

Review the curriculum to find where your content and methods of teaching and learning already support your vision. Look beyond "environmental studies" to the whole curriculum. Ask how you can build on what you have done so far.

Find data wherever you can—utility and water bills, expenditures for school vehicles, office supply invoices, or payments for waste hauling. Many local utilities, businesses, government agencies, and other resource people have already developed relevant audit tools and will happily assist. Make the audit part of learning about sustainability.

4. PLAN. Create a strategy and move from vision to action.

The real world is the optimal learning environment. Make the campus a hands-on laboratory for addressing real issues around sustainability. Set high goals, but take manageable steps. Identify the actions that can have the most impact and the issues that most stir the community. Inspiring, challenging goals that lead to substantial change are important, but so are more immediate achievements that allow people to experience success and receive recognition, encouraging them to stretch for higher goals. Start with one achievable project; you do not need to do everything at once.

Recognize that change can be very difficult. Anticipate the education and training that students and staff will need in order to change behavior, adopt new practices, and use new tools. Make it fun. Games, competitions, and rewards for creative problem solving can feed motivation and lead to surprising solutions.

Create partnerships with community organizations. Locate opportunities for civic engagement and service education where students can make a difference in nature and the local community.

5. REFLECT. Close the feedback loop: monitor, evaluate, and celebrate progress.

Nature is our teacher. Natural ecosystems and social systems maintain themselves, "learn," and evolve through networks of feedback. Set up processes to candidly evaluate progress toward your goals as a basis for your next steps. The process is cyclical. Be honest about how well you are doing, but also be prepared to go back and reconsider both your vision and your action plan. Remember that the community is involved in a learning process and that you cannot perfectly predict or manage change in complex systems. Keep the local community informed about your progress. Plan events to celebrate your successes. Pay attention to what you're learning and keep a record for the next time around.

IT'S LUNCHTIME AT SCHOOL: WHAT IN HEALTH IS GOING ON HERE?

The way we eat represents our most profound engagement with the natural world. It can also be the occasion for deepening our appreciation of that engagement, for the benefit of the natural world and our relationship with it.

—Michael Pollan

By the time today's kindergartner finishes high school, she may have eaten well over 4,000 school meals—that's 4,000 opportunities to strengthen her body and mind, introduce food pleasures that will make her a lifelong healthy eater, and deepen her engagement with the natural world. Multiply that child by the 30.5 million children in the National School Lunch Program, and we have the ingredients for a movement that could remake the way we grow, prepare, eat, and think about food; reduce healthcare costs; revitalize agricultural communities; and raise a generation of children with the prospect of a healthier, more vibrant future. Berkeley restaurateur-educator Alice Waters calls this the "Delicious Revolution."

The Delicious Revolution is being waged with knives and forks, hoes and shovels, seeds and compost as educators, parents, citizens, and farmers across the country seize the opportunities presented through the 5.5 billion lunches that U.S. schools serve every year. These quiet revolutionaries have helped children discover that tomatoes and onions and carrots, picked fresh and prepared with love, can taste even better than junk food. They have used food as a focus to teach ecological principles, explore sustainability issues from world hunger to energy use, and awaken children's wonder at the natural world unfolding in a school garden. They have built community by sharing meals around a common table and redirecting some of the billions

OUR SUPERSIZED KIDS: A GROWING CONCERN

U.S. surveys indicate that the percentage of overweight children 2 to 19 years old increased dramatically between 1976–1980 and 2003–2004.

1976–1980

2003–2004

Data from two National Health and Nutrition Examination Surveys (1976–1980 and 2003–2004) show that the prevalence of overweight increased from 5 percent to 13.9 percent for children aged 2–5, from 6.5 percent to 18.8 percent for children 6–11, and from 5 percent to 17.4 percent for children 12–19.

of dollars spent on school food toward supporting local farming and sustainable agriculture.

As stories in this book show, school food reformers often face formidable challenges—otherwise, we wouldn't need a revolution. They must contend with school calendars out of synch with growing seasons, rising food costs, contradictory government mandates, beliefs that gardening is just "digging in the dirt," and competition from food advertising directed at children.[1] The very encouraging news is that committed change agents are meeting these challenges with energy, persistence, and imagination. Their stories highlight a variety of strategies, including year-round gardens in even the coldest climates, farmer co-ops and farm-to-school programs, farmers' market salad bars, local tax measures, partnerships with community organizations, and creative revamping of schools' daily schedules.

Turning Crisis into Opportunity

The Delicious Revolution emerged during a time of crisis. The past three decades have seen an epidemic of overweight children, on their way to becoming permanently obese adults at risk for diabetes and other illnesses. The costs of treating nutrition-related illnesses and their consequences impact families, communities, and the economy.

Would-be school food reformers had become accustomed to the "snicker factor," an "Oh, please, you can't be serious" response from administrators overwhelmed by low academic achievement, high dropout rates, and discipline problems on campus. The lunch period has long been treated as a break from the school's responsibilities for teaching and learning.

But the magnitude of the current epidemic is so great that school authorities, along with government and the media, have had to pay more serious attention to schools' impact on the health of children and their communities. This has created opportunities for innovative rethinking of school food, from the meal on the plate, to the ambience of the lunchroom, to the function of food in the curriculum.

The Context for Reform: A Public Health Catastrophe of Diet-Related Illness

About 16 percent of children ages two to nineteen are overweight, triple the percentage thirty years ago.[2] Half of overweight children stay overweight through adulthood, and most overweight teenagers will also be overweight adults.[3] A boy born in the United States in 2000 had a one in three lifetime risk of being diagnosed with diabetes by the age of fifty (closer to two in five for African-American or Hispanic boys). A girl born that year had a two in five chance (nearly one in two if African-American or Hispanic).[4]

Children are never too small to learn big ideas about the wonders and pleasures of working with nature.

AT RISK FOR DIABETES

A boy born in the United States in 2000 had a one in three lifetime risk of being diagnosed with diabetes...

...two in five if he was African-American or Hispanic.

A girl born that year had a two in five chance...

...nearly one in two if she was African-American or Hispanic.

Undernourished children are more likely to be hyperactive, absent, or tardy; have more behavioral problems; repeat a grade; and require more special education and mental health services.[5] Nutrient deficiencies, refined sugars and carbohydrates, pesticide residues, preservatives, and artificial colorings in food have all been associated with altered thinking and behavior and with neurodevelopmental disorders such as Attention Deficit/Hyperactivity Disorder.[6]

In 1960, Americans spent about 17.5 percent of their income on food and 5.2 percent on health care. Today, they spend less than 10 percent on food and 16 percent on health care.[7] A 2004 report estimated the annual costs of providing medical treatment to obese Americans at $75 billion, of which taxpayers paid more than half through Medicare and Medicaid.[8]

At the same time, a growing body of research has connected better nutrition with higher achievement on standardized tests; increased cognitive function, attention, and memory; and an array of positive behavioral indicators, including school attendance and cooperation.[9] In response, many schools have begun to heed the call for more holistic approaches that integrate nutritious school food, nutrition education, and health care.[10]

Food-focused Learning Environments

The Center for Ecoliteracy, in working with school food systems for more than a decade, has observed food's potential as a focus for education that is Smart by Nature. The greatest impacts on children's knowledge, behavior, and attitudes come from combining hands-on and minds-on experiences, especially in four settings: school gardens, instructional kitchens, lunchrooms, and classrooms.

School gardens. Parents and educators who want to incorporate food into the curriculum and immerse children in nature often start with a garden. Especially in cities, gardens may be young people's only connection to the natural world. Michael Ableman, founder of the Center for Urban Agriculture, writes: "[Gardens] are not just a little break from the endless, mindless stretch of pavement; they become gathering places, sanctuaries, cultural and social centers, and they are as important to the health of our civic life as are art museums, theaters, and great restaurants. They are part of a city's soul."[11]

Tracing the paths food follows from the seed in the soil, to the vegetable on the vine, to the meal in the cafeteria teaches basic ecological literacy concepts—the flow of energy from the sun to plants and animals, planetary cycles of water and weather, the interdependent web of relations embodied in every bite we take. Gardens allow students to be more physically active and to use all their senses. Children literally dig in to projects that matter and want to learn the skills to tend living things in their care. Gardens support different learning styles; children who aren't engaged in the classroom often become leaders in the garden.

Studies confirm that children who garden score better in science, reading and writing, and independent thinking; have increased self-esteem and better attendance; and better appreciate safe water and healthy soil, and the importance of conserving them.[12]

Instructional kitchens. Some highly evolved programs, such as the renowned Edible Schoolyard in Berkeley, include separate kitchen classrooms and teachers that reach all students. Other schools build ovens—fueled by propane or wood— or install kitchens with simple hot plates in their gardens. In yet others, the "kitchen" is a portable cart that can carry cooking equipment and supplies to any classroom.[13]

Students will almost always try food they have cooked, particularly if they have grown it in the garden. They discover that healthy food can be delicious and will often take recipes home to suggest (or even teach!) to their parents. The kitchen classroom provides an excellent venue for taste-testing dishes before they become part of the lunchroom menu. Students can also experience history and other cultures by using the techniques and foods of other ages or peoples. They use math to measure portions, calculate waste, and solve problems in the kitchen. They may gather around a table brightened with fresh garden flowers and spread with a tablecloth—and experience the pleasures of a different style of eating.

Lunchrooms. Children learn important lessons in the lunchroom—whether intended or not. Low-quality lunches, junk food sales, and hallway soda machines can become the most memorable les-

CONNECTING GARDEN TO CAFETERIA

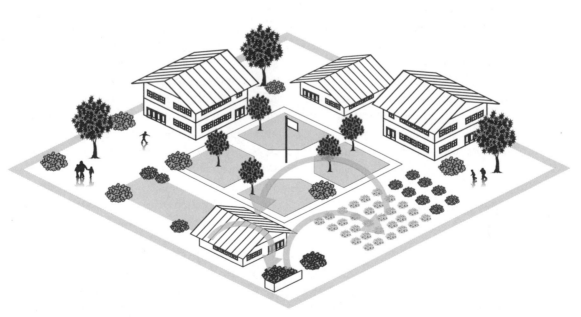

Students learn ecological concepts by tracing the path of food from the garden to the cafeteria, and back to the garden as compost.

Smart by Nature

sons about schools' attitudes toward nutrition and student health. The Center for Ecoliteracy became involved in school lunch reform after realizing how often unappetizing, minimally nutritious meals, served in unattractive settings, undermined successful garden and cooking programs.

Food educator Antonia Demas argues, "We need to quit viewing [the lunch program] as the 'school *feeding* program' and start thinking of it as the 'school *dining* program.' There is a clear analogy to animal feedlots: herd them in quickly, and feed them high-density foods in a short amount of time in crowded conditions. As concerned parents and teachers, we must give serious attention to the eating environment of the school and appreciate the fact that changing the environment could be a way to foster social skills in children."[14]

Lunchroom learning continues after the eating stops. When leftover food is composted, children can follow it back to the soil as it completes the cycle begun in the garden. They learn other lessons when they reuse or recycle packaging, plates, and utensils rather than sending them—out of sight, out of mind—to the landfill.

Classrooms. Food is so central to human survival and experience that nearly any subject can be integrated through it—science, health, history,

Children learn social skills and discover the pleasures of good food when they share a meal in the kitchen classroom.

social studies, geography, art, economics. Nutrition education makes more sense when studied in the context of how nature provides.

How we grow, process, transport, market, prepare, and dispose of food is critical to the central issues of sustainable living: resource use, energy, pollution, water and soil conservation. Food serves as an ideal entry point for understanding the interrelations of such world issues as hunger, trade policy, energy use, and climate change. Students can track the sources of the food in their lunches and calculate the resources and energy used to bring it to them. They can research what types of foods would and would not be available to them if they were to adopt a regionally oriented "hundred-mile diet"—eating only food grown within a hundred-

mile radius in order to emphasize fresh and seasonal ingredients, support local agriculture, and reduce the energy and expense needed to preserve and ship food over long distances.

Changing School Food Systems

Recognizing the importance of improving school food and using it as a focus for teaching sustainability is one thing. Changing complex, entrenched food systems is another. It can take time and require ingenuity and commitment.

Based on its experience with school food systems, the Center for Ecoliteracy developed a plan-

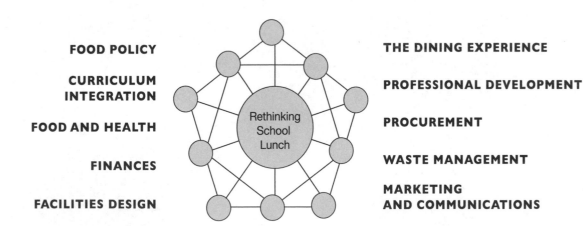

CENTER FOR ECOLITERACY
PLANNING FRAMEWORK FOR FOOD SYSTEMS

FOOD POLICY

CURRICULUM INTEGRATION

FOOD AND HEALTH

FINANCES

FACILITIES DESIGN

Rethinking School Lunch

THE DINING EXPERIENCE

PROFESSIONAL DEVELOPMENT

PROCUREMENT

WASTE MANAGEMENT

MARKETING AND COMMUNICATIONS

Change can begin at any place in this framework because the elements of the school food system are all connected.

Food service staff members help children make healthy choices from the salad bar.

ning framework, "Rethinking School Lunch." This framework identifies ten different aspects of school operations that relate to food change: food policy, curriculum integration, food and health, finances, facilities design, the dining experience, professional development, procurement, waste management, and marketing and communications. These areas are explored in depth in a downloadable 175-page guide, available on the CEL website (http://www.ecoliteracy.org/programs/rsl-guide.html).

The web of connections formed within this framework is key. Change in one area leads to change in others. Attempting to alter everything at once can be daunting, but those who wish to

affect school food can begin at some point where they have resources, interests, and opportunities, understanding that the change process will eventually lead them to other areas. And just as a spider's web becomes stronger when more of its strands connect, any group's efforts will become stronger when connected to others' work in the different areas.

For instance, Santa Monica, California, food service director Rodney Taylor wanted to offer better food choices for the sake of children's health. That led to him to experiment with a new dining experience, the salad bar, which required changing the procurement process and purchasing from farmers' markets. Adding the new menu items depended on training existing staff in new food-handling procedures, as well as increasing staff. This required additional financing, which Taylor addressed by reaching out to PTAs and launching a marketing campaign to attract more "customers" for school lunch.

Anyone interested in changing school food needs to understand the fundamentals that create the context in which change will occur. Rodney Taylor calls these fundamentals "Food Service 101." Among them:

● *School food service is a business.* School districts are usually divided into two domains, business and instruction, "that don't have much communications circuitry established between them," says former California Department of Education official Ann M. Evans.[15] Food service is lodged firmly on the business side and is often expected to operate in the black, or even to generate a surplus for the district's general fund, after paying for everything from food and salaries to serving trays and delivery trucks. "When I was hired," says one director, "my boss said, 'I don't know anything about food service, and I don't want to know anything. Just put $50,000 a year on the bottom line.'"[16]

● *Government reimbursements don't cover costs.* The major income source for most school food services is federal and state reimbursement for meals offered free or at reduced cost to children from families below federally defined income levels.[17] The School Nutrition Association reported in 2008 that the 2005–2006 subsidy (cash reimbursements plus commodities) averaged $2.49 per meal while the cost to produce a reimbursable meal was $2.91. That gap has since grown.[18] Food services are forced to further reduce costs or find other sources of income. The need for revenues has made soft drink machines and sale of "a la carte" items such as candy and junk food attractive to many school districts. School organizations, including PTAs and booster clubs on some campuses, sell pizza, candy, and sodas to support sports, computer labs, music, art, and other programs.

● *The National School Lunch Program has mixed objectives.* Since the first national U.S. school lunch program was launched during the Depression, the programs have been intended simultaneously to support children's health and to create a market for American agriculture. As long as the country's chief nutrition problem was malnourishment, the dual objectives were a win–win. Once the problem became too many calories, and healthy advice became "eat less," USDA's mandate to both support health and push American agriculture created a conflict of interest, which still persists.[19]

● *Reformers need to know who has authority to make the changes that matter to them.* The national school food system is a complex hierarchy, with responsibilities stretching from the local campus to the U.S. Congress (see "Levels of Authority for School Food Systems"). In theory, working from both bottom up and top down works best. In practice, change agents must understand where decisions get made and where authority lies.

LEVELS OF AUTHORITY FOR SCHOOL FOOD SYSTEMS

This is a partial list of typical food system responsibilities.

Federal Government

- Sets reimbursement and income level requirements for national breakfast and lunch programs
- Determines minimal nutrition requirements for federally supported meals
- Creates policies for commodity foods offered to schools

State Government

- May supplement federal reimbursements
- Sets regulations for foods served in schools not participating in federal programs
- Administers food stamp nutrition education fund programs in schools
- Creates academic state-level standards and testing procedures

School Board

- Approves district operating budget
- Sets priorities for superintendent
- Approves federally mandated wellness policies for local districts
- Proposes tax measures for approval by voters

District Superintendent/Administration

- Establishes expectations and priorities for food service, guided by federal requirements (break even, maintain surplus, and so on)
- Recommends budget, may propose allocating additional funds to supplement food service income
- Determines where savings achieved by food service, such as reduced trash-hauling fees, will be applied, guided by federal requirements
- Oversees design, construction, and maintenance of kitchen facilities and resources
- Secures additional resources, such as funding to staff garden and kitchen classes

Food Service Director

- Creates and manages food service budget, determining how funds will be allocated among food purchases, personnel, equipment, and so on
- Sets menus and documents adherence to required nutritional standards
- Procures and oversees preparation of food; locates and negotiates with farmers, distributors, and vendors
- Determines food service staff roles; oversees staff training
- "Markets" food service to students and families

Principal

- Sets the tone for campus regarding openness to change and spirit of cooperation
- Determines the level of support and encouragement for faculty and staff experimentation and innovation at the school site
- With teachers, creates class schedule (e.g., amount of time for lunch, order of lunch and recess)

Teachers and Staff (sometimes constrained by union contracts)

- Choose whether and how to incorporate food and nutrition into classroom lessons
- Determine how food may be used outside of meals (for instance for treats and celebrations, or as reward and punishment), within local and state requirements
- Can model attitudes toward school food
- Usually maintain the most direct communication with parents

Creative Solutions to Food Service Challenges

Schools across the country have devised inventive responses to many of the obstacles to improving school food and creating learning opportunities around food. Schools are successfully experimenting with innovative techniques, including building affordable structures to permit year-round gardening even in frigid climates, and producing garden harvests bountiful enough to make their programs self-supporting.

It is encouraging to note that children are not hopelessly addicted to junk food. To the utter surprise of parents, students will try, and often come to love, unfamiliar food, especially if they've grown it, cooked it, or encountered it in the right setting. "I had one kid whose mother called him a 'picky eater,'" recalls a teacher in Berkeley's Edible Schoolyard. "Over the year, that took on a new meaning, because he was picking—and eating—everything in the garden."[21] Instead of lining up for lunch at Lopez Island School in Washington, children sit at tables that offer bowls of fresh vegetables until their classes are called. The kids are less fidgety, the lunchroom is quieter and more pleasant for everyone, and the vegetables get eaten. Other schools make fresh fruits and vegetables available throughout the day.

Scheduling can be an obstacle. In many schools, lunch periods are short, and students race through lunch to get to the playground. Schools such as John Muir Elementary in Berkeley, California, are reaping multiple benefits from simply reversing the order of lunch and recess. Students arriving at different times, often because of bus schedules, can complicate serving breakfast, so schools in several states offer breakfast in the classroom while teachers take roll and complete other tasks.

Funding creates another issue. A majority of food service directors polled by the School Nutrition Association ranked money as the most pressing problem facing their programs. Ultimately, citizens and legislators will have to confront the skewed calculus by which society pinches pennies for school food, then spends billions of dollars to treat nutrition-related illness. Looking at funding questions systemically, one study calculated that New York City schools could be losing as much as $28 million a year in state attendance-based funding merely through excess absences by overweight students.[22]

In response to these issues, schools, including those profiled below, have developed some successful strategies for increasing income and lowering expenses without compromising quality: creating self-supporting gardens, implementing citizen self-taxation, lowering waste-hauling expenses by increasing recycling and composting, or raising funds by selling compost to the community. Others schools aggressively market meals to students and teachers, form partnerships with other community organizations, or provide fee-based services to clients outside the school. Schools often fear they must choose between healthy food and adequate income. The opposite may be the case; as the Richland, South Carolina, district discovered, when less-healthy foods were abolished, students often simply bought school lunches or healthier drinks instead, resulting in higher food service income.[23]

GROWING VEGETABLES AT 10 BELOW

What: The Garden Project

Where: Troy Howard Middle School
                 Belfast, Maine

Initiators: Middle school teachers

Key Strategies: Four-season school garden in student-
                 built greenhouses

                 A garden-centered curriculum

                 A program that pays its own way and
                 serves the wider community

"This week we took all of our student gardeners snowshoeing before picking greens for market," wrote Steve Tanguay in a January email. "If we can grow at school throughout the winter here, it can be done by schools in every state." "Here" is Belfast, on the coast of Maine, where winter temperatures sometimes dive to 10 below.

Students at Troy Howard Middle School (THMS) in Belfast aren't just picking greens; they're growing 8,000 pounds of produce a year, winning prizes for heirloom vegetables at the country's largest organic fair, enjoying freshly harvested foods in the cafeteria year-round, and learning about sustainability in garden-based courses that meet state standards in a half-dozen areas from math to social studies.

That's not bad for a public school whose one-acre garden site had been a bed of gravel slated to become a bus garage. In 2001, teachers led by history, economics, and agriculture teacher Steve Tanguay, proposed building a school garden there instead. They wanted to immerse students in outdoor learning and ensure that every student ate at least some fresh food throughout the year. (Most of the school's food was being shipped in from the South or California.)

Tanguay and Jon Thurston, the school district's agricultural coordinator, had worked in experiential education for more than two decades. Fellow teacher Don White, who was gardening successfully with his special education students, inspired their garden efforts, as did their close neighbor, four-season organic gardening guru Eliot Coleman, who consulted with them as they launched their project.[24]

The gravel bed had no topsoil, so the Troy Howard crew brought in whatever organic material they could collect or scrounge: seaweed from the ocean, a mile away; manure from local farms; leaves and yard clippings collected by city work crews; table scraps from the school lunchroom. The first year's harvest, grown almost entirely from seed bought from Maine companies, yielded 80 varieties of vegetables, including onions, Savoy cabbage, peppers, and multiple varieties of tomatoes—fall crops that students could harvest and enjoy at the start of the school year.

Wintertime Gardening

To garden during the winter, the school initially used a grant to build a 30-by-45-foot state-of-the-art commercial greenhouse that is heated at night by an oil furnace (the furnace is rarely needed during the daylight hours, when solar heat gain captured in the growing beds maintains the temperature).

Education for sustainability at THMS, however, also includes devising tools and techniques for making whole communities more self-sufficient,

The hoop house, designed and built by students using local hardware and materials, is an affordable structure for all-season gardening.

and many homeowners and small farmers cannot afford commercial greenhouses. So students and teachers began to look for inexpensive alternatives that others in their community could build for themselves.

In 2006, students researched designs, costs, and locally available supplies, then constructed scale models of "hoop houses," simple 12-by-20-foot portable greenhouses invented by their neighbor, master farmer Eliot Coleman. They built the school's first hoop house using local hardware and materials. Math, science, language arts, industrial arts, and economics teachers all designed lessons that related to the project.

The prototype hoop house confirmed their hypothesis that crops could be grown in low-cost structures that needed no supplementary heating. Students have since built two more, substantial

The hoop house lets students grow fresh produce in any climate.

enough to survive heavy snowfalls, using steel tubing purchased from a New Hampshire farmer and locally acquired scrap lumber, for less than $1,000 each.

Farmers' Market Boot Camp

The experimental garden evolved into the Garden Project, which now serves as the core of the academic program for about half of Troy Howard's 150 seventh-graders and a handful of students from other grades. The project's goal is "to engage all students in a journey of discovery through gardening projects that achieve Maine science, math, technology and social studies learning results, produce nutritious food and pioneer action-research for sustainability. At the heart of the gardening program are the young people excited by making a real difference in their school and community."[25]

"One hundred percent of the kids eat vegetables without prompting," says Tanguay. "You can teach nutrition all you want, but they really need to be directly involved with the food before they'll make it part of their lives." The Garden Project is also helping to change the Belfast food culture, which was historically based on fishing and chickens. "We get twelve-year-old rural kids here who've never tried a tomato," Tanguay adds. Now, he says, parents report that students are asking them to start their own gardens, to shop at the Belfast Co-op, and to cook with fresh produce.

Garden Project seventh-graders begin the year with a week-long "Farmers' Market Boot Camp," in which they experience as many aspects of the project as possible, before serving eight-week ap-

The greenhouse is also a laboratory for learning the science behind natural methods of pest management.

prenticeships. Then each student applies for work as an "employee" in one of three divisions of the Garden Project: Compost, Seed, and Garden Stand, where responsibilities range from planting, picking, and packing to financial management, advertising, and distribution. Each of the divisions is run like a business. There are real consequences if students don't meet their responsibilities.

Besides supplying fresh food for all of Belfast's schools and regularly donating food to the local soup kitchen, the program sells produce and seeds at its own farm stand, by mail order, and at the Belfast Co-op. Students also manage a "restaurant" that serves pizzas made from scratch using almost entirely ingredients they have grown. But first they develop a business plan that is reviewed by a committee, including the chief investment officer of a local bank, which evaluates their re-

search and projections for income and expenses, competition, inventory, quality control, and potential locations.

Garden Project sales now cover all the expenses of the program except for Jon Thurston's salary. Project leaders are determined to succeed without sacrificing the school's commitment to its community. "Before we began selling produce and seeds at the Co-op," says Tanguay, "we met with local farmers to find a niche we could fill without competing with them. We want to support local farmers and businesses and help them expand their markets, not take away from their sales. So we decided to grow Swiss chard, which stores were importing from California. It's on the shelves within an hour of being picked, and it's all gone by the same afternoon. We sell seeds at bookstores, which don't normally have seed racks, but not at the Co-op or hardware stores, where selling bulbs and seedlings is a big part of their business."

Sustainability Education in the Garden Project

The Garden Project's stated purpose is to grow academically empowered, successful young people who integrate sustainability into their lives by producing and learning to satisfy their needs locally.[26] Students learn where food comes from; how to grow, harvest, and prepare vegetables and fruits organically; and the keys to building healthy soils.

Especially, they learn about cultivating relationships with place and community. Everything the

Art meets commerce when students design packets to market seeds from the school garden.

Garden Project does reinforces those connections, whether reestablishing orchards with native trees, saving heirloom seeds, buying seeds from Maine companies, or taking the extra step to work with, rather than compete with, local farmers and seed savers. It's important not only that students contribute produce to the local soup kitchen, but also that they get to know the members of their community served by the kitchen. In turn the community reciprocates: local businesses give discounts to the project, residents patronize the garden stand, local families volunteer to help maintain the garden over the summer.

Part of sustainability education, says Tanguay, is teaching students that they have the skills to run a business that provides a living, and ensuring that they understand what it entails. They learn both that self-sufficient local agriculture is an alternative to the industrial food system, and that it requires someone's getting up and getting out there seven days a week.

"What they learn," says Tanguay, "is that they have the power to really manage something that they're proud of and that can extend into their lives as adults. If they want to learn something, Jon and I won't always be available to them. We want learning to be more like you'd learn from your grandfather. Once you pay attention, you'll get it."

THE GARDEN-CENTERED CURRICULUM

Almost any aspect of the Garden Project can be integrated into the curriculum. Garden-based lessons account for about 90 percent of Garden Project students' seventh-grade social studies curriculum, 30 percent of their art, and 20 percent each of their math, language arts, and science instruction. Students learn about their region and its history, good nutrition, local food production, small business management, and conducting good science. The garden is a laboratory where students experiment in germination and propagation, nutrients and control, orchard development, aquaculture, weather studies, and soil amendments. Saving heirloom seeds becomes an occasion for studying Maine's agricultural and social history, as well as making a contribution to its future. Students explore the origins of vegetables and their impact on world history. They compare the nutritional value of spinach from the garden to store-bought products. They investigate the pathways of food from garden to table, including the effects of processing and the consequences of globalization (the pizza project, for example, requires them to trace how typical pizza ingredients came to be available in the United States).

The project mixes traditional low-tech practices with the use of sophisticated tools. Automated probes track temperatures inside and outside the greenhouses twenty-four hours a day. Students use digital microscopes and laptop computers to photograph eggs, larvae, and adult pests found on their plants, then determine the most effective control method for each intruder.

The Garden Project curriculum is highly inquiry based, encouraging students to research the questions that arise in the course of operating the garden and running their businesses.

Running such a program while attending to state standards requires flexibility on teachers' parts. For instance, says math teacher Katie Coleman, "Jon may call me in the morning and say that they're laying out garden beds, and I'll build in a lesson about X and Y coordinates." When the time comes to do soil amendments in the spring, math lessons include performing measurements, consulting tables, and calculating the formulas that will be used for tilling later that day.

"Katie can do that," says Tanguay, "because she really knows her subject and can recognize how an activity can be turned into a lesson that meets the needs of the students and standards. Some people think that teaching in a program like this one is mostly digging in the dirt with the students. You really need to know the curriculum much better than a regular teacher does, in order to be prepared to make a lesson out of whatever comes up."

FARM TO SCHOOL, SOUTHERN STYLE

What: The New North Florida Cooperative

Where: Tallahassee, Florida

Initiators: Small-scale African-American farmers

Key Strategies: Farm-to-school programs combine
                 healthy food with nutrition education

                 Farmer collaborative serves the needs of
                 small-scale farmers, making food more
                 affordable to school districts

Minority farmers with limited access to markets, a depressed economy, and underfunded schools in the region of the country with the highest obesity levels—these conditions are not exactly the recipe for a healthy-children, healthy-farms success story. Since its founding in 1995 by African-American farmers, though, the New North Florida Cooperative (NNFC) has provided income to farmers and delivered fresh produce to over a million students in more than 70 districts in Florida, Georgia, Alabama, Mississippi, and Arkansas.

Eight of the ten states with the highest obesity rates in the United States are in the South.[27] Blame it on a cultural predilection for biscuits and gravy and fried chicken, but it's no coincidence that the states with the highest obesity rates also have the highest poverty levels. Researchers hypothesize that limited economic resources may shift diets toward processed foods with refined grains and added sugar and fat, which provide maximum calories per dollar.[28] Offering children in the region healthy alternatives through school food, then, becomes even more important.

A Farm-to-School Strategy

When the New North Florida Cooperative began, its area in the Florida panhandle was economically depressed, with high unemployment and struggling farms. NNFC's founders sought to help each other and to seek markets that could offer stability and profitability for their small-scale operations.

After trying unsuccessfully to generate sufficient revenue through local farmers' markets and roadside stands, the cooperative found a niche as one of the nation's first farm-to-school programs (see "What Is a Farm-to-School Program?"). The farmers wanted business relationships with buyers on whom they could rely and with whom they could negotiate equitable prices. Gadsden County School District food director J'Amy Peterson wanted to introduce more fresh produce into school meals and to support local farmers. Farm-to-school proved a winning solution for both.[29]

Farmers and Schools Meet in the Cafeteria

As a farm-to-school pioneer with no track record, the New North Florida Cooperative had to persuade food service directors that a newly formed cooperative of small farmers could dependably deliver high-quality produce, in the quantities ordered, at the agreed-upon time, at reasonable prices. The farmers, who had not always had good experiences with government programs, needed to know they could count on timely payments and on their crops reaching markets in good condition, freeing them to do what they do best, farm.

Start-up funds for the cooperative consisted mostly of sweat equity from the farmers. A few loans from local banks and the Jackson County Development Council funded the purchase of a cutting/chopping machine and a refrigeration storage system. By washing, chopping, and bagging produce, NNFC could serve districts not equipped to handle fresh, unprocessed greens. Because the cooperative assumed labor and equipment costs, schools on tight budgets found their offerings affordable. Farmers—who lacked the time or means to make small deliveries to

Farmer-run education programs teach students about the importance of small farms to the local economy.

THE NORTH FLORIDA CORPORATIVE FARM

Sponsored By:
WEST FLORIDA
R.C.&D. USDA.
FAMU 1890
OUT REACH PROGRAM
NATURAL RESOURCE
CONSERVATION SERVICE

THE NET WORTH IS FOUND *in the* LAND

numerous schools—could drop produce off at the cooperative for processing and delivery.

During its first year, the cooperative provided 3,000 pounds of leafy greens as free samples, to demonstrate its competence as a supplier of local agriculture. Food service managers reported increased School Lunch Program participation, more sales to teachers and staff members, and reduced after-meal waste.[30] Word of mouth has helped NNFC grow since then.

Melanie Payne, food service director for the Opelika, Alabama, city schools, became an early out-of-state client. She had made news in 1993 as one of the first Alabama directors to banish fried food from her district's menus. She began replacing canned fruits and vegetables with frozen options, but labor costs limited the amount of fresh produce she could offer. Working with NNFC allowed her to add fresh vegetables such as collards, peas, butterbeans, and sweet potato sticks to her menus. "I am not going to the farmer down the street and personally picking up 50 cases of cabbage," she explained. "There needs to be supervision; someone checking on the farms for reliance, transparency, and credibility....We need a system of certification that the product is produced under acceptable conditions. I trust [co-op director] Glyen Holmes because of his strict procedures and knowledge of the USDA regulations."[31]

The cooperative hosts field trips where children can see how food is grown and prepared, and it has designed posters for cafeteria walls showing the life cycle of crops, from production to consumption, to help educate children while promoting the NNFC brand.

At any time, sixty to a hundred farmers work with the NNFC, which is now a multi-state processing and marketing network. It funds itself almost completely through sales and consulting, and has established a working capital fund to help farmers cover bills between harvest and receipt of customers' payments.

Farmer-writer Wendell Berry talks about solutions that create cascading sets of other solutions. The New North Florida Cooperative is one of those. It began as a project to address one problem: farmers struggling to make a living in a tough economy. Its solution has cascaded into healthy and fresh food for children, increased participation in lunch programs, reduced waste, money savings, assured quality control, nutrition education opportunities, and a flow of cash through local economies.

Co-op farmers deliver farm-fresh produce to the school kitchen—washed, chopped, bagged, and ready for cooking.

WHAT IS A FARM-TO-SCHOOL PROGRAM?

More than eight thousand schools in forty states participate in farm-to-school programs to improve student nutrition, provide health and nutrition education, and support local farmers. There is no farm-to-school program blueprint. Projects are locally designed and are "as different as the communities in which they exist," according to the Community Food Security Coalition, which manages the National Farm to School Network, (www.farmtoschool.org).[32] Depending on climate, participants, and local desires and needs, programs can operate year-round or for as little as two months a year. Some are focused on single crops, such as the NH Farm-to-School Program, which began as a project to introduce local apples and cider into New Hampshire schools.[33] Others offer a dozen or more crops. Some provide food every day or several times a week. Others highlight local foods at special events, such as Wisconsin Homegrown, which initially featured Wisconsin products at one meal per season.[34] Various farm-to-school programs have been initiated by farmers, parents, schools, and local agriculture and health advocates. Some like that at Santa Monica-Malibu, California, were launched as full-blown efforts led by district food services. Others began as small projects, such as Missoula (Montana) County Schools Farm to School, coordinated by two University of Montana graduate students.[35]

Most farm-to-school programs help students understand where food comes from and how it gets to them. Visits by farmers to classrooms or field trips to farms or farmers' markets put a face on the food. Some ambitious programs go even further: Fresh from the Farm in the Chicago area has designed eight-week curriculum modules that focus on nutrition, earth-friendly agriculture, and global food traditions, and use all five senses to experience food. The program offers professional development sessions to help teachers and parents use the curriculum.[36] Vermont Food Education Every Day (FEED) brings together teams of teachers, farmers, food service staff, and local leaders to create a "curriculum of place" within the school curriculum, with standards-based lessons that offer students an introduction to Vermont's farm life, agricultural cycles, nutrition education, and local history.[37]

The National Farm to School Network, initiated in 2000, is managed by the Community Food Security Coalition and the Center for Food & Justice of the Urban & Environmental Policy Institute at Occidental College. Its services include helping groups to start and sustain efforts, raise funds, and locate informational resources. It also offers professional development.

Farm-to-school programs help students appreciate where their food comes from and the rich web of interdependence connecting them to farmers.

THE SALAD BAR MAN

What: Santa Monica and Riverside Salad Bars

Where: Santa Monica and Riverside, California

Initiators: One parent, one food service director

Key Stategies: Fresh, "user-friendly" produce
                Politely persistent parent persuasion
                "Marketing like mad," running the
                food service as a business

Rodney Taylor asks his audience to picture the scene at an elementary school salad bar: "The kindergartners are in line, as cute as they can be. They've cleaned their little hands and lined up on both sides of the self-serve bar. First there's green lettuce fresh from local farmers, cherry tomatoes, broccoli—chopped so it's user-friendly for the small kids, cauliflower, cucumbers. Then there's turkey ham, turkey, yogurt, cottage cheese. And the fruits—plums, watermelon, pears. Imagine the color, the crispness because it was delivered from the farm and cut up just this morning. By the end of the line, you've seen a young kid build this beautiful, colorful salad. And you've seen a five-year-old learning to become a lifelong healthy eater.[38]

"We hope each kid will have access to this kind of meal in the very near future," continues Taylor, who directs nutrition services in the Riverside, California, Unified School District, where he serves three-quarters of a million farm-to-school salad bar lunches a year.

Taylor's groundbreaking salad bar work has won him widespread recognition, including a Regional Social Justice Award, praise from the American Cancer Society, and appointment to the University of California President's Advisory Committee on Agriculture and Natural Resources. But he admits that he was a reluctant convert to the notion of salad bars as a school lunch centerpiece. "You're looking at an inner city kid," he says. "Do you really think I dreamed about being a salad bar man? That is not what I grew up wanting to be."

Food service director Rodney Taylor (left), principal John McCombs, and students celebrate the arrival of fresh salad bar greens at Emerson Elementary School.

The Power of One Persistent Parent

Taylor's salad bar conversion illustrates the impact one parent can have. In 1997, Taylor directed food and nutrition services with the Santa Monica-Malibu Unified School District, when a district parent named Bob Gottlieb approached him. Gottlieb applauded the presence of salad bars in the district, but was dismayed that his daughter would not eat at her school's, with its processed fruit from a can, white and filmy carrots, and lettuce and celery that were turning brown. Why not buy from local farmers, asked Gottlieb. Why not buy from the local farmers' market?

"He pitched the idea of supporting local farmers, and I can tell you, that was the furthest thing from

my mind," Taylor says now. He was positive it wouldn't work. Gottlieb is a professor at Occidental College in Los Angeles and director of the Urban Environmental Policy Institute, though Taylor didn't know that at the time. "I thought he was just another affluent parent with a little too much time on his hands." Taylor assumed that Gottlieb, like most of the rest, would go away when his idea wasn't immediately embraced. Instead, he kept coming back, politely but persistently presenting the case for farm-fresh food and asking, "What can I do to help?"

Taylor finally gave in and agreed to a two-week trial during a summer childcare class. "I just knew that four-year-olds were not going to eat this food," he recalls. "When I walked in the first day and saw the youngsters grabbing food off the salad bar, I was changed forever. I didn't even need to go back the next day."

The new convert became a farm-to-school salad bar evangelist. The Occidental College Community Food Security Project helped secure a start-up grant from the California Endowment and found farmers willing to give discounts to launch a pilot in one school. Taylor also "marketed like mad."[39] He brought salad bar samples to parent back-to-school nights, offered discount coupons to attract teachers, and preached his new gospel to principals and PTAs. The next year, the district secured a state grant to expand the program into less-affluent schools, and Taylor persuaded PTAs at better-off schools to commit $5,000 a year for two years, promising them that the program would be self-supporting after that.

He also turned to PTAs for volunteers. When farm-to-school programs are implemented, the food frequently costs less than processed, packaged, and trucked-in alternatives. On the other hand, labor costs go up.[40] "Had we not had parent volunteers, I wouldn't be talking today about the farm-to-school program," says Taylor. "It was the parents that came in that first year and did all of the chopping and everything else that needed to be done."

The salad bars competed successfully with pizza and sloppy joes. At some schools, average salad bar participation was 10 times what it had been the year before. The program expanded to every school in the district and became almost completely self-supporting, as Taylor had promised. It also extended beyond the lunchroom to include school gardens, classroom visits by chefs, and field trips to farms and the farmers' market.

Running the Food Service as a Business

In 2002, Taylor moved from the affluent Santa Monica-Malibu district to Riverside, a district with high needs, where he felt he could make an impact. Fifty-three percent of Riverside students came from at-risk homes. Riverside had no farmers' market offering access to fresh food, so he had to locate and negotiate with local farmers. Most parents worked and weren't free to volunteer. PTAs weren't able to make sizeable contributions. The food service was in debt.

"When I said I'm going to put salad bars in all the elementary schools, people who knew the challenges laughed and said, 'This isn't Santa Monica-Malibu.' But I knew from Santa Monica that the salad bar creates a kind of excitement, that once you get it going, it's a vehicle that drives itself. The custodians were talking to each other and saying it's not the mess that they think it is. One principal started talking about it, and then it was two, and then three, and now I've got principals jockeying to get up the list for salad bars."

Taylor is often asked how much it costs to add a salad bar program. He says that that's the wrong question. Instead, the food service as a whole—both expenses and income—needs to be thought of as a business. Many food service directors are nutritionists by training or have always worked in school programs. Taylor feels that those like himself, with backgrounds in marketing and private industry, may be better at seeing the school food service as a business that must constantly redefine itself, understand its competition, and respond to its customers. "We talk a lot about growing our business," he says. "At first, no one truly understood what I was talking about. They said, 'Wait a minute, our enrollment is declining.' I said, 'We feed 51 percent of our 43,000 kids. That means 21,000 a day who aren't eating with us.'"

Today, the food service feeds 65 percent of Riverside's students. Taylor is still marketing like mad: soliciting students' preferences, holding tastings of new items, taking the extra effort to make the salad bar user-friendly by cutting whole apples, oranges, and broccoli into bite-sized pieces that small children can manage. He also refuses to be a food purist. "Those items that children like, that you and I grew up with, don't kill us. They'll draw kids into the cafeteria. So I advocate keeping the hamburgers and corn dogs and hot dogs, but once they pick up the hot dog, they pick up the rest of their meal at the salad bar, so they get a well-balanced meal and their minimum of fruits and vegetables."

He also targets teachers. "One of the huge benefits of the salad bar is that I'm getting ten to fifteen teachers at a school where they didn't used to eat at all. We're talking about maybe $13,000 times thirty-two schools. But here's something even more important. When children see fifteen teachers a day eating at the salad bar, that sends a powerful message. And then on back-to-school night when a parent asks a teacher, 'Should I pack my kid a sack lunch this year?' the teacher can say, 'Oh, no, we have an internationally famous salad bar. I eat there myself.'"

How else to grow the business? The Riverside Meals on Wheels program was being serviced by a private company that raised its prices more than 60 percent. "I read in the newspaper that Meals on Wheels had predicted they'd be bankrupt within a year. So I took that article to my boss and said, 'We can make a little money, and look like heroes doing it.' And that's exactly what is happening. We service twenty accounts—little private schools, for-profits, and nonprofits. During a time of declining enrollment, our participation is growing, because of the dollars that we find within the community."

Treating the food service as a whole system underwrites the costs of buying and preparing fresh salad bar food. "If you ask me, 'Does the salad bar pay for itself? Does it make money?' I don't know that it does in and of itself, but that wasn't my intention. My intention was to get your kid at five, and teach her to be a lifelong healthy eater. Now the extra money that I'm going to spend on that is the price to bring healthy food in. The extra work that we do is our commitment to serving our kids the very best that we can. I tell my employees we serve more than food. We serve love. I like to think of the salad bars as one of my greatest expressions of love to the kids. There's nothing like walking into a store in your community and having someone say, 'I know you. You're the salad bar man.' That's pretty cool to me."

RECONNECT, REVITALIZE, SUSTAIN

What: Lopez Island Farm Education

Where: Lopez Island, Washington

Initiators: Parent/donors, school officials, farmers, community groups

Key Strategies: Community-based farm-to-school program
                School-sponsored community meals
                Support for local farmers
                Island intelligence

What if they gave a party and no one came? That question sat heavy on the minds of organizers of the January, 2008, "Hungry Moon Winter Harvest Dinner" at Lopez Island School, located on Lopez Island in Washington's San Juan Islands. The dinner, the first of what the planners hoped would become monthly events, had multiple purposes: providing seasonal organic food for hungry people, supporting local farmers, publicizing the Lopez Island farm-to-school program, and strengthening connections between the school and the community.

The tables were set, the room decorated. White bean chili with pumpkin, Lopez lamb sausage, tricolor cabbage slaw, red velvet beet cake—prepared fresh from local products by prominent island chefs—were arrayed and ready. But would people turn out on a cold, wet mid-week evening, with snow still on the ground after a rare snowstorm? "Maybe we'll get a hundred. Maybe fifty. We know that the basketball team is practicing that night, so at least we know they'll be there," remarked Michele Heller, a Lopez parent and civic leader who was one of the event's organizers.

When the doors opened at 5:30, a line snaked out the door and around the building. People kept coming. And coming. The room filled. Volunteers gently urged eaters to move along after finishing their suppers, to make room for others. Eventually, three hundred people—children, parents, old-timers, new arrivals, the well-to-do, and those barely getting by—showed up. The food ran out before the line did. People kept remarking that they couldn't remember an event with such a cross section of the island's population. "I'm seeing people I've never seen at the school," said Superintendent of Schools Bill Evans.

The school served another full-capacity crowd the following month (on what local Native Americans call the "Moon of the Opening Buds"), and every month during the school session since. Under the theme "Nourish Ourselves, Nourish Our Community," the meals are coordinated by the Lopez Locavores, whose mission is to create a sustainable local food system on the island. Their goals—"reconnect, revitalize, and sustain"—also reflect Lopez Island School's aim to use school food as a means to cultivate community as a key component of schooling for sustainability.

Practicing Island Intelligence

Community is central to what Hawaiian social entrepreneur James Koshiba calls 'island intelli-gence.' "As an island people," he says, "we have an intuitive understanding of the power and fragility of nature. We know that resources are limited, we know they can only be taxed and pushed to a certain degree, and we know they're shared."[41] Island people also know, experience, and respect economic and cultural diversity, he continues, and the world is entering an age in which island intelligence will be of greater value than perhaps in any other time in history.

That's the kind of thinking that drives schooling for sustainability at Lopez Island School, the only public school on Lopez, a 30-square-mile island with a population of two thousand. "We are a microcosm of a larger system," agrees Michele Heller. "There's more pressure on careful use of resources. There's a sense of wanting to support each other. We're more vulnerable than most, so

Fresh greens, ready to eat, from the school garden.

there's heightened awareness about the need to create local systems."

San Juan County, in which Lopez is located, has the highest housing costs and the lowest wages in Washington State.[42] Before huge public works projects irrigated the Columbia River Valley, Lopez was an important food supplier to the Puget Sound region. Apple and pear orchards still produce, but the fruit falls to the ground unpicked because there isn't enough market for it. Over the last two decades, the island has become a popular destination for wealthy and hyperwealthy immigrants from Microsoft, Boeing, and other Seattle-area companies, helping to drive up property values and drive out families and small-scale farms. Forty to forty-five percent of the school's students qualify for free or reduced-price meals. School enrollment is declining. Limited natural resources, especially water, affect the community, the economy, and the schools.

A Community Partnership for Farm to School

From the beginning, the local farm-to-school program, Lopez Island Farm Education (L.I.F.E.), has been a collaborative community project extending beyond the school district to include local agricultural institutions, the Lopez Community Land Trust, the Lopez Family Resource Center, and the Lopez Island Education Foundation.

The superintendent of schools signaled the L.I.F.E. program's importance to the community by serving as its chair, as well as serving on the board of the Lopez Community Land Trust, whose man-

dates combine land stewardship with affordable housing, renewable energy, and sustainable agriculture. On an island such as Lopez, with limited resources and land for development, the health of the schools is closely tied to the availability of housing that young families can afford.

Farm-to-school education at Lopez began at S & S Center for Sustainable Agriculture, about ten minutes from the school, where Henning Sehmsdorf and Elizabeth Simpson practice biodynamic farming. To them, growing food, facilitating education, and serving their community are inseparable. The farm is a Community Supported Agriculture (CSA) site. When one of its members repeatedly referred to CSA as "Consumer Subscription Agriculture," Sehmsdorf forcefully corrected him:

"I think you've misconstrued the term. It means community support. It's great that the vegetables are cheap, but we want you to be a subscriber because it's healthy for you, and it's a sustainable way of growing food in the community." In 2002, Sehmsdorf and Simpson proposed to teach ecological food production and supply a modest stream of fresh vegetables for the school cafeteria. When the district couldn't afford to support the program, they taught the course for free.

In 2006, Michele and Steve Heller, who own a 15-acre farm on Lopez, donated a 12 × 20 × 48-foot "high tower tunnel" greenhouse to the school to grow produce year round. It was erected at the S & S Center instead of the school because the water available on campus was insufficient.

(Island intelligence includes learning not to tap into groundwater at levels that exceed the amount recharged each year.)[43]

Believing that programs that depend wholly on volunteers are not sustainable, the Hellers also funded a paid staff position to create a farm-to-school program, which became L.I.F.E. Besides reviving the on-campus garden, which had fallen into disuse, the program sponsored training for food service staff and teachers with nationally prominent food educator Antonia Demas and organized a forum, open to the whole island, on local food.

Kindergarten through fifth-grade students now spend at least two sessions a week in the garden

Community dinners promote school food, support local farmers, and strengthen community connections.

and cooking classes, with lessons integrated into their regular curriculum. Every middle-school student gets his or her hands dirty, working in the school garden or the greenhouse. Meanwhile, students in Huck Phillips's Green Building and Design class are putting their lessons to use, working on a Lopez Community Land Trust project to build affordable housing with straw bale walls, wind power, and solar water heating and electricity. They're learning the fundamentals of green building firsthand, while making a much-appreciated contribution to their community.

Says Michele Heller, "The work that we're doing is about academics, but it's also about our connection to each other. We've tried every step to have the whole thing be about our relationships—to each other, other creatures, and the soil and the water that we use." Program leaders take care to consult everyone who will be affected by decisions. Before beginning the evening meal project, organizers conferred with local restaurants to avoid competing with them. They asked the head custodian for his recommendations for the garden program. No one, he replied, had ever

The school garden is a place of beauty and joy.

before asked his opinion when making maintenance or capital expense decisions.[44]

The school principal, lunchroom chefs, administrative staff, and community volunteers received financial support to attend Rethinking School Lunch and Educating for Sustainability seminars at the Center for Ecoliteracy. Supporting their attendance as a team was the best move their funder ever made, says food service director Dana Cotten. She returned more firmly committed to including organic and local food in school meals. As important, attending the seminars together, away from day-to-day responsibilities, deepened relationships and improved the L.I.F.E. team members' ability to work together.

A Standing Ovation for School Lunch

Improving food at the school has paid unexpected dividends. The number of adults buying lunch at the school doubled. Says Dana Cotten, "They will ask, 'Is this Lopez beef?' and they'll have it. All the people that used to get the veggie burgers now will have a regular hamburger, because it's Lopez beef." The track team, which went to the state meet, and the football team, which won its league title, publicly credited their success to the improved food. After a lunch of stir-fry teriyaki and campus-grown Asian greens, the football team gave the kitchen staff a spontaneous standing ovation—possibly a first in the history of school lunch.

The food service now purchases as much locally grown food as possible and pays market prices rather than asking local farmers to offer discounts (though some farmers do). The community has reciprocated. Money raised through donations at the evening meals has bought kitchenware, an industrial food processor, and other equipment for the school kitchen. Throughout the launch of the L.I.F.E. program, says Michele Heller, "So much money came to us in ways that we never expected. And so much came in the form of in-kind service—donations of equipment, topsoil, straw for the garden, manure, compost. Whatever we needed, it would appear. One of our local farms told us that we could have all the potatoes that we could get out of the field, so the little kids can go out and pick them. If you have something that is of benefit to others, and the time is right, then resources will flow to it."

A SWITCH IN TIME

What: John Muir Elementary School

Where: Berkeley, California

Initiators: Elementary school principal, then staff

Key Strategies: Reversing lunch and recess

                Teachers joining their classes in
                the lunchroom

                Counting lunch clean-up as class time

Before 2005, lunchtime at John Muir Elementary School in Berkeley, California, was not so different from most other schools. The nondescript, greasy, and calorie-heavy food had often traveled thousands of miles before arriving in preprocessed heat-and-serve "units" bearing corporate logos. For students, lunch was a detour on the way to their real goal: the playground.

Muir fifth-grade teacher Stephen Rutherford reports: "Children would claim to be done with their lunch in five minutes, with a huge amount of food waste, bag lunches uneaten, school lunches just tossed, because the only mind-set was to get out on the playground and have fun. Children would pour waste into this or that bin, in an atmosphere of chaos and neglect." Despite rushing through lunch, children spent as few as five or ten minutes playing during the thirty-five-minute lunch/recess because aides spent much of the time trying to calm them down and march them to the playground.

A former Muir teacher described the noisy lunchroom as, "Just not the place where you wanted to be." Tussling and shoving there carried over into bullying on the playground and sometimes into classes afterward.

No more. In 2004, Muir's principal learned of plans to launch the Berkeley School Lunch Initiative (SLI), a collaboration of the school district, the Chez Panisse Foundation, and the Center for Ecoliteracy to implement curriculum and food service innovations. Though it was summer, she urged teachers to attend the first meeting and make John Muir an SLI pilot school.

The enthusiastic Muir representatives generated lots of ideas for improving lunch, but many of them—

such as overhauling the district food service or radically redesigning the lunchroom—were expensive, time-consuming, or out of their control. They needed a starting place, something they could do themselves that didn't require extra money but had high visibility and prospects for early success.

Muir representatives attended a series of SLI workshops offered by the Center for Ecoliteracy. At one, they reviewed research that found those elementary students who ate after recess were more focused, behaved better in the lunchroom, wasted less food, and consumed more vitamins and minerals (see "The Healthy Results of Reversing Lunch and Recess").[45]

In 2005, Muir made the reversal, and added ten minutes to the lunch period. Having exercised, and with no incentive to rush through their food, children began to eat more, drink more water at lunch, and throw away less. The new schedule also prompted less-expected changes. Many schools—faced with mandates to raise test scores—are reducing time for both physical education and meals, despite evidence that children who exercise and eat well can learn more. With the schedule change, Muir students spent more time playing *and* more time eating than before. Playground supervisors reported less fighting. Students returned to class ready to learn. "I never have students coming back into the classroom angry and upset," as they had before, says one teacher.

Clean-up Time Is Teaching Time

The changes didn't stop with scheduling. The district food service also began to improve. Previous reform efforts had foundered as teachers be-

came cynical about promises of better food. Said one, "The mantra was, 'Why are we doing this? It's counterproductive. We teach children about healthy eating, and then they go to lunch, and get the chocolate milk and predone hot dog.'" Seeing the food actually improving made teachers more willing to support other changes.

More teachers began eating in the lunchroom, but even those who didn't began joining their classes for the last ten minutes of lunch and clean-up. This ten minutes is designated as instructional time, a precious commodity in the face of pressures to devote more minutes to subjects covered on standardized tests.

Starting in first grade, students learn to clean their plates into gray bins ("recycling"), green bins ("compost"), and galvanized cans (labeled "landfill" to remind students that whatever they throw "away" goes somewhere). These distinctions are now part of Muir's vocabulary, lessons, and practice. "Even the kids who are bringing lunch aren't just throwing things into the landfill," reported a first-grade teacher. "They're taking them back to reuse them. And they want to reuse their little baggies."

Changing the Structure Requires School-wide Buy-In

Inspired individual teachers can make a difference, but school-wide innovation almost always depends on a core of committed faculty and staff members as well as the support of the principal. "If we're going to do this," said Muir staff, "it has to be our initiative. Not the Berkeley School Lunch Initiative. This has to be the John Muir School Lunch Initiative."

Making the plan work required the cooperation of the full Muir staff, including custodians, playground and lunchroom aides, and others it affected. While preparing to present the plan, faculty members realized that Muir's "staff" meetings were usually held at times when only teachers could attend. They went to considerable effort to schedule meetings when the full staff could come and worked to get everyone, including parents, to the meetings.

"If we hadn't done that," says Rutherford, "I don't think that the staff would have weathered the program's rocky start, because, of course, our first plan needed tweaking, really fast." Staff and students were confronted with substantial new responsibilities, in a system being designed on the fly. Then the plan had to be *redesigned* when the county waste management authority revised its own procedures.

Not everyone supported the changes; Muir had to negotiate a special "side agreement" with the teachers union after one teacher filed a complaint over designating part of lunch as instructional time. The "tweaking" took several months, but the staff stuck with the program because it had agreed that the changes were important and committed to them.

The lunchtime innovations built on Muir's longtime dedication to hands-on experience. Every class, kindergarten through fifth grade, regularly spends time in a lovely instructional garden built by students and in a cooking classroom. Classroom teachers use garden and kitchen experiences to teach topics from math to history.

With this start, the Center for Ecoliteracy secured a grant from the S. D. Bechtel, Jr. Foundation to pre-

THE HEALTHY RESULTS OF REVERSING LUNCH AND RECESS

In a Western Washington University study, elementary students who ate lunch after recess:

• Ate more fruit, vegetables, and milk

• Wasted 30 percent less food by weight

• Ate 14 percent more iron

• Consumed 35 percent more calcium

• Consumed 13 percent more vitamin A

Source: Ethan A. Bergman et al., "Relationships of Meal and Recess Schedules to Plate Waste in Elementary Schools," *Insight* 24 (Spring 2004), p. 5.

parc for more deeply integrating the curriculum around food, health, culture, and the environment. Dr. Carolie Sly, now the Center's education program director, introduced the project at a Muir faculty meeting. The principal asked for planning team volunteers to participate on their own time. "I think he was shocked," Sly reported, "when more than half the faculty volunteered."

Change often comes slowly, especially in public schools. As in any organization, some members embrace change more eagerly than others. Even for supporters, enthusiasm can wane after years of only modest progress. Still, the major structural innovations begun by the simple act of switching lunch and recess are now considered "just the way things are" at John Muir Elementary.

Recycle, compost, or landfill? Cleaning up after eating is a time to learn.

LESSONS LEARNED FROM

- Changing food systems structures and practices will probably take at least three years.

- Establishing policies helps keep changes in place when activists move on.

- Introducing food-based education in the garden gets students involved quickly in hands-on activities with easy-to-experience results.

- Gardens are usually more effective when they're the "property" of the whole school, rather than one classroom.

- A teacher shouldn't be expected to oversee the garden—scheduling, maintenance, and so on—on top of a full teaching load. Freeing someone (it could be a reliable volunteer) from other responsibilities improves the chances that the garden will continue after the initial enthusiasm wears off. Someone needs to maintain the garden during weekends or school breaks.

FOOD SYSTEMS EFFORTS

● Inviting the local community into the garden makes it a local resource and increases security. School gardens with unlocked gates often experience less vandalism and theft than those that bar the neighbors.

● When teachers participate with their students in garden and cooking classes, the educational value increases.

● Roaming chickens, rabbits in hutches, beautiful flowers, medicinal plants, and plants that attract pollinators to gardens enhance the garden experience.

● Food service success depends on knowing and satisfying its "customers'" desires and preferences. Offering taste tests before introducing new menu items is crucial.

● The ambience of the lunchroom can make a difference in attracting students.

WHAT YOU

● Experience lunch at your school. Is the food healthy and appealing? Is the lunchroom atmosphere conducive to good eating? What are children "learning" from the food and its presentation?

● Read your district's wellness policy. Does it reflect your beliefs and hopes? If you have concerns about school food, who else (parents, students, teachers, nurses, administrators, board members, health or waste management agencies, civic organizations) shares them? Agree to work together.

● Identify the levels of authority responsible for the areas that concern you. Who can make the changes that matter most to you?

CAN DO

- Meet with the district's food service director. Ask how you can help. Be persistent. Be polite. Listen, but be clear that you're not going away.

- Start a garden. They're highly visible and popular. They also allow community members and businesses to engage by making donations in the form of cash, services, or in-kind contributions.

- Identify the farm-to-school lead agency for your region and investigate programs, such as Harvest of the Month, to introduce fresh foods into your school.

- Rethink the school day. Imagine a schedule with recess before lunch, adequate time to eat lunch, and quiet time after lunch.

- Start a composting program for lunchroom "waste." If you have a garden, use kitchen and table scraps to enrich its soil.

- Support legislation to get junk food and commercial advertising off school campuses.

CHAPTER 3

THE SMART BY NATURE CAMPUS

We shape our buildings, and afterwards our buildings shape us.

—Winston Churchill

The campus begins to teach before a student or visitor ever walks into a classroom. It is the most visible symbol of the school's relationship with the natural world. That symbol can be dramatic: the 2,358 photovoltaic panels covering rooftops and the hillside behind San Domenico School in San Anselmo, California; the Living Machine for natural wastewater treatment at Darrow School in New Lebanon, New York; the living roof at the Tarkington School of Excellence in Chicago.

Less dramatic but no less important symbols and tools for teaching include school gardens, on-campus habitats, publicly accessible energy meters, and recycling containers placed next to trash cans labeled "landfill." The campus can communicate that the school is a fortress designed to keep kids in and the rest of the world out—or it can reveal itself as a place of wonder that draws children to appreciate their relatedness to the world.

Schools take in energy and resources, which they use, transform, recycle, or discharge into the systems that surround them. By the materials they use; the suppliers and other organizations they support; and the pollution, waste, and greenhouse emissions they generate or eliminate, schools make those larger systems either more or less sustainable. Schools impact the environment through the resources and energy needed to transport people to them, the open space they occupy, and the burden they place (or reduce) on community infrastructure, such as water systems.

Healthy school ecosystems are healthy for the people who study and work in them. A substantial body of research connects daylighting, air quality, temperature, acoustics, ventilation, and other elements of the campus environment with students' and teachers' short- and long-term health, ability to learn, productivity, and performance.[1]

Designed and operated with imagination, a Smart by Nature campus becomes a place where learning about sustainability comes alive, where the school manifests its respect for the environment and its commitment to the stewardship of resources. It serves as a laboratory for exploring solutions to twenty-first-century environmental problems, a model of sustainable practice, and

an inspiration to the surrounding community and to other institutions. This chapter looks at the campus from five related perspectives: design and construction, how campuses teach, green and healthy schools, provisions and purchasing, and money matters.

Design and Construction

Buildings account for one-third of the total energy, two-thirds of the electricity, and one-eighth of the water used in the United States. School construction is the largest construction sector of the economy, with more than $33 billion spent annually by K–12 schools.[2] The nation's public school districts spend more than $8 billion annually on energy alone—more than they spend on computers and textbooks combined.

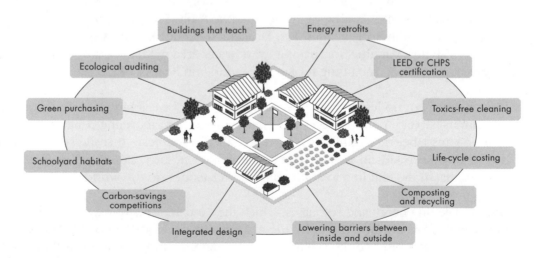

GREENING THE CAMPUS

Buildings that teach · Energy retrofits · Ecological auditing · LEED or CHPS certification · Green purchasing · Toxics-free cleaning · Schoolyard habitats · Life-cycle costing · Carbon-savings competitions · Composting and recycling · Integrated design · Lowering barriers between inside and outside

The campus offers multiple opportunities for schools to demonstrate sustainable practices that also become vivid lessons for students.

Smart by Nature

The standards of the two primary programs that evaluate green school design and construction– LEED for Schools[3] and the Collaborative for High Performance Schools (CHPS)[4] (see sidebar)—offer an instructive overview of the many elements of a sustainable campus. Their ratings apply only to new construction and major modifications but can provide a snapshot of current thinking about what constitutes a green, sustainable, or "high-performance" school.

CHPS defines a high-performance school as one that protects the environment, reduces operating costs, and enhances teaching and learning. The attributes CHPS considers include:[5]

- ● Healthy

- Thermally, visually, and acoustically comfortable

- Efficient use of energy, materials, and water

- Easy to maintain and operate

- Commissioned (a process for checking the efficiency of building systems during design and construction)

- A teaching tool

- ● Environmentally responsive

- Safe and secure

- A community resource

- Stimulating architecture

Anyone interested in specifics can access the detailed LEED for Schools and CHPS manuals,

LEED AND CHPS: WHAT ARE THEY?

Sidwell Friends School in Washington, D.C., where Sasha and Malia Obama attend, proclaims that it is "the first K–12 school in the United States to have a LEED Platinum rating." The Los Angeles Unified School District boasts that it was the first California district to adopt the standards of the Collaborative for High Performance Schools (CHPS). What exactly does that mean?

The Leadership in Energy and Environmental Design (LEED) program of the U.S. Green Building Council and the Collaborative for High Performance Schools (CHPS) are voluntary programs that rate the greenness of major construction projects. Both systems were developed in conjunction with educators, industry professionals, government agencies, and nongovernmental organizations. They award points (up to 79 for LEED for Schools, 116 for CHPS) according to benchmarks for health, safety, and sustainability. For instance, buildings must meet a minimum level of energy efficiency, and they earn additional points for exceeding that standard. Schools can receive points for water-efficient landscaping, low-flow bathroom fixtures, locating near public transportation, providing bike racks or preferred parking for carpools, and so on. LEED certification is granted at "Certified," "Silver," "Gold," and "Platinum" levels based on the total points earned. CHPS certification is about the equivalent of LEED Silver.

It is possible to create a brilliantly green campus without ever considering CHPS or LEED, but their seal of approval often matters to schools and districts that care about reputation and compete for attention, students, and funding. The programs' criteria are similar, but different enough that schools usually choose to apply for just one rather than invest time and money in pursuing both.[6]

available on their websites. To give some sense of the weight given to different concerns, about half of the possible LEED and CHPS points awarded concern energy efficiency and indoor environmental quality. A quarter take into consideration construction and materials, waste management, and sustainable sites (including transportation, stormwater, joint use of facilities, and school gardens).

LEED or CHPS certification verifies that school sites and buildings were designed, constructed, and evaluated according to detailed standards. What matters next is what happens once the campus opens, and what students learn about sustainability from it.

How Campuses Teach

Properly understood, the campus can act as both the classroom and the lesson. Schools discussed here consciously incorporate their campuses into the curriculum.

The best school design includes a deeper knowledge of place, considering architecture, landscaping, and open space appropriate to the history and geography of the site. Planners for Willow School, for example, conducted a survey of their New Jersey region and then constructed the campus using materials and methods described in historical documents discovered in their research.

Landscaping can invite students to explore and learn before they even enter the building. Environmental educator Herbert W. Broda calls the outdoors "the most powerful audio-visual tool around."[7] Some schools, such as the School of Environmental Studies in Minnesota, are within walking distance of wild places that become de facto extensions of the campus, but even city schools can incorporate nature through gardens and on-campus habitats.[8]

Instead of a grass lawn on its Washington, D.C., middle school campus, Sidwell Friends constructed a wetland, pond, and water garden. The wetland adds nature to the campus, treats and recycles water from the school's kitchen and bathrooms (helping to cut the school's use of municipal water by 90 percent), and serves as a hands-on lab for learning biology, ecology, and chemistry. A living roof captures rainfall, moderates the temperature inside buildings, and teaches about nature's cycles. Urban schools that lack financial resources can still create natural oases of nature in the schoolyard; share space with city parks, as at Tarkington School of Excellence in Chicago; or even design science lessons around plants growing through cracks in the asphalt.[9]

"You can build a gorgeous green building," says Bryant, Arkansas, assistant superintendent Debbie Bruick. But "kids will never notice it if you do not teach them why it was done the way it was done." Willow School posts signs around the campus noting building elements made of recycled materials. Displays on the wall proclaim that Tarkington is the first green school in Illinois. Parents and teachers and siblings mention it. But what does it mean to be green? What purposes do the floors made with recycled glass, waterless urinals, rooftop garden, and white reflective roof serve? Those questions provide springboards for investigating conservation, water cycles, reflection and absorption, urban heat islands, the relationship of building temperature to ozone production, and related subjects. The green campus isn't necessary for studying these topics, but the lessons become more real when they grow out of curiosity sparked by students' experiences.

Green campus features and practices allow a school to demonstrate that it means what it says about sustainable living and to inspire students to join the effort. The Living Machine at Darrow School isn't the least expensive way to treat wastewater, but this valuable resource teaches students about accepting responsibility for the waste they and their school generate.

Other schools leave conduits, ducts, and other structural elements exposed so students can understand how sustainable buildings work. Some offer real-time measurements of energy, water, or resource use, accessed through centrally located monitors or from students' computers, as at Northfield Mount Hermon School in Massachusetts.

Students really come to understand their school's sustainable features when they become tour leaders for visitors or create Web pages and presentations to explain the campus to other students. Green Team members at Tarkington, in the Bryant schools, and elsewhere teach other students—and their teachers—when they supervise recycling, patrol for left-on lights and computers, or brainstorm about saving resources and energy.

Student research can also shape the campus. Northfield Mount Hermon banned dorm minifridges on the basis of a physics class's study of campus energy use. A sustainability audit by staff and students can serve as a tool for planning, goal setting, and measuring progress. It's also an opportunity to learn how sustainability issues arise in day-to-day decisions, and to deliberate about responses that will have the largest impacts.

Green and Healthy Schools

Just as school food bridges individuals' health and community sustainability, so do campus health concerns. A sustainable society protects its most vulnerable members. Schools with the most health problems are often in the poorest neighborhoods, making healthy schools a matter of environmental justice. Harmful products such as toxic cleaning supplies, pesticides, and asbestos make their way into the water, air, and food web on which plant and animal life depend. For these

A wall plaque that teaches while reminding students of their school's commitment to sustainability.

The insulation in the interior and exterior walls of this building is natural cotton fiber insulation. It is made from 100% natural cotton fibers, 85% of which is recycled. The cotton plant is a rapidly renewable building material, planted and harvested within a ten year cycle.

and other reasons, many champions of sustainable schools now phrase their objective as "green and healthy schools."[10]

Schools present particular challenges. The fifty-five million students and more than six million adults in U.S. schools typically spend 85 to 90 percent of their time indoors, where the concentration of pollutants is as much as 10 to 100 times higher than outdoors. Children breathe, eat, and drink more per pound of body weight than adults. Exposures and injuries at a young age can disrupt normal development. Schools, more densely occupied and used more hours a week than most offices, require more cleaning and maintenance.

Administrators and parents for whom "sustainability" seems an abstraction will often respond to campus health issues. "When administrators are handing out pink slips to teachers," says Green Schools Initiative executive director Deborah Moore, "they don't care to talk about recycling or what kind of paper or dye they're using. But health falls under their responsibilities for keeping kids safe at school. We're not going to talk to parents in East L.A. about polar bears and global warming, but we can talk to them about asthma in the community and chemicals that their kids are exposed to, and that can lead to saving energy and less toxic pollution."

CAMPUS HEALTH ISSUES

- Custodians and teachers experience some of the highest rates of occupational asthma.

- An average janitor uses 23 gallons of cleaning products a year. Twenty-five percent of the chemicals in cleaning products used in schools are toxic and contribute to poor indoor air quality, smog, cancer, asthma, and other diseases.

- Of the forty-eight pesticides most commonly used in schools, the EPA classifies twenty-two as possible or probable carcinogens.

- Six out of one hundred custodians are injured each year. Twenty percent of the injuries are serious burns to the skin or eyes. Twelve percent are the result of inhaling chemical vapors.

- In the United States, 9.9 million children under the age of eighteen have been diagnosed with asthma. Children between the ages of five and seventeen miss nearly fifteen million days of school a year because of asthma. Children in low-income families are 30 to 50 percent more likely to have respiratory problems.

- More than 25 percent of children attend structurally substandard or dangerous schools.

Sources: U.S. Environmental Protection Agency, Green Schools Initiative, National Collaborative Work Group on Green Cleaning and Chemical Policy Reform in Schools, Planet Green, Centers for Disease Control and Prevention, "Greening America's Schools: Costs and Benefits."

Provisions and Purchasing

Not every school or district will undertake new construction or major renovations, but every school will buy office and school supplies, cleaners, pesticides, fertilizers, food, playground equipment, vehicles. The billions of dollars spent and the millions of tons of materials that pass through schools provide opportunities for schools to act sustainably and teach through their actions.

Per capita waste generation in the United States is twice that of any other country, and the amount of garbage we produce is rising. The Environmental Protection Agency estimates that within five years, one-third of all landfills in the nation will reach capacity.[11] The Oregon Resource Efficiency Program calculates that each student in the state produces about 240 pounds of waste per year.[12] California schools collectively dispose of more than 750,000 tons of waste yearly, of which nearly half is paper and another quarter organic material.[13] A campus trash audit is an eye-opening exercise that offers students immediate feedback about the school's contribution to its community's waste stream and provides a baseline for redesigning the school's waste management system.

Recycling is an obvious response and is a popular step toward sustainable action on many campuses, but the sustainability theme song is still "Reduce, Reuse, Recycle," in that order. For example, first find replacements for paper (electronic memos and email newsletters, online writing assignments), then write on both sides of the sheets of paper you do use, and then recycle used paper and purchase paper made with post-consumer waste.

When it comes time to buy, many schools exercise "environmentally preferable purchasing."

The EPA defines "environmentally preferable" as "products or services that have a lesser or reduced effect on human health and the environment when compared with competing products or services that serve the same purpose."[14] That definition implies that "effects" are always bad and should be minimized. In fact, the enormous collective purchasing power of schools can also create markets for products that benefit the environment, create jobs, and raise the quality of life of communities.

Products are rarely completely virtuous or completely undesirable.[15] When considering a purchase, ask:

● What are the environmental and social impacts over the lifetime of the product or service?

● Is the product reusable or more durable?

● Is there an available product with recycled content that performs just as well?

● Does it conserve energy or water?

● Is it less hazardous than alternatives?

● What happens at the end of its life? Can it be recycled? Will the manufacturer take the product back? Will it need special disposal?

● Is a similar product grown or produced locally?

● Under what conditions is it grown, extracted, or manufactured? Are the people who produced it fairly compensated?

As environmentally preferable purchasing becomes more prevalent, resources proliferate. The Green Schools Initiative's "Green Schools Buying Guide" contains information on a wide range of products, tips on buying green, and sample purchasing policies.[16] Among other agencies, the U.S. EPA[17] and the California Integrated Waste Management Board[18] supply extensive information. A number of organizations, such as the Green Purchasing Cooperative Program at Rutgers University,[19] offer advice to K–12 schools or permit schools to purchase through them.

Money Matters

Studies repeatedly show that campus greening, especially reducing energy, water, and resource use, is cost-effective, often within a short time. According to the U.S. Department of Energy, an energy-efficient school district with 4,000 students could save $1.6 million in energy costs over ten years.[20] Ohio's School Facilities Commission, after determining that it could save $1.4 billion in energy costs on schools it was rebuilding, adopted a resolution requiring all future school buildings to achieve LEED certification.

It doesn't matter how much a project can save in the long run, though, if it never gets built. In a tough economy, schools need creative strategies for campus greening.[21] The Green Schools Initiative's "Greenbacks for Green Schools"[22] and the U.S. Department of Energy's "Guide to Financing EnergySmart Schools"[23] outline a variety of options for new construction and for retrofits. Among them:

Begin with efficiency. The easiest way to "raise" money is not to need it. The Department of Energy estimates that simple technological and behavioral changes—such as turning off computers, copiers, and lights when not in use—can reduce energy use by as much as 33 percent.

Raise funds internally. Sometimes greening enhances fundraising, enabling schools to tap alums who have not given previously. Some schools create revolving investment funds in which savings from green projects are earmarked for future projects.

Consider grants and loans. Besides such expected government sources as the Department of Energy, other sources offer funds, including the Homeland Security Grant Program for buildings that can be used by the public in case of a disaster. Many local utilities offer reduced-interest loans, rebates, and technical assistance for energy savings. North Carolina State University maintains an extensive database of state, local, federal, and utility grants and incentives.[24]

Explore leases or power-purchase agreements. A private firm installed the 412 kW photovoltaic system at San Domenico School in California. It sells the energy generated by the system to the school at a rate lower than the local utility's. The company paid the up-front costs, and the school gets 85 percent of its electricity through solar energy—while reducing its energy costs.[25] Private companies can often take advantage of tax credits that schools, which do not pay taxes, cannot.

Enter into performance contracts. Many schools have found it worthwhile to hire a high-performance or energy expert to navigate the

Right: Moving to greener energy sources (here, photovoltaic panels) saves money over time while benefiting the environment.

requirements of incentive programs or to negotiate performance contracts or lease-purchase agreements. With or without such help, a school may enter into an agreement with a company that will guarantee energy savings over a specified period. On the basis of that guarantee, the district can take out a loan or sell bonds, to be repaid from the savings.

Consider expenses and benefits from a different perspective. Overcoming perceived cost obstacles sometimes requires shifts in perspective that characterize systems thinking, which many schools are not used to or structured to support.

One shift is from minimizing first costs to optimizing life-cycle costs—from focusing on getting the building up and the kids through the doors to weighing the expenses of operations, insurance, maintenance, and ultimately replacing worn-out equipment and structures. Emphasis on first costs reflects fragmented thinking that is reinforced by the school system organization. Capital and operating budgets are usually segregated into different departments, included in the job descriptions of different administrators, and funded from separate sources.

"For every dollar you put in to move toward grid neutrality or higher energy efficiency," says California State Architect David Thorman, "you're going to save ten to twenty dollars on the operating side over time. If you were a business you would look at it from that standpoint. Unfortunately, schools don't look at it that way. They look at it in terms of, if you take a dollar away from my operating side and put it into building, that's a dollar out of our teachers' salaries."[26]

The logic of life-cycle costing seems unassailable. In practice, superintendents and business managers will come and go during the life of a school. Architects are rewarded for minimizing first costs. Cash is tight today; tomorrow's costs are hidden. It takes foresight to make decisions with benefits that will not be realized for decades. Software programs are available for estimating life-cycle costs, including free programs from the Federal Energy Management Program.[27] Says Willow School's Mark Biedron, "Whoever is going to be head of school here in 50 years, when I'm dead and buried, is going to say, 'Thank you very much. Because you spent money on a stainless steel roof and built with a stone exterior, I don't have to replace them now.' But it's just so hard to convince people of that."

A second shift is to integrated design, a "whole building" approach applied in Bryant, Arkansas, and elsewhere. This process convenes stakeholders to consider the project and its components and technologies as an interconnected system. When employed as early in the process as possible, it optimizes efficiency, cost, and the building's effect on teachers and students.

A third shift is to look at the total costs and benefits to the wider community. A much-quoted 2006 study, "Greening America's Schools: Costs and Benefits," analyzed thirty schools in ten states built to LEED or CHPS standards between 2001 and 2006. It dramatically concluded that green schools cost on average less than 2 percent more than conventional schools to build, but provide financial benefits twenty times as large.[28]

The additional costs of building green, such as more expensive (but often more durable) materials, more complex mechanical systems, and additional costs for design and planning, ranged from zero to 6.27 percent, with an average of 1.65 percent, or about $3 per square foot. A more extensive 2008 survey of nearly 150 green school and office buildings yielded similar results: a median "green premium" of 1.6 percent (members of the public polled in this study estimated the added costs of building green to be 10 times as high).[29]

For the $3 per square foot invested in up-front costs, the 2006 study calculated the following benefits, projected over twenty years (a conservative estimate given that school buildings are typically in service forty years or more):

Energy	$9
Emissions	$1
Water and wastewater	$1
Asthma reduction	$3
Cold and flu reduction	$5
Teacher retention	$4
Employment impact	$2
Increased earnings	$49
Total	$74

The largest payoffs came from projecting increased earnings by graduates who would learn more, score higher on tests, and get better jobs. Those numbers are, of course, speculative, but the energy and water savings alone are more than three times the expenditure for building green.

Many other benefits—from lower health care costs to reduced demand on water systems to higher tax revenues—accrue to the community as a whole rather than to the school. Still other benefits include fewer teacher sick days, lower insurance risks, reduced social inequity, educational enrichment, less air and water pollution, and the creation of more green collar jobs. The fact that we don't normally consider such factors in the economics of school campuses says less about their importance than about the inadequacy of the metrics we use to measure our collective well-being and, ultimately, the sustainability of our society.

A BEACON FOR SUSTAINABILITY

What: Willow School

Where: Gladstone, New Jersey

Initiators: Two parents

Key Strategies: The inside flows out; the outside flows in
                 Buildings that teach
                 The woods are the playground
                 Design that gives back to the
                     environment

While explaining her intentions for the design of Willow School, cofounder Gretchen Biedron brought the campus architects to their knees. Literally. She wanted to ensure that the view through the windows in the new building would help children connect to the woods outside. "I didn't want the children to see clouds and treetops," she says. "I wanted them to see the chipmunk running to the tree. 'Sit down or kneel on the ground,' I told the architects. 'Okay, we get it,' they said. 'No, no, go ahead and get down. Now you know what it's like to be a kindergartner. Your perspective has to be from this angle.'"

Breaking down separations between inside and outside (as well as seeing the world through others' eyes) permeates the approach of Willow, an independent K–8 school in Gladstone, New Jersey. Each classroom has many tall windows and opens to the outdoors. "We go in and out a lot," says Head of School Kate Walsh. "The buildings are designed so that the inside flows out and the outside is brought in." Students spend as much time outdoors as possible. The school has no playground with swings and climbing walls; the kids play in the woods.

Willow School boasts one of the greenest campuses in the country, including Gold and Platinum LEED-rated buildings that are constructed mostly from salvaged material and honor regional history. Buildings use up to 70 percent less energy than codes require, wastewater is treated in a constructed wetland, materials and design optimize indoor air quality and minimize

Right: Lots of windows, natural daylighting, and views of the outdoors help students feel connected to nature even when they're inside.

noise and light pollution. Buildings teach earth stewardship and sustainability.

Care for the earth–not initially part of the school's mission–emerged organically through a series of aha! experiences. Mark and Gretchen Biedron founded Willow in 2000 after finding no school that offered the combination they wanted for their children: academic excellence, joy of learning, mastery of language, and a focus on virtues and ethical living. They purchased a 34-acre site on former farmland in the region of New Jersey where Gretchen had grown up.

The first aha!, says Mark Biedron, "was to realize that if we're going to mentor ethical relationships between humans, we can't do that without mentoring an ethical relationship with nature, because it's all one. We need to show the children that we care about the earth as much as we care about each other. What does that mean, we asked, and started reading people like William McDonough and David W. Orr."

At the beginning, recalls Gretchen, "I told the landscape architect, 'This is not about the environment. This is about academic excellence.' But I started to think about why I'm here and doing what I'm doing. I love this place, the way the air feels, the way the weather patterns move in and

A bathroom partition that teaches.

The partitions in this bathroom are 100% recycled and are made from approximately 6,728 plastic detergent bottles fabricated in Scranton, PA

out, and the way the birds sound. It's very visceral for me. This is part of why I'm doing this, and these things aren't separate at all. They're inextricably intertwined."

Although construction drawings for the first new building were already 75 percent complete, the founders told the architect and engineer, "Take a two-month time-out. Then come back and tell us what it's going to take to meet sustainability standards."

For every construction material, says Mark Biedron, "we determined whether we could buy salvaged. If we couldn't, could we buy it new but with a huge recycled content? Can we recycle it once this building is demolished? And we considered what it is made of. What's the environmental impact when it's manufactured and thrown away?"[30]

Kate Walsh compares sourcing the building materials to a scavenger hunt. Douglas fir for doors and windows was salvaged from dismantled vinegar vats at a Heinz ketchup factory. Ceiling tiles were made from old newspapers and computer printouts. Framing came from abandoned harbor pilings, posts, and beams from a cotton mill in North Carolina and a toothpick factory in Maine. The few trees that had to be cleared to make space for the building were crafted by Amish furniture makers into classroom desks and chairs. Light posts are discarded telephone poles. The school's stonemason made curbing from granite disposed of at a Connecticut Turnpike cloverleaf. Bluestone was retrieved from sidewalks being demolished for Boston's "Big Dig" tunnel megaproject.

The design team also initiated an in-depth regional survey: What was here before? How did New

Jersey's first people, the Lenape Indians, address erosion, soil management, and crop generation? What patterns and recurring themes from this place can be brought into the campus design and curriculum?

Willow's builders clad the first building in limestone, because historical records showed that limestone was once milled in Gladstone. They patterned buildings on old barns that had characterized western New Jersey and eastern Pennsylvania. They built according to plans uncovered by their research, down to constructing entirely with mortise and tenon joinery, using no nails or metal in the buildings' superstructures.

Build It and It Will Teach

The next big aha! was the realization, as David W. Orr writes, that "buildings have their own hidden curriculum that teaches as effectively as any course taught in them."[31] The Willow team was determined to expose students to the campus's design and systems. Signs posted throughout the campus announce things like, "The partitions in this bathroom are 100% recycled and are made from approximately 6,728 plastic detergent bottles fabricated in Scranton, PA." A window cut into an interior wall reveals the cotton fiber insulation inside—mostly recycled blue jeans. Mechanical, plumbing, and photovoltaic systems connect to a monitor in the school's lobby, so students can observe the real-time state of the systems and see the consequences of using water or turning lights or air conditioning on and off. Students participate actively in systems that collaborate with nature. When the outside temperature is between 65 and 80 degrees, heating and air conditioning systems shut down and green lights flash in classrooms, alerting students to open the windows.

Giving Back to the Earth

"Our next aha!," says Mark Biedron, "was to ask whether doing less bad is good enough." They wanted to move beyond minimizing damage to the environment, to engage in practices that replace the degeneration of past practices—a philosophy called "regenerative design."[32] "As designers in the field are increasingly prepared to acknowledge, our design practices not only need to do no harm, they must initiate regenerative processes to replace the degeneration resulting from past practices," argues the Regenerative Design Institute. "We envision humans as a positive, healing presence on Earth, creating more abundance on the planet than would be possible without them."[33] Hundreds of years of farming on the school site had left an unhealthy forest with invasive species on the floor and badly depleted topsoil. The school has since replaced turf grass, planted some 60,000 drought-resistant native grasses and perennials, helped to build topsoil, created habitat, and encouraged the forest's natural succession toward greater species diversity and long-term prospects for evolutionary health.

The school's water recycling and treatment system combines twenty-first-century technology with natural processes that conserve water and soil and create habitat. Rainwater falling on 95 percent recycled stainless steel roofs is collected in a 57,000-gallon, recycled-plastic tank, disinfected with ozone, and used for irrigation and flushing toilets. Wastewater flows to a constructed wetland (the first in New Jersey), where hydroponically grown plants clean it before it is pumped back onto the site through an infiltration field.

Willow intends that all storm water be recharged into groundwater onsite. Vegetated swales of deep-rooted grasses and perennials have largely replaced curbing on roads, creating a natural "sponge" that slows down water, cleans it, and opens up soil. Any runoff flows to a constructed marsh wetland whose evolution students are chronicling. Each year students inventory invertebrate species, which are indicators of wetland health, comparing their findings with previous years' observations. They share their data online with students around the world, allowing the students to participate as scientists in a long-term study of wetland evolution that will remain as a legacy when they graduate.

Willow's work has opened the way for innovative practices in its region. When Mark Biedron went to state officials for approval of the water management system, "The first guy whose office I sit down in looks at me and goes, 'You're going to treat septic water in a plant bed in a pool? Don't even talk to me.' He basically threw me out of his office." Eventually, at considerable expense, they got their approval, and demonstrated the value of the system. A while later, leaders from Duke Farms visited the school, were impressed, and decided that they too wanted to become a "beacon of sustainability." When they sought approval for their systems, "The guy looked at him and said, 'Is this the same one as the Willow School has?' and he said, 'It's going to be exactly the same.' 'No problem, then, go right ahead.'"

An on-campus wetland and pond make studying science an adventure.

A Continuum of Consequences

Rather than give students "do this" or "don't do that" absolutes, Willow's founders want them to understand consequences and then take responsibility for their actions and decisions. They practice that philosophy as well. Green building is a compromise, says Mark Biedron. Take for example the seemingly counterintuitive decision to install synthetic rather than natural turf playing fields on their very green campus. Biedron knows that people have raised serious health and environmental questions about synthetic turf, but he says that his research convinced him that it is on the whole better for students and the environment in his school's geographical location.

"If you mow and play on a turf field for two years," he says, "it's basically as impervious as a gravel driveway. When it rains, the water sheets off and ends up creating erosion and downstream pollution. Then there's fertilizer, pesticides, herbicides, pollution from two-stroke combustion mowers, and the water it takes to keep that thing green and shaped so you can play on it. Our field recharges local groundwater 100 percent better than a natural turf, because the turf matting is perforated with holes and underneath is about 20 inches of gravel, so when it rains, water slowly percolates into the ground. We have to figure out how to make the synthetic turf better with better materials. I couldn't argue that. It's not natural grass, but is it safer than natural grass? The studies I've seen show it's much safer."

Ethics, Ecology, and Place-based Learning

The curriculum weaves together challenging academics, ethical grounding, ecological awareness, place-based learning, and hands-on experience. When Biedron and Willow's landscape architect Anthony Sblendorio describe the goals of the curriculum, they use a systems-thinking vocabulary: "learning to recognize patterns, understand relationships, and make connections."[34]

Each grade level is organized around an academic theme, a virtues theme, and an environmental theme. Themes begin with the self in kindergarten (linked with the virtues of joy and respect and the environmental theme of trees). They spiral outward to community (wonder and patience, seeds) in first grade, diversity (gratitude and generosity, soil) in second grade, place (stewardship and loyalty, habitat) in third, up to patterns and systems (responsibility and wisdom, Earth) in eighth grade. History, social studies, science, music, art, and the rest of the curriculum hang on that framework (described in detail at www.willowschool.org/academics/curriculum.pdf).

The final aha!, says Mark Biedron, was that "we've done a really lousy job of telling our children over the past seventy-five years what it takes to live on this planet. It's important to teach kids two plus two and history and social studies, but if we don't teach them how that applies to living on the planet and the alignment with the systems that support us, we're not doing our job."

GREENING CHICAGO, ONE SCHOOL AT A TIME

What: Tarkington School of Excellence

Where: Chicago, Illinois

Initiators: Mayor and board of education

Key Strategies: Green urban campus spurs curriculum
                     Living roof
                     School–park district collaboration

Under Mayor Richard M. Daley, Chicago (whose motto is *Urbs in Horto*, "City in a Garden") is committed to becoming "the most environmentally friendly city in the world," with a mandate to achieve Leadership in Energy and Environmental Design (LEED) certification for all new city facilities, including new schools. Tarkington School of Excellence, a public pre-K–8 school in Marquette Park, an ethnically diverse, industrial neighborhood in Southwest Chicago, opened in 2005 as the first embodiment of this intention.

The features that make Tarkington healthier for students and better for the environment are important. As important is the greening throughout the curriculum that the campus is inspiring.

According to the mission statement of the 1,100-student school, "Tarkington students are intrinsically motivated to positively influence our world and become catalysts for social and environmental change"–a reminder that the two go together. Additionally, Tarkington's ambitious published goals include becoming Chicago's first "90/90/90 school," where 90 percent of the students served are minority, 90 percent are below the poverty line, and 90 percent meet or exceed state standards.[35]

A Green School in a Green Space

When Tarkington was under development, Daley ordered the school district and the Chicago Park District to collaborate to build schools on parkland, and to make school facilities more centrally located within existing neighborhoods. Tarkington, whose masonry facing and offset brick pattern evoke the appearance of the brick and limestone houses surrounding it, is situated on a ten-acre park district site with spacious green views out many windows and a huge playing field.

At Principal Vincent Iturralde's insistence, Tarkington became one of the few schools in the city with daily recess. "I was very passionate about how important it is for brown and black children, that they don't get that anywhere, and the union voted yes. It's fantastic How much more green can you get than being able to play outside?"

Most of the site had been an open trash-strewn field, says seventh-grade science teacher Angela Sims. Her students tell her, "Wow, they really changed this. It used to be really polluted, and we couldn't do anything there. Our neighbors would dump their trash, and now we're picking it up and cleaning it up." The park is becoming a place where people can go to play and where they want to be. Meanwhile, the school's competition-sized gym is open to the community after school hours, with yoga, fitness, and dance classes available to the public.

The living roof, planted with tundra vegetation, captures rainfall, reduces summertime building heat, and teaches about nature's cycles.

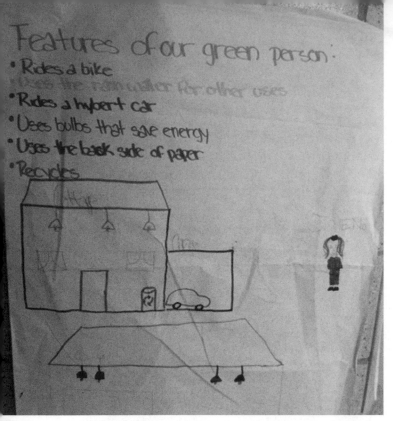

Features of our green person:
- Rides a bike
- ~~Uses the rain water for other uses~~
- Rides a hybert car
- Uses bulbs that save energy
- Uses the back side of paper
- Recycles

Students imagine the qualities of "our green person."

The building's east-west orientation and double-story windows help fill the space with natural daylight and give the interior a feeling of airiness. In the classrooms and hallways, sensors dim lights or turn them off when sunlight is sufficient. "Some days, I don't turn the lights on at all," says eighth-grade science teacher Kathy Bailey.

A quarter of the building materials came from within a 500-mile radius, 90 percent of the structural steel is made of recycled metals, floors are terrazzo made from recycled glass. Eighty-two percent of the construction waste was recycled. Low-flow toilets and waterless urinals cut water use by 20 percent.

"I think that the best part is that there's not pollution," student Alfredo Favela tells a reporter.[36]

Low-emitting materials, including paints, carpets, wood, and sealants, used throughout the building improve air quality, while the ventilation system maintains a mixture of outdoor and filtered air. The school is in an area with some of the highest asthma rates in the country. Schools in most areas with high levels of asthma report elevated absenteeism, but attendance at Tarkington remains high. Principal Iturralde cites a student with asthma who reported that he had frequently missed classes at his previous school but had not needed his inhaler a single time in a year and a half at Tarkington.

The school's most dramatic green element is its roof, a third of which is planted with drought-resistant tundra vegetation chosen for its ability to withstand Chicago winters. Windows facing the roof garden make it visibly accessible as a teaching tool. The living roof captures rainfall, returning water to the air through evapotranspiration, while a stormwater management system delivers naturally filtered runoff water to a lagoon adjacent to the school. The rest of the roof is covered by a reflective white coating rather than a typical black tarred surfacing. Together with the rooftop garden, it reduces the urban heat-island effect and lowers the need for air conditioning.

As one of the first large green school projects, Tarkington serves as a prototype, teaching lessons that will inform future construction elsewhere. The maple ceilings, sustainably harvested within 50 miles of the school, are gorgeous. They proved to be too expensive for a public school construction budget, though, and have been dropped from plans for future Chicago Public Schools buildings. The living roof lacks sufficient support and safety railings to allow hands-on exploration by students, a missed opportunity in Iturralde's eyes.

South-facing windows were designed with horizontal stripes that let sunlight in while reducing the flow of heat, so rooms would not be as hot in summer or as cold in winter. Unfortunately, viewing moving objects such as swaying trees through the striped windows induced vertigo in many students, so the school had to move tables away from the windows and install shades, reducing the windows' effectiveness. Based on these experiences, future windows will be designed with a different pattern.

Greening the Curriculum Step by Step

As a former science teacher, Iturralde was eager to incorporate the green campus into the formal curriculum. He cautions educators, though, not to try to do everything at once. Students had come to Tarkington from two other schools, one where just 24 percent of the students met state standards, another at the 50 percent level. Moreover, says Iturralde, "they really hated to read." He determined that the school's first two years needed to lay a foundation in literacy and math. Otherwise, he says, "We'd just be known as a green school where students weren't learning to read and do math well."

So the faculty concentrated for two years on developing consistent instruction in math and literacy, then began increasing attention on environmental issues. This curricular strategy, combined with the fact that healthier schools generally serve as better learning environments, seems to be paying off. After a year, Tarkington's students were at the 61 percent level, a number that has increased by 5 percentage points each year since. Test scores

aside, teachers see that students are better able to learn. Compared with other schools where she has taught, says sixth-grade science teacher Lori Stenger, "I just feel like students are able to focus more in class. It was always a challenge in the past to give kids some written material, and actually have the room get quiet and have everyone focus on that. That's something that I really appreciate here."

Just knowing that theirs is a "green school" is a conversation starter. When asked what that means, at first students may not know. "They had heard that this was a green school," says Kathy Bailey, "but then when I asked the boys about the urinals, they said, 'Oh, yeah, we never paid attention to that.' They knew that the floors were from the recycled glass, but they didn't understand why. Now they're starting to see why things are the way they are."

The next step involved using the campus as a springboard for more complex lessons. "You ask them why we have a rooftop garden," says Lori Stenger, "and their immediate response is, 'Because we're a green school.' So then you have to break it down, and ask the question in a different way: 'Why is our rooftop garden good for the environment?' We walk down to the rooftop garden. Kids make drawings in their notebooks and brainstorm ideas about why that would be good for the environment, and then go back and research rooftop gardens on the Web."

"The kids know more about the building than I do," says the principal. "When the school first opened, there were loads of folks coming in. They kept asking, 'You know all of this stuff. What about the kids? What do they know?' I got tired of those questions, and I just recruited kids from the Student Council and Green Club. They're the ones that do the tours now. People love it. I love it. Now they know more than me."

In 2008–2009, the faculty began to take sustainability to a deeper level. "We didn't really want to be just about recycling and just about conservation, but to be about choices, and how everything interconnects," says fifth-grade teacher Natasha Schaefer. Teachers identified four sustainability-related "essential questions" around which they could organize science lessons, and wove them into the social studies curriculum as well: How does the land affect a culture? How does technology affect a group of people? How does our economics affect culture? How do we affect other people?

So, for instance, a field trip to study river invertebrates or a study of the rooftop garden and

Terrazzo floors made from recycled glass and ample daylight create a welcoming entryway that helps teach about living more sustainably.

the campus water management system converge around common questions: What is a watershed? How do humans affect watersheds? What does it mean to conserve a watershed? How do economics influence what people do for the environment? A study of materials and technology—what things are made of and how they are made—overlaps with both colonial history and economics lessons about scarcity, opportunity costs, and decisions about resources.

Practice What You Teach

Seeing the school practicing its own lessons makes a huge difference to students, who are keenly tuned to inconsistencies between adults' words and actions. "It's not just something that we're talking about," says Angela Sims. "It's not one of those things where we're saying 'You should do this,' and little happens. They see it being done. It inspires them and makes them want to do those things." Students do take lessons about personal choices to heart. "They hold each other accountable," says second-grade teacher Rachel Galán. "They'll tell you right away, 'You could write on the front. Instead of making one mistake and crumpling it up and throwing the paper out, you could write on the back.'" They take lessons home with them. "I've even gotten calls from parents,"

says Sims. "'What is this about? My kid says they don't want me to drive! We've got to walk!'"

Creating that consciousness also keeps the school on its toes; students notice when it fails to meet their expectations. They comment when the kitchen uses disposable instead of reusable trays, or when teachers don't recycle the paper in their classrooms. Schooling for sustainability is an ongoing education process at all levels. At least three times a year, Galán says, the faculty Green Committee reminds teachers, "Here's how to separate trash. Don't forget to turn your lights off."

"A lot of times, you think kids don't absorb or they don't understand," says Vincent Iturralde. "They really do. It's so inspiring for me to see that they take things to the next step. If you ask me what legacy I'd like to leave here, I'd like to see the kids be motivated and sparked by something here, and then come back years later and say, 'You know, this is what I became because of what I learned there.'" As the years have gone by, says Angela Sims, some students have begun to take the school more for granted, because it's what they know. That may in itself be a sign of progress. In 2008, the Collaborative for High Performance Schools chose "Working toward the day when a healthy green school is just called a school" as the theme for its annual conference. For the students at Tarkington, that day has begun to dawn.

WHEN I WALK INTO THIS BUILDING, IT JUST MAKES ME FEEL GOOD

What: Bryant School District

Where: Saline County, Arkansas

Initiators: State senator, district superintendent,
                  school board

Key Strategies: LEED-certified construction
                  Life-cycle costing
                  "Integrated design" process
                  Campus-inspired curriculum

When Bethel Middle School in Bryant, Arkansas, opened in 2006 as the first Leadership in Energy and Environmental Design (LEED)-certified school in the state, officials met with some surprising complaints. Some citizens thought that the lovely, airy, light-filled building was too beautiful, unnecessarily extravagant, for a school. Researchers David Gruenewald and Gregory A. Smith report that a community often bases a school's legitimacy on how it conforms to adults' memories of their schools, even if those memories aren't necessarily pleasant.[37] Adults who remember schools as windowless fortresses may have trouble accepting the value of educating children in attractive sunlit buildings. Fortunately, the Bryant district has the data to show that beautiful design can save energy, materials, and dollars while serving students and teachers better.

In 2003, the Bryant district, located about 20 miles west of Little Rock, was well along on plans for a new middle school. Voters had passed the bond measure to finance construction when State Senator Shane Broadway suggested to Superintendent Richard Abernathy that Bryant consider building a green school. "At the time, I didn't know what a green school was," remembers Abernathy. He agreed to join a delegation of educators and legislators to visit some green projects. After touring a recently opened school in Austin, Texas, Bryant officials were intrigued enough to further research green schools. They were convinced, especially by the evidence for improved student health and academic achievement.

Right: High windows, ceilings of reflective material, and hanging acoustical panels that double as light reflectors diffuse daylight throughout the buildings and create a spacious feeling in the Media Room.

In choosing to design for improved air quality, natural daylighting, acoustics, and other green-building qualities, they decided to also pursue LEED certification, in spite of increased costs. They believed validation from a nationally recognized certification program would demonstrate to taxpayers–who would have to approve future bond measures–that the district was accomplishing its goals. Publicity about LEED certification would raise public interest and create an opportunity to educate the community about the virtues of building green. And they hoped that constructing Arkansas's first LEED-certified school would enhance economic development, placing Bryant on the cutting edge and piquing the interest of companies thinking of locating in the region.

Life-Cycle Costing

Their budget was already set, though, and the Bryant planners didn't feel they could go back to voters and ask for more money. Arkansas law at that time allowed districts to borrow money for energy-efficiency retrofits if they could acquire performance contracts from manufacturers that guaranteed sufficient savings to pay back the loans within 15 years, but the law did not apply to new construction. In 2004, Senator Broadway shepherded a bill through the legislature extending those provisions to new projects, and Bryant signed a performance contract with the manufacturer of its heating and air conditioning equipment.

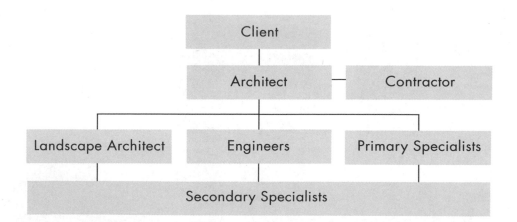

CONVENTIONAL CONSTRUCTION SILO

In a conventional "silo" process, the client–such as a school district–works mostly with an architect, while various engineers (electrical, civil, structural, mechanical, etc.) and specialists in acoustics, lighting, stormwater management, seismic design and so on work in isolation from each other.

Smart by Nature

That shift was one piece of the broader transition, changing the primary objective from minimizing first costs to optimizing life-cycle costs. Such perspectives have implications throughout school operations. Take something as humble as floors. Schools have traditionally used vinyl composite tile (VCT), which Bryant architect "Bunny" Brown calls "one of the least expensive front-end materials you can use, and one of the most expensive life-cycle materials." Traditional floors have to be stripped with chemicals (a potential health cost to workers that will never appear in the capital budget) and need frequent rewaxing (a recurring maintenance cost), sometimes as early in the school year as Christmas. They also need to be replaced more often. A polished concrete floor, such as the one installed at Bethel, might cost $1.00 per square foot more at the front end, but could save $12.00 per foot or more in maintenance costs over ten years.[38]

Design through Teamwork

A second transition is from traditional design processes to what designers call "integrated design." In a traditional "silo" design process, the school or district employs an architect, who lays out the plans. Then engineers and other specialists design the various mechanical, electrical, and other systems, followed by contractors who oversee the construction. An integrated design process, in contrast, involves collaboration by as many of the special-

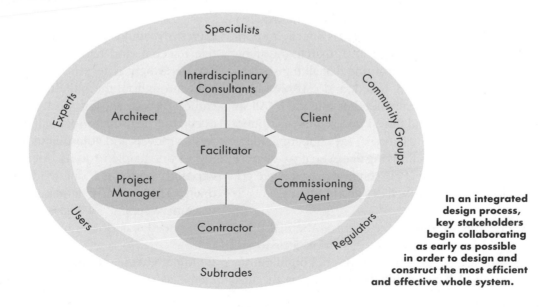

GREEN CAMPUS STAKEHOLDERS

In an integrated design process, key stakeholders begin collaborating as early as possible in order to design and construct the most efficient and effective whole system.

ists as possible, as early as possible. "The most important step," says Willow School cofounder Mark Biedron, "is to have all the stakeholders sitting around a table, and to design the building slowly and take advantage of the reciprocal relationships that exist, for example, between insulation, heating, cooling, and lighting. If you don't have that conversation and you just slap green things on a building, it's going to be a mess and it's going to cost 30 percent more than a conventional building. But if you have the conversation, you can say, 'Okay, I'm willing to spend $20,000 on super-insulated windows if I can cut my air conditioning and heating systems in half and save $60,000.' That's when the numbers work out."

LEED certification requires the use of a design team, though standards don't specify the team's membership. The Bryant team included, among others, district administrators, architects, construction consultants, landscape architects, and electrical, mechanical, structural, plumbing, civil, and acoustical engineers. Additionally, a new position—commissioning agent—has emerged as systems have become more complex and is now required for LEED certification. The agent is directly responsible to the school district (rather than to the architect or contractor) for ensuring that all the systems are designed, installed, tested, and capable of being operated and maintained as intended. "All in all, we probably had fifteen people that sat around the table on a regular basis," says Superintendent Abernathy. "I recall thinking that even if we weren't able to achieve the LEED certification, we were going to have a really well-designed building."

There are, of course, trade-offs. Abernathy estimates that the design process took four to six months longer than a conventional building design would have, partly because it was the first LEED building for most of the team. He is convinced, however, that the extra time and expense were worth it. For example, by participating in discussions of everything from the physical orientation of the building to the glaze on the windows and the types of light bulbs, the HVAC technician calculated that the cooling equipment required by the building could be cut by 130 tons, or nearly a third. Abernathy would not want to build another building without such a team, whether or not the district planned to seek LEED certification.

Bethel Middle School and Hurricane Creek Elementary School, which the Bryant district opened a year later, are appealing, healthy, and good for the environment. The buildings, oriented on east/west axes, have window overhangs based on sun angles, in order to optimize the natural sunlight coming into the building while controlling for glare and for heat during the summer. Two-story construction reduces the buildings' footprints, leaving more undisturbed natural space on campus while creating a spacious feeling in high-ceilinged hallways and rooms, such as the library.

Clerestory windows, angled ceilings of reflective material, and hanging acoustical panels that double as light reflectors combine to diffuse daylight throughout the buildings. Light sensors and carbon dioxide sensors work in conjunction with occupancy sensors to maintain optimal light and fresh-air levels and adjust lights and air conditioning in unoccupied rooms. Air circulates through exposed, perforated ductwork without causing drafts. The grounds, landscaped with drought-resistant weeping lovegrass, native to Arkansas, won't need watering or mowing.

Building green also inspired the district to increase its use of more environmentally friendly

Smart by Nature

chemical and cleaning products. "Back in 2003, we had zero green products," says Abernathy. The products used now are not yet 100 percent green, but they are getting closer, as more products become available that are less toxic without sacrificing effectiveness.

Bethel, which achieved a LEED Silver rating, cost $11.7 million to build. The district projects that it will save $11.3 million over the life of the school in energy, water, maintenance, equipment that won't need to be replaced, and other expenses. Similar savings are projected for Hurricane Creek. Those numbers helped to convince the school board and reassure voters, but the real beneficiaries, says Abernathy, are students and the environment. Energy use is expected to be reduced by 40 percent. Reports of asthma-related incidents are down by 50 percent. More intangibly, students, teachers, and visitors all report that the buildings are places where they want to be. Attendance is up. Teachers who leave to teach elsewhere want to come back. Abernathy reports that parents tell him, "When I walk into this building, it just makes me feel good."

Green Grow the Lesson Plans

The green campuses are also helping to inspire a greener curriculum. In 2006, Debbie Bruick, a high school principal writing a doctoral dissertation comparing LEED and non-LEED campuses as environments for teaching and learning, was hired as assistant superintendent, with responsibilities for curriculum. Superintendent Abernathy wanted to do more than just have green buildings, and supported her collaborating with teachers to integrate sustainability into the curricula. She began by working with faculty members from Bethel and Hurricane Creek, but teachers from other schools said, "We need to do this for all the schools."

A forty-person district-wide Green Team emerged, with representation from every campus. Green Team members are creating lesson plans—cross-referenced to meet existing state standards in science, social studies, language arts, math, art, library skills, and other subjects—for sustainability topics such as climate change, ecosystem health, and resources conservation. They circulate and post the lessons for use by their colleagues, and have formed a team that offers professional development in sustainability education for other Arkansas districts.

Meanwhile, student green teams have also blossomed at each Bryant school. Hurricane Creek students produced a PowerPoint presentation to introduce the green features of their campus to other students. Teams at other schools have launched outdoor habitat projects and recycling competitions. A high school science teacher designed lab kits for teaching environmental issues at elementary schools, and her students created podcasts to demonstrate their use to elementary teachers. "Our goal," says Bruick, "is to go beyond add-on lessons, and make sustainability part of our daily practice—to work from a philosophy where daily lessons are written with great thought and great research, and sustainability ideas and green practices are integrated into the normal curriculum we would do anyway."

WASTE-BASED LEARNING

What: Darrow School

Where: New Lebanon, New York

Initiators: Head of school, then board and faculty

Key Strategies: Place-based learning

A Living Machine on a two-hundred-year-old campus

Eighteenth-century values guide twenty-first-century sustainability

Sustainability indicators to orient new faculty

No one promised that education for sustainable living would never get messy. Take the experience of Darrow School in New Lebanon, New York. Darrow is firmly committed to sustainability education and to a place-based curriculum. Its "place," though, is the Mount Lebanon Shaker Village Historic Landmark, a collection of buildings whose exteriors cannot be altered from their historic condition.

"Two-hundred-year-old Shaker buildings make for a great logo, but with many windows and little or no insulation, they are not green buildings," wrote Stacey Giordano, former codirector of Darrow's Samson Environmental Center. "We embrace the dichotomy of living in drafty old buildings while preaching energy efficiency. We share with our students the complexity of our real world and ask, 'Do we bulldoze these buildings in the name of sustainability? Would we be the same school if we did not live and work in these pieces of history?' The answer to both is, 'Of course not.' And then we ask, 'What can we do, given the limitations and opportunities of our community, to live as sustainable a lifestyle as possible?'"[39]

"It's a huge opportunity to connect historic preservation and sustainability in a way that's not happening anywhere," adds current Samson Environmental Center director Craig Westcott. "The historic preservation people say, 'Don't touch it, don't change it,' and the sustainability people say, 'We want to keep the heat in.' At some point, those two things need to come together."

Right: The Living Machine processes wastewater using nature's methods and teaches the community about taking responsibility for the waste it generates.

The campus, known affectionately as "the Mountainside," comprises 385 acres of sugar maple and mixed hardwood forest, fields, streams, and ponds in the foothills of the Berkshire Mountains. Settled in the 1780s, it was one of the first North American communities of the United Order of Believers in the Second Coming of Christ—aka the "Shakers." Seventeen of the buildings the school occupies are pre-Shaker or Shaker structures. Darrow, an independent high school that opened in 1932, was never formally affiliated with the Shakers, but the Shaker culture of community, stewardship of the land, respect for hard work, and voluntary simplicity pervades the Darrow approach to sustainability education. So does a philosophy of using modern technology based on the processes of nature.

The Living Machine

Darrow's most visible symbol of this combination is the Samson Environmental Center, with its Living Machine, a lovely name for a waste treatment system that uses natural ecosystem processes. Darrow's system treats 7,000 gallons of wastewater a day from the school's dorms, dining hall, and academic and athletic facilities. This system of interlinked 3,000-gallon tanks, housed in a 1,800-square foot greenhouse, looks and feels as much like a tropical-plant conservatory as a wastewater treatment facility.

Solar energy warms the building and fuels photosynthesis of the plants in it. As wastewater flows through the system, in much the same way water flows in a river, a diverse community of microorganisms, snails, oxygen, fish, and basic plant life break down and digest organic pollutants. Dense beds of tropical plants growing in the tanks absorb nutrients from the water and provide surfaces on which bacteria live. A bed of porous lava filters out solids and provides a habitat for aquatic invertebrates that consume pathogenic bacteria. A constructed wetland adds a final "polishing," which further filters the water before it passes through a fish pond where healthy koi and frogs ("our canaries in the coal mine") confirm that the water is fit to be returned—safe for fishing and swimming—to the Hudson River watershed.

The Living Machine was an educational solution to a very real, and smelly, environmental problem. The head of school's residence and an adjacent pond lie at the end of an ancient delivery system that carried wastewater down the mountainside from most of the campus. The system had become dilapidated by the 1990s. Craig Westcott relates, "Every day Mike Clark, the head of school, would go into his basement and be up to his knees in wastewater and come out and look at the pond, this beautiful gem in the middle of campus, and see a wastewater cesspool." Clark knew of Dr. John Todd, inventor of the Living Machine.[40] Clark reasoned that a Living Machine could help Darrow simultaneously solve its wastewater treatment and delivery issues, put itself on the map, and reenvision itself as a sustainable school featuring a college prep academic program that also reflected Shaker ideas of natural processes, simplicity of design, and stewardship of the land.

Darrow's Living Machine, installed in 1998, was the first on a school campus; a handful of others have appeared since. They are not for everyone or every school, cautions Westcott. "Schools need to embrace the fact that not everyone wants to be elbow-deep in wastewater or a swamp. To make them work best, schools need to wrap their collective minds around the idea of a community-based wastewater solution, where the waste is dealt with by those who create it. There are much cheaper and less complex ways to move waste away from campus, but none of them come close to approaching the institutional mind-set-changing potential of a Living Machine."

The Living Machine would not be worth it, says Westcott, if it did not act as an anchor for a broader sustainability program. In addition to processing the school's wastewater, the Living Machine provides learning opportunities to Darrow students and organizations from outside the school. Students monitor levels of bacteria, phosphorous, nitrogen, and other biological and chemical levels. They examine plant life growing in the treatment tanks and explore possibilities for basing environmental sustainability on the processes of nature. They also lead tours for the hundreds of visitors who come to Darrow to see the Living Machine.

The Canvas on Which the Program Is Painted

As Mike Clark had predicted, creation of the Samson Environmental Center with its Living Machine served as the catalyst for making sustainability education one of Darrow's pillars ("the canvas on which the program is painted," affirms current head Nancy Wolf). The school's mission statement was rewritten in 1999 to emphasize "a unique combination of classroom instruction, hands-on learning, and environmental consciousness." An exhibit posted in the Samson Center since 1999 reads,

> To live sustainably we must live in ways that use only the amount of renewable resources that can be replenished naturally and in ways that do not overload the capacity of the environment to cleanse and renew itself. Current human actions jeopardize the ability of Earth to sustain future generations by using resources faster than they can be renewed and by overloading life support systems with more waste than they can filter and recycle. In a sustainable world, environmental protection, economic objectives and social justice should be linked in harmony.

The "Sustainable Decision-Making Paradigm," pictured beneath this intention, takes the form of a triangle with "Sustainable Decision Making" at the center and "Human Welfare," "Environmental Health," and "Economic Objectives" at the points.

"We are not going to crank out environmental educators or environmental lawyers, or anything like that, though we'll get a couple," says Westcott. The school wants all its graduates, whatever professions they follow, to have absorbed that paradigm, and to be able to act on it. "We've been thinking about making that triangle a tetrahedron, and the birds-eye point of the tetrahedron would be civic responsibility: 'What is my responsibility to act on the fact that I know how to make decisions based on sustainability?'"

Sustainability Indicators

Darrow has set out a sophisticated set of "sustainability indicators" as a way to orient new faculty members to the understandings, values, and skills that they hope graduates will acquire across the curriculum:[41]

- Understand systems as the context for decision making

- Take intergenerational responsibility

- Become mindful of and skillful with implications and consequences

- Develop awareness of driving forces and their impacts

- Assume strategic responsibility

- Acquire the capacity to shift paradigms

In practice, the curriculum is as place based as possible. The four-year science sequence begins with a field-based environmental science course, where students learn about the scientific method and study natural cycles in the Living Machine and the natural environment of the campus. The senior capstone courses include advanced environmental science and stream ecology, taught around Kinderhook Creek, a direct tributary of the Hudson. For five years, Darrow has hosted the Clean Water Congress, where students from schools in the Hudson River watershed stream compete to identify stream fauna, analyze mystery water samples, show off their water-testing sites, and present data that goes directly to the state Department of Environmental Quality.

Courses outside science study how relationship with the natural environment shapes people and events. An English class reading *Ethan Frome*, set over the mountain from Darrow, examines place as a character in the novel. Math classes devise formulas for tracking food waste in the dining hall. History students reflect on the relationship between societies' use of resources and their longevity. Multicultural studies students compare different countries' use of environmental resources. Photography students document the change of seasons on plants in the Living Machine.

"Hands to Work, Hearts to God"

One of Darrow's oldest traditions is the Hands-to-Work program, in which the entire school—

THE DECISION-MAKING PARADIGM

Human Welfare

Sustainable
Decision Making

Environmental
Health

Economic
Objectives

Darrow envisions sustainable decision making as a three-part process.

Smart by Nature

students, faculty, and staff—devotes every Wednesday morning to the work needed to maintain the campus and community life and to reach out beyond the campus. Mother Ann Lee, revered by Shakers as a female counterpart to Christ, coined the phrase "Hands to work, hearts to God," sanctifying hard work as the way to holiness. The Hands-to-Work program began the week Darrow opened in 1932 and has remained a mainstay.

Craig Westcott calls the program "the 'sustainability corps' that gets done the practical work of sustainability on campus and beyond." Participants work at everything from cutting and hauling downed wood in the forest to maple syrup production to computer maintenance to volunteering on local Habitat for Humanity projects. Students learn to recognize the dignity of all work and to appreciate those who do the work that keeps communities functioning. "Kids here may not enjoy their Hands-to-Work deal that day," says Tom Seamon, director of facilities, "whether it's shoveling snow or picking up trash along a road or recycling or raking leaves.

But they learn that you work and you get it done. There are chores to be done. And somebody's got to do them." In 2005, the campus magazine queried alumni about their Hands-to-Work memories. Many felt that the program had not made them particularly more godly, but they repeatedly cited its role in deepening their connection to community, service, and the natural world.[42]

Sustainability education is a work in progress at Darrow, constantly being renewed and refined. Discussions about incorporating civic responsibility into the Sustainability Decision-Making Paradigm are one example. A plan to replace plastic water bottles with cups that students would tote with them didn't catch on, and is being rethought. The advanced environmental science course may evolve into "science and sustainability" to better reflect its intentions. "I get board members who ask me, 'When are we going to be done with our sustainability plan?'" says Westcott. "Well, we're never going to be done. We're going to always be working on it."

Darrow honors the history of its campus site and the community that once lived there.

ECOLOGICAL ACCOUNTING

What: Northfield Mount Hermon School

Where: Mount Hermon, Massachusetts

Initiators: Faculty and head of school

Key Strategies: Thorough sustainability audit
Task force on sustainability
WorkJob program
Green Cup Challenge energy-saving competition

Could you say exactly how much petroleum or electricity your campus requires in a year, how much water you use and where it comes from, or how much food is wasted in the dining room? You could know all that and a lot more if you attended Northfield Mount Hermon School (NMH), an independent high school in Mount Hermon, Massachusetts. For the record, according to an exhaustive sustainability audit completed in 2007, statistics for the previous year for the school included consumption of 27,722 gallons of vehicle fuel; 331,766 gallons of low-sulfur #6 fuel oil; 4,0899,064 kW of electricity; 58,000 gallons of water a day from an aquifer 1.3 miles from the campus; and "post-consumer" dining hall food waste of 18 percent.[43]

Those numbers were compiled for a reason—as baselines for measuring progress toward sustainability targets for 2012 and beyond. The ambitious sustainability goals and the decision to undertake such a thorough and public review of school operations reflect an institutional commitment to environmental stewardship. That commitment is based, according to the Northfield Mount Hermon Task Force on Sustainability, on "a communal sense of moral duty and concerned citizenship."[44]

Terms like *moral duty* are taken seriously at NMH. In a short conversation about sustainability initiatives with Head of School Tom Sturtevant, *ethical orientation*, *ethical implications*, and *ethical decisions* arise a half-dozen times. NMH's history may help explain this perspective. The school was founded by famed nineteenth-

Right: Maple syrup production—a WorkJob assignment that increases self-sufficiency.

century evangelist Dwight L. Moody as two institutions that later merged: Northfield Seminary for Young Ladies and Mount Hermon School for Boys. Moody wanted to provide an education for young men and women denied that opportunity, usually because of financial hardship. The schools turned no student away for lack of money; in fact, students who could afford to attend other schools were often encouraged to go elsewhere. The schools were among the first in the country to accept Native Americans and former slaves as students.

All students contributed manual labor, such as assisting in the kitchen, doing laundry, or working on the school's small farm. In that tradition, a required WorkJob program for 4.5 hours a week continues today. Students may still help in the dining hall or on the farm, but they might also work as library aides, computer lab monitors, or as "EcoLeaders" helping to further the school's sustainability goals.

The days of required chapel or expectations that students are preparing for Christian service have long passed. Today the school prides itself on its rigorous academics and its graduates' success at top colleges and universities. Not every student develops environmental fervor (and some resist what they see as a liberal political agenda being forced on them). Still, something of the school's original ethos is reflected in its approach to schooling for sustainability. In the required ninth-grade humanities course, students use literature and religious studies to investigate their own identities and the nature of place through an environmental lens.

From its beginnings, NMH's mantra has been "head, hands, and heart." Says one faculty member, "All of it—the head, the heart, and the hands; the inclusivity; the WorkJob program—is part of a global perspective and a values system that includes our environment as well as social justice and economic sustainability." "And," adds another, "the heart is really at the center of all of those things."

THE GREEN CUP CHALLANGE

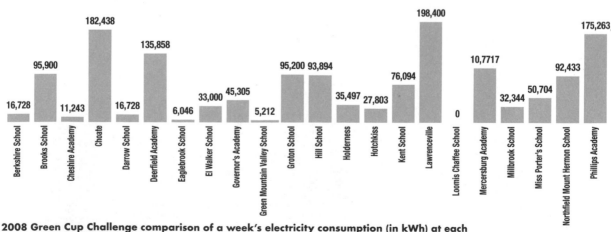

2008 Green Cup Challenge comparison of a week's electricity consumption (in kWh) at each of the participating schools.

Smart by Nature

A Task Force for Sustainability

"A close connection with the land has been a consistent theme since the school's founding, and farm-to-table efforts and outdoor education are central to NMH programs," according to the sustainability audit report. "In recent years, faculty, staff, and administrators recognized that while we had been making many schoolwide sustainability decisions for decades, this was not translating into a transparent, unified approach to sustainability across campus."

Environmental responsibility was identified in 2004 as one of the school's five key strategic goals. Working with faculty and administrators, Tom Sturtevant created the Task Force on Sustainability in 2005 to promote environmental responsibility within the school community, advise him and trustees about sustainability practices and priorities, identify opportunities for research on environmental issues, and explore sustainability-related learning opportunities in and out of the classroom.

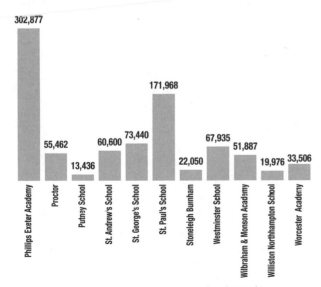

302,877

55,462
13,436
60,600
73,440
171,968
22,050
67,935
51,887
19,976
33,506

Phillips Exeter Academy
Proctor
Putney School
St. Andrew's School
St. George's School
St. Paul's School
Stoneleigh Burnham
Westminster School
Wilbraham & Monson Academy
Williston Northampton School
Worcester Academy

Source: www.nmhschool.org/sustain/gcc_charts/index.php#week1

Sturtevant assigned key administrators to the task force, including the assistant head of school, the chief financial officer, the director of facilities, and the director of dining services. Faculty members, students, and alumni joined them. "I've been around here fifty years, and there's never been a committee with that breadth of community representation–top to bottom, front to back, up and down," says retired teacher Walt Conadrin, who serves on the task force. "That has definitely made a big difference, and people are listening to it."

The task force became involved almost immediately in discussions about a new 43,000-square-foot Center for the Arts, the next building scheduled to be built on the campus. Assisted by a solar engineer, they generated suggestions for making the project a symbol of the school's intention to incorporate state-of-the-art sustainability practices. The building received a gold-level LEED certification upon completion in 2008.

Meanwhile, individual classes have gotten into the sustainability act. In 2006, students in a freshman physics class monitored dormitory energy use as a class project. They concluded that mini-refrigerators in dorm rooms were leading energy hogs and recommended they be banned from campus. The office of the dean of students said, "No more mini-fridges on campus." The community balked at first, and the refrigerators were given a one-year reprieve; by fall 2007 they were gone.

Competing to Cut Carbon

Alongside invocations of moral duty, NMH looks for ways to make acting for sustainability fun. In 2006, biology teacher Becca Leslie, who was then coordinator of the Task Force for Sustainability, helped found the Green Cup Challenge, an energy-reduction competition between NMH, Phillips Exeter Academy in New Hampshire, and Lawrenceville School in New Jersey.[46] The schools vied to record the largest reduction of electricity use compared with the same month the previous year. The contest grew to fifteen schools in 2007, thirty-three (primarily on the Eastern seaboard) in 2008, and one hundred and fifty in twenty-four states and Canada in 2009. The 2009 competitors collectively reduced total CO_2 emissions by 1,216 tons over four weeks.[47]

Many students become engaged and empowered, says Leslie, when they see their actions result in millions of pounds of carbon dioxide kept out of the atmosphere. Wanting to win draws others not swayed by moral exhortation or desire to save the planet. Organizers also play on the "cool kid factor," cultivating leaders whom other students want to associate with. Still, keeping interest up from year to year requires creativity. NMH won the inaugural Green Cup Challenge in 2006, reducing its electricity use by nearly 11 percent. Having accomplished that the first year, further percentage reductions have been harder to come by; in fact, the contest has been won each year by a school participating for the first time. So NMH leaders have added different twists, such as competitions between dorms or among day students and staff living off-campus. The competition has kicked off with a "dinner in the dark," when the NMH community dines by candlelight and glow sticks to glamorize saving electricity. Green Cup Challenge leaders are looking at ways to expand the competition to other areas, such as water and solid waste.

Auditing for Sustainability

This desire to devise a campus-wide approach resulted in the biggest project of the task force, the 2007 sustainability audit, which was designed to document practices already in place, present a vision for a sustainable campus, and articulate action steps and targets for later assessments. Some faculty members had suggested such an audit as early as 1996. "It really went nowhere," says science teacher and current Task Force for Sustainability coordinator Craig Hefner. "We needed administrative buy-in before things started to happen. It's important for schools to realize that you have to keep chipping away at it until you do get that buy-in from the administration, and that until then, you may feel like you're spinning your wheels."

"I just can't imagine how their faculty had time to do that audit," says the sustainability coordinator at another independent school. "Becca says it took them an hour a week. There is no way on God's green earth that our faculty is going to come in an hour a week to do a sustainability audit." Areas in the audit included energy, water, chemicals, consumption, curriculum, and food. The proposals called for a combination of educational initiatives, changes in attitudes, and technological fixes. A few examples:

Vision

● NMH will cut back on total vehicle fossil fuel use by 25 percent.

● Every member of the community will be aware of the number of gallons used per minute by faucets, toilets, and showers.

● More trees will be strategically placed on the central campus, creating shade, habitat, and water and soil retention.

● Heavy metals and toxic chemicals will be minimized, if not eliminated completely, in the science department, art department, mechanical rooms, and throughout the rest of the campus.

● Twenty-five percent of the annual dining service budget will be dedicated to purchasing locally grown foods.

Action

● Timers and water-use charts will be installed in all public showers.

● NMH will install pumps from the Connecticut River to use river water instead of treated aquifer water to water all athletic fields.

● The science department will be committed to microlabs, in which the quantities of chemicals used will be minimized.

● All students should have the opportunity, during freshman orientation, to use clay from the Connecticut River to produce their own bowl and mug. These dishes would serve as their in-dorm dishes, allowing dining hall dishes to stay in the dining hall.

● Sheep raised on the NMH farm will be made available on a rotating basis to maintain grass length on faculty lawns during the summer months.

The committee continues to meet biweekly and to create monthly action steps to move in the direction of the sustainability audit goals and of its vision that "all members of the NMH community must share a collective responsibility and awareness of the way their actions impact the local and global environments."[48]

LESSONS LEARNED FROM

● Language matters. Some audiences who find sustainability too distant a concept become engaged by talking about health, student performance, savings, or whatever addresses their deepest desires and concerns.

● Kids love clipboards and happily participate in sustainability audits, goal setting, and monitoring progress toward sustainability goals.

● Students can be the most effective ambassadors, tour guides, and interpreters for green campuses. They learn the most that way too.

● Trustees and boards of education can be moved by well-prepared, informed presentations by children.

● People are more likely to recycle when recycling containers are placed next to trash receptacles than when they're in separate locations.

CAMPUS PRACTICES

● Changing ingrained habits and mind-sets—of students, staff, parents, and citizens—often requires nudging, cajoling, repeating the same thoughts and reminders. It's like any other kind of teaching: the lesson probably won't take the first time.

● The easiest money to "raise" for campus greening is the money that's not spent. Address energy and resource conservation before looking for technological solutions.

● Emphasizing low initial costs and quick paybacks can result in lower quality, less satisfaction, and much higher long-term costs for campus projects.

● On a large project, employing a commissioning agent can save time and expense in the short term, and prevent much grief in the long term.

● Fun is good. Games and competitions often work where moral suasion and invocations of responsibility don't.

● Form a campus green team to brainstorm about processes and projects.

● Do an audit of your current sustainability practices. What are you already doing? How can you build on that? What more do you want to do?

● Find the places, even if they're small, where nature is present on your campus. Get out of the classroom and into those places. Then make more of them.

● Practice integrated planning—get as many stakeholders to the table as early and as often as possible—at whatever scale is appropriate for your project. Include maintenance and custodial staff, and others who will be responsible for ongoing upkeep after the initial burst of enthusiasm for the project wears off.

CAN DO

- Involve teachers early in the planning process and design a new or renovated campus around what you want to teach and what kind of community you want to be.

- Calculate and consider life-cycle costs of projects.

- Make your green efforts visible. Use exposed parts of the campus infrastructure, signage, computer-accessible monitoring, online and print publications, and other means to inform your internal community and the public about what you are doing and why.

CHAPTER 4

SUSTAINABILITY:
A COMMUNITY PRACTICE

To all peoples practicing bioregional self-sufficient economies, the realization that the total community must be engaged in order to attain sustainability comes as the result of surviving together for thousands of years.

—Okanagan wisdom keeper Jeannette Armstrong

The school is far more than a building and classrooms. Schools contain the networks of relationships in which students spend much of their time, and develop the values and attitudes they carry into adulthood. The relationships they share at school affect how and what they learn, and deeply shape their capacity to contribute to the creation of sustainable communities.

Jeannette Armstrong of the En'owkin Centre in British Columbia has profoundly influenced the Center for Ecoliteracy's understanding of sustainable living. She has shown how traditional societies have survived for millennia, despite meager resources, by ensuring the cooperation of the whole community. But she goes further: "The word 'cooperation' is insufficient to describe the organic nature by which community members continue, well beyond necessity, to cultivate the principles basic to caretaking for one another and for other life forms."[1] These communities foster sustainability by helping their members realize their full physical, emotional, intellectual, and spiritual potential.

According to our guiding Smart by Nature principles, sustainability is a community practice. Many of the most pressing problems facing us—climate change, the end of cheap energy, resource depletion, loss of biodiversity—require actions by citizens who are willing and able to collaborate effectively in organizations, communities, and societies.

Successful schools act as "apprentice communities" for learning the art of living in an interdependent world.[2] By example and by design, children learn through shared experience about cooperation, tolerance, empathy, caretaking, and support for others. The adults model collaboration, and students learn from joining with faculty, administrators, and board members in meaningful decision making. Sustainable schools affirm students as individuals while helping them recognize their responsibilities to others. And they celebrate the joy of community along with the responsibility.

In "What Makes a Principal Great," North Carolina teacher of the year Cindi Rigsbee says, "There is an air of connectedness that any visitor can sense when walking into a school that is led by a great principal. I've heard it referred to as a 'community of caring,'…and just as good teachers maintain a family atmosphere in a classroom, good principals establish that same feeling in the school as a whole. There are frequent celebrations and the work is fun for everyone in the building."[3]

Students serve their local community by helping to restore its habitat.

Schools also teach sustainable community behavior by their institutional practices. They are part of larger geographical, political, and economic communities. They depend on those communities for tax revenues and other resources, and they impact them when they provision themselves, contribute to public affairs, form partnerships, support other institutions, and set examples. Schools use their larger communities as real-world classrooms, laboratories for civic engagement, and opportunities for learning through service.

Cultivating Community

The definition of "environmental studies" at the School of Environmental Studies (SES), in Apple Valley, Minnesota, transcends natural science. Its multidisciplinary effort explores the complex networks of relationship within the natural and human worlds. The curriculum and the experiences it offers prepare students to serve the community, both locally and globally. The organization of the student body and faculty and even the school's architecture aim to nurture self-aware individuals who feel strongly connected to others. Students apply to SES from throughout the district; the challenging curriculum and unique on- and off-campus learning experiences draw the applicants, but administrators say that the culture of the community—freedom and responsibility, knowing and enjoying each other, and developing mutual respect among students and teachers—is one of its strongest appeals.

The process of becoming green offers huge opportunities for members of a school to practice working in community. Organizations that work with schools place the dynamics of the green-school coordinating committee at the heart of the entire project: "The committee organizes and directs the school activities and consists of the stakeholders of the school environment, namely pupils, teachers, custodial staff, caretakers, parents and even representatives of the municipality or local authority. The sense of democracy involved, and the motivation in resolving initiatives brought forth by the students themselves, are products of this process."[4]

"To create better health in a living system, connect it to more of itself," writes organizational dynamics maven Margaret Wheatley.[5] The more the entire school community gets involved in greening efforts, the better the chances of success. It makes sense to bring as many stakeholders as possible to the table, according to Liz Duffy, head of Lawrenceville School in New Jersey. You never know, she says, where you will find the passionate leaders in your community. One who emerged at Lawrenceville, to Duffy's surprise, was the director of food service. At Princeton Day School it was a ceramics teacher. In Davis, California, buy-in by custodians proved crucial.

Recycling at Lawrenceville School: a practice of the whole school community.

The recommendation to create a sustainability committee (or green team, eco-council, or whatever name it takes) is of course excellent advice. In practice, making that happen and keeping the team involved and motivated will probably require at least one highly motivated, doggedly persistent person who can work behind the scenes to cultivate interest and cooperation. Schools that can appoint a faculty or staff member to coordinate sustainability efforts have an advantage, but even those schools need to generate broad campus-wide support before the work will take off. For example, before she had a network in place, Princeton Day School English teacher Liz Cutler spent months organizing meetings and dinners, buttonholing colleagues over lunch, taking long walks with trustees, and meeting with parents. Only then was she ready to propose a formal sustainability initiative to the administration.

When the Eco-Council at Marin Academy in San Rafael, California, began, says parent/trustee Mimi Buckley, its chief booster, "We had maybe eight kids and four or five faculty at the most. Some weeks they'd come, and some weeks they didn't." But she kept convening meetings, providing good food and a welcoming place to meet, until the Eco-Council took hold.

The well-established Sustainable Schools Project in Burlington, Vermont, bases its work on four Cs: campus ecology, curriculum connections, community partnerships, and collaboration. Collaboration is perhaps the most important, according to Jen Cirillo, director of professional development at Shelburne Farms, one partner in the project.[6] Because cooperation is essential for citizens working to create sustainable communities, she says, the process of designing programs that teach cooperation should also be collaborative.

4Cs
campus ecology
curriculum connections
community partnerships
collaboration

The "Four Cs" of the Sustainable Schools Project in Burlington, Vermont, are all about making and maintaining connections.

The project originated with a teacher's suggestion that her school address new state sustainability standards by implementing a school-wide sustainability curriculum rather than expecting teachers to devise plans individually. With assistance from Shelburne Farms staff, the teachers collectively identified a framework for integrating the curriculum and generated "essential questions" to link sustainability concepts across grade levels and between subjects. To deepen their collaboration, they practiced participatory discussion, engaging multiple perspectives and cooperative problem solving.[7]

Collaboration often means extra work for teachers. Teaching in three-person cross-disciplinary teams at the School of Environmental Studies can require two or more hours of joint planning a day, as teachers stretch themselves and learn new material. "If you wanted to live in a very teacher-directed modality, to lecture, and to be the expert, it just wasn't going to happen here," says teacher Todd Carlson, one of the school's founders. "The movement, the noise, the lighting, everything is built to prohibit that, and that was intentional." But turnover is low, and teachers say that they and students gain from the effort.

Collaboration can also take place between schools through outside organizations, such as the Marin Green Schools Alliance in California or the Princeton-area Organizing Action on Sustainability in Schools. Groups of schools support each other, exchange information, brainstorm ideas, and research possibilities such as joint purchase of green supplies. The National Association of Independent Schools offers a variety of resources to help its members help each other, including a sustainability listserv and an annual summer sustainability leadership institute.[8] The Bay Area Teachers Collaborative offered a fellows program in sustainability education, facilitated by the Center for Ecoliteracy.

Extending community beyond schools to include neighbors benefits everyone. Marin Academy, an independent school with mostly well-off students, began a partnership with the Canal Alliance, which serves one of the city's poorest neighborhoods. The program became more meaningful because the students jointly chose projects and worked as peers rather than Marin Academy students "helping" their poorer neighbors. Even more important, students moved beyond service projects to connect as people, glimpse their city through others' eyes, and get together to enjoy each other and to affirm their differences as well as their commonalities.

Making connections and joint planning requires time, often a chief obstacle to collaboration. Again, outside organizations such as the Center for Ecoliteracy, Shelburne Farms, or the Farm to School Connection in Davis, California, can help. For example, the Center for Ecoliteracy has secured funding to support release time for teachers to plan together. Shelburne Farms contributed to the Sustainable Schools Project by connecting teachers with people and organizations in the community. These contacts were very willing to speak to classes, assist teachers, and work with students on community-based projects, but teachers had never found time to do the research and make the connections. Efforts in Davis took a significant turn when the Farm to School Connection brought together the district food service, leading chefs, and the Davis Farmers Market.

Civic Engagement: The Community Is a Teacher

For a number of educators, the essence of sustainability education is civic engagement—"working to make a difference in the civic life of our communities and developing the combination of knowledge, skills, values, and motivation to make that difference."[9] Many schools require student involvement in service learning or volunteer projects beyond the campus. Civic engagement goes a step further in its attention to community-wide needs and citizen involvement in addressing public concerns.

Students can understand a community better by seeing it through the eyes of the people who live and work there. In the Sustainable Lawrence community organization in New Jersey, for example, students and staff from Lawrenceville School take their cues from the local residents, who define the sustainability priorities. Students have a greater incentive to learn when their actions matter to others. Those in the Green Building and Design class at Lopez Island School in Washington work on an affordable housing project, studying green building techniques, working alongside the people who will live in the houses, and learning about the social issues that make expansion of affordable housing necessary.

Fourth- and fifth-graders participating in Healthy Neighborhoods/Healthy Kids, a program within the Sustainable Schools Project, brainstorm about indicators of the quality of life in their Burlington neighborhoods, then create community report cards, make recommendations to local government, and initiate community improvement projects. Teachers report that these students become more engaged in all their schoolwork, and their scores in standardized reading and math tests improve.

One of the first projects for new students at the School of Environmental Studies is an investigation of the water quality of ponds and lakes in the region. Students take the assignment particularly seriously because they present their analyses to local water boards, which use the findings in future planning. They also complete projects in conjunction with a variety of regional and state agencies. Their careers conclude with a legacy community service project and a public presentation that demonstrates their ability to persuade citizens about the importance of a public issue.

Facilitating Change: Findings from Recent Science

Becoming a more sustainable society requires new attitudes, practices, and structures. Anyone who wishes to change schools must first understand how change occurs in communities and recognize that schools are notoriously resistant to change. "Schools are among the more conservative of our society's democratic institutions, and therefore among the slowest to change," says former California Department of Education official Ann M. Evans. "Perhaps that's for good reason: they are designed to resist experimentation on our most precious natural resource, our children." Says an administrator at an independent school, "I compare it to turning a supertanker. You've got to plan your turn about six years in advance, and even when you turn the wheel five hundred times, it only goes two degrees."

But schools can and do change, sometimes dramatically, as examples presented here show. Fritjof Capra describes recent scientific research into living systems that gives insight into change in even seemingly entrenched organizations.[10] Living natural and social systems, he says, generally remain in a stable state, even while energy and matter, communications and ideas, flow through them. That's why they're hard to change. Every now and then, however, a system will encounter a point of instability that precipitates either a breakdown or the appearance of new forms. This spontaneous emergence of order, often simply called "emergence," is a key property of all living systems and is the origin of development, learning, and evolution.

In a human organization, says Capra, the event that instigates emergence can be as simple as an offhand comment, which may not seem important to the speaker but has meaning to people within the community. As they circulate the

When Troy Howard Middle School students in Bethel, Maine, sell the produce they grow to support their Garden Project, they first make sure that they are not competing with local farmers.

information, it may get amplified and expanded. If the system cannot integrate the new information into its existing order, it must give up some of its old structures, behaviors, or beliefs. The new order that appears is not designed by any individual, but emerges as a result of the organization's collective creativity.

Facilitating emergence requires a different kind of leadership: one that supports the institution's capacity for creativity by building up and nurturing its networks of connection and communication, by creating a climate of trust and mutual support, and by encouraging questioning and rewarding innovation. Leaders need to be able to recognize the emergent novelty, articulate it, and incorpo-

rate it into the organization's design. Doing so sometimes requires that they loosen their control and take the risk of dispersing authority and responsibility more widely.

We see this process at work at Marin Academy, which experienced what its head at the time, Bodie Brizendine, later called a top-to-bottom "change of consciousness" around sustainability. The seemingly minor event that sparked the process was a new trustee's observation about the lack of recycling at a school event. Brizendine responded with, "Wonderful! What do you want to do about it?" and a recognition, as she reflected later, that "there are moments of leadership where what you do is just allow good things to happen."

Fourth- and fifth-grade students participating in the Healthy Neighborhoods/Healthy Kids program issue report cards on the quality of life in their Burlington, Vermont, neighborhoods.

But she did more than that. She demonstrated her support of the resulting student/faculty/trustee Eco-Council by attending early meetings and gave it status and authority by appointing key administration members to it.

Change can begin anywhere—from the initiatives of students, teachers, principals and heads of school, trustees, and boards of education. Ultimately, lasting change will evolve from informal networks to formal structures. Brizendine joined with Marin Academy alumni to raise funds for an endowed faculty chair to give the emerging structure a formal place within the school's organizational design. During a difficult transition for the Lopez Island Farm Education program in Washington, Superintendent of Schools Bill Evans stepped up to chair the program, empowering it while signaling the school district's commitment. Lawrenceville head Liz Duffy helped to institutionalize the school's Green Campus Initiative by proposing that the board of trustees establish a sustainability committee, the only board committee that includes students, faculty, and local citizens.

Be Prepared to Be Surprised

Margaret J. Wheatley and fellow organizational change theorist Deborah Frieze write that large-scale emergence occurs when a number of small local actions connect with other local actions. Three things, they say, are guaranteed with these emergent phenomena: "Their power and influence will far exceed any sum of the separate parts. They will exhibit skills and capacities that were not present in the local efforts. And their appearance always surprises us."[11] The following stories bear this out: When the Marin Academy Eco-Council formed, no one expected that it would lead to the board of trustees' tearing up the plans and starting over on a major construction project. Davis school administrators did not anticipate going to voters to ask for taxes for fresh produce in school lunches. And few at Burlington's Barnes School –which parents had tried to keep their children from having to attend—foresaw that schooling for sustainability would contribute to Barnes's becoming the "cool school" or that parents would apply for waivers of residence requirements to get their children into the school.

LEARNING IN COMMUNITY, FOR COMMUNITY

What: School of Environmental Studies

Where: Apple Valley, Minnesota

Initiators: School district planners

Key Strategies: Environmental studies as the study of
                 relationship

                 Architecture and student body
                 organization emphasize community

                 Expectation that graduates will become
                 effective citizens

                 Research projects collect data that public
                 agencies will use

An "admirable graduate," according to the School of Environmental Studies, "will serve the community...inform the community about issues that inspire their passion... demonstrate a high level of self-knowledge...[and] begin their lifelong answer to the question, 'How, then, shall we live?'"[12]

Virtually everything about this eleventh- and twelfth-grade public school in suburban Minneapolis—its curriculum, architecture, class schedule, and network of community partnerships—reinforces its intention to prepare self-aware, competent graduates who accept responsibility for the local and global communities in which they live.

"Environmental study" as understood by the school could as easily be called "community study" or "relationship study." The core of the curriculum is interdisciplinary investigation of the relationships that constitute the natural and human worlds. Explorations range across biological and cultural diversity; social, economic, and technological determinants of human and environmental health; and the effect of human institutions on sustainability. They culminate in a senior capstone in which students demonstrate skills needed for active citizenship.

The school opened in 1995 as an experiment in school–community partnership. Instead of building a fifth 2,000-student high school for its growing region, the District 196 school board proposed creating several theme-based "schools of choice" to which any student living in the district could apply.

Right: Students combine ecology lessons with community service by compiling data on buckthorn and European earthworms to help eradicate invasive species at nearby Fort Snelling State Park.

Each would enroll up to 400 students, be linked to a major community partner, accept a population of students as diverse as the rest of the district, and offer a program distinct from those of the district's other schools, while costing no more per pupil to build and operate.

Planners examined a range of possible themes for the proposed schools, including health, business, the fine arts, humanities, and environmental studies. Population growth in the area slowed, though, and the School of Environmental Studies, a partnership with the Minnesota Zoo, is the only one to have opened to date. From the beginning, the venture required an unusual, complex community collaboration. "There were more lawyers in the room than you could shake a stick at," recalls one of the school's founders. The site, 12 acres of zoo property, belongs to the state and county. The city of Apple Valley owns the building. The furnishings are the property of the school district, which has jurisdiction over the staff, students, and program.

SES students collaborated with the state Department of Natural Resources to monitor water-quality data and restore habitat at Birch Pond, which now serves as a teaching station for the school.

A Campus Designed for Learning in Community

School of Environmental Studies planners chose to design a campus that would support the curriculum and the student experience they wanted, rather than conforming the experience to fit the building. Before hiring an architect, they spent two years researching how students learn; consulting with educators, parents, and the community; and creating a curriculum and organizational structure. They hoped that students would see themselves as self-motivated agents of change rather than containers for information. They intended that students would become self-aware and at the same time understand their relationship and responsibility to others. The organization of the student body and the structure of the campus are both designed to serve these ends.

Students in traditional classrooms typically occupy a desk for 50 minutes or so, then move to another room, period by period throughout the day. Each School of Environmental Studies student has a personal workstation with a desk and storage space to use when not in class. The workstations reinforce the notion of the school as a place where students come to be productive. Each station has space for personal pictures, posters, and decorations, affirming the student's identity as an individual, but each is set within larger communal spaces. Students are organized into "pods" of ten students. Each pod has a shared space in which its members arrange their workstations, and each sets its own rules for behavior and working norms.

Ten pods make a "house" of a hundred students and three teachers. A house's ten pods are physically arrayed around a central classroom space that can be arranged to accommodate all one hundred students or broken into smaller working groups. The four houses, on the building's second floor, overlook the school's largest meeting space, whose doors open to the wider "campus," which stretches from an adjacent pond to the zoo next door, a 3,000-acre park across the street, and the surrounding communities beyond.

Environmental Study: The Study of Relationship

Students and their house's three teachers—who teach language arts, social studies, and environmental science—meet for half of each day for studies organized around overarching interdisciplinary questions that explore natural and human relationship. The other half of the day is devoted to electives, Advanced Placement study, and independent projects.[13] Junior year may begin with "What is your role in creating a successful community?" The question "What are the relationships between organisms and water?" might be addressed through immersion—literally—in local wetlands, but also through literature such as *A River Runs through It*. Studies regularly extend beyond the campus. "How do organisms interact with and adapt to their environments over time?" can take students to the zoo for comparative study of primate evolution or on a midwinter wilderness expedition to study adaptations to climate.

Senior year, the emphasis shifts to the interaction of humans and the natural environment. The first trimester explores the dynamic relationships between species diversity, genetic diversity, and cultural diversity. Other organizing questions include "What are the relationships between changes in population and quality of life?" "Is it possible to manage for what we value? With what tools?" or "How do governmental, legal, and political systems affect sustainability?" And, finally, the big summarizing question: "How, then, shall we live?"

The normal academic calendar doesn't provide the best fit for all subjects, so the school cracks the calendar open for an extended study during the last two weeks of every trimester. Intensive elective courses include poetry workshops, field ornithology in local parks and refuges, eco-architecture, and winter outdoor recreation, as well as optional six- to twelve-day field trips to unique places (paid for by student fundraising projects): tramping in New Zealand, comparing the geology and ecology of Scotland and Minnesota, canoeing the Boundary Waters Canoe Area Wilderness, dogsledding with Arctic explorer Will Steger.

Whenever possible, challenging projects requested by someone in the wider community ground studies. Students' two years start and end with rites of passage, the junior year pond profile and the tripartite senior project.

The "big, arduous" pond profile, first trimester of the junior year, sorts out who will stay at SES and who will not, say graduates Will Black and Inga Strinz. "If you can stick out the pond profile and get something from it, you know that you're in the right place." Student teams analyze ponds or lakes chosen by local city officials. They do chemical and biological testing and compare factors such as water quality, pollutants, pH value, and biodiversity against measures of pond health. They learn about watersheds through the historical society and trace how water gets to the ponds and where human actions affect it along the way. At the end of the project, the teams organize their data into extensive primary research documents and offer their findings and recommendations in public presentations before city water commissioners, who use the information in planning decisions.

The school has neither the expectation nor the desire that all of its graduates will pursue "environmental" careers. It does hope that graduates will become engaged citizens with the knowledge and skills to address environmental issues. "If you have arsenic in the playground equipment that's affecting your children's neurological development, you'd better be able to go in front of city hall and speak to that," says teacher Steve Hage. Adds fellow teacher Craig Johnson, "I want you to be an autonomous, thinking, motivated citizen. If I see you at a public hearing, I don't care what you think. I want you *to* think. You can know all kinds of things, but if you sit in your room and don't go out and have the courage or tenacity or motivation to do something with it, then it's for naught."

Toward that end, students' programs culminate in a three-part senior capstone. Part one is a community service project that will remain as a legacy after the student graduates. "It's really magical to see what they embrace," says Johnson. Two students started their own foundation to raise money for African villages that lacked resources to put roofs on their mud houses. Other students have restored habitat, built trails, and constructed peregrine falcon boxes. Students created a repair shop where bicycles are reconstructed and then donated to children who need them. One major project—a wind turbine and solar array near a public trail that crosses the campus—required the work of teams of seniors over three years. They persuaded the utility company and city to cooperate on the project, obtained permits, secured funding, and created a display to educate the public about alternative energy generation.

Part two is a forum to which students invite family and friends. They dress up and present as if to a city council—demonstrating their skill at persuading a public audience on an issue they feel strongly about. Part three is an articulation of students' environmental ethics, the answer to the "How, then, shall we live?" question. "We ask them to say, 'Here's who I think I am at the tender age of eighteen in relationship to people on the planet,'" says teacher Todd Carlson, who calls this "the gutsiest part" of the capstone. "They sit down with a group of their peers, and say who they are. That takes a lot of courage." When they have finished, they are ready to take their place among the School of Environmental Studies' admirable graduates.

HOW TO BECOME THE COOL SCHOOL

What: Sustainable Schools Project

Where: Shelburne Farms and Burlington School
                District, Burlington, Vermont

Initiators: Educational nonprofit and schools

Key Strategies: Whole school collaboration to
                integrate curriculum

                Education for civic engagement

                Outside organization makes
                community connections on behalf
                of time-pressed teachers

                Students identify quality-of-life indicators
                and issue neighborhood report cards

Barnes Elementary School had a horrendous reputation, says its former principal Paula Bowen. "It's in the inner city, with high poverty. It's where refugees are first resettled. Anybody who had the wherewithal to get their kids into some other school typically did. Now Barnes is the groovy school, the cool school. Test scores are up. Parents are asking for variances to get *into* Barnes."

The spark behind the turnaround at the Burlington, Vermont, school, says Bowen, was the Sustainable Schools Project (SSP), a collaboration with nearby Shelburne Farms (see sidebar). SSP combines place-based learning, school-wide curriculum planning, partnerships with organizations in the surrounding community, and hands-on civic engagement in which students learn that they can make a difference.

In 2000, Shelburne Farms helped organize several months of forums around the state to ask, "If we want to prepare students for the twenty-first century, what are the gaps in our state education standards?" The forums resulted in Vermont's becoming the first state to incorporate sustainability and understanding place into its standards:

Sustainability: Students make decisions that demonstrate understanding of natural and human communities; the ecological, economic, political, or social systems within them; and awareness of how their personal and collective actions affect the sustainability of these interrelated systems.

Understanding Place: Students demonstrate understanding of the relationship between their local environment and community heritage and how each shapes their lives.[14]

The mural at Barnes School includes a quote from Matthew Fox: "Sustainability is another word for justice, for what is just is sustainable, and what is unjust is not."

In response to educators requesting assistance in teaching the new standards, Shelburne Farms designed a series of professional development workshops and contributed the bulk of the writing of the "Vermont Guide to Education for Sustainability," still one of the best introductions to the topic.[15] The state standards had intentionally left the definition of "sustainability" broad, out of a belief that communities should create their own definitions based on their needs and visions. The for-

mulation that Shelburne Farms chose, "Improving the quality of life for all—socially, economically, and environmentally—now and for future generations," partly reflects the work of the Burlington Legacy Project, a citywide effort to envision a sustainable Burlington.[16]

For Shelburne Farms, civic engagement, defined as hands-on involvement to address issues identified as important by the community, links

SHELBURNE FARMS

Shelburne Farms, located seven miles south of Burlington on the shores of Lake Champlain, is a 1,400-acre working farm, a National Historic Landmark, and a national leader in schooling for sustainability.[17] Founded in 1886 as a model estate to demonstrate innovation in agriculture, the farm is managed today as an example of sustainable farming and forestry. Income from farm operations, catalog sales, and an inn and restaurant in historic buildings on the site is cycled back into education programs, which are more powerful for being rooted "in the reality of grazing cows, crafting cheese, tapping maples, sawing lumber, and planting seeds."[18]

Shelburne Farms, a working farm, model of sustainable agriculture, and leader in schooling for sustainability.

The farm's dozens of onsite and outreach programs include numerous publications, ecology and agriculture classes and camps, consultation and professional development for educators and community organizations, and workshops and resources to help farmers offer agricultural education on their farms. Shelburne Farms, the collaborator par excellence, has founded and participated in a dizzying array of national and regional partnerships, including the Burlington School Food Project, Vermont Education for Sustainability,[19] Vermont FEED,[20] A Forest for Every Classroom,[21] Place-based Landscape Analysis and Community Education,[22] the Conservation Study Institute,[23] the Place-based Education Evaluation Collaborative,[24] and the Foundation for Our Future.[25]

sustainability and schooling. "Students must not get lost in the complexity of the world," writes former Sustainable Schools Project coordinator Erica Zimmerman, "nor become simply rooted in compassion for it. They must have some measure of control and power within themselves to effect the changes they now understand are needed."[26]

Zimmerman identifies three elements essential to making education based on civic engagement successful:

1. **Understanding connections.** Learning gains meaning and depth and students begin to comprehend how human and natural systems work when they see the networks of interconnection within their community.

2. **Connecting to place.** Students need to know their own place before they can make the leap to thinking globally. Writes Zimmerman, "They become literate in their local place. They gain names and stories for the world around them—the source of their water, the long-ago business owner who built the big brick house, the name of the bird that sounds their wake-up call. With such knowledge, they have more reason to care for this world and become stewards of it."[27]

3. **Making a difference.** In order to become motivated and engaged citizens, students need to know that they can make a difference. Therefore, schooling for sustainability depends on hands-on projects that are meaningful, have academic integrity, are developmentally appropriate, and can be completed by students with the time and resources available to them.

Big Ideas and Essential Questions: The Birth of the Sustainable Schools Project

Colleen Cowell, a dynamic fourth- and fifth-grade teacher at Champlain Elementary School on Burlington's suburban fringe, attended one of Shelburne's workshops on teaching sustainability. She thought that the emphasis on community was very important. Taking that a step further, she questioned the impact of individual teachers putting the ideas of sustainability in practice, one by one. What if a whole school worked together? In 2001, with Cowell's enthusiasm, and strong support from principal Nancy Zahnhiser, Champlain launched the Sustainable Schools Project in collaboration with Shelburne Farms. Three years later, the project migrated to inner-city Lawrence Barnes Elementary School.

Teachers at the schools, working with Shelburne Farms consultants, identified nine "big ideas of sustainability" as a framework for integrating the curriculum: diversity, interdependence, cycles, limits, fairness and equity, connecting to place, ability to make a difference, long-term effects, and community. SSP staff assisted the faculty to create "curriculum maps" of the progression of these ideas from grade to grade and from the classroom to the schoolyard, to the neighborhood, and eventually to the wider community. They identified "essential questions" to tie the concepts of sustainability together while crossing subject-matter boundaries. For instance:

● What do all living things need in order to live a safe, healthy, and productive life?

● What does it mean to be a citizen in our community?

● What connections and cycles shape our Lake Champlain ecosystem?

● How do we take care of the world, and how does the world take care of us?

The big ideas and essential questions helped recapture portions of the curriculum that testing mandates, such as those of No Child Left Behind legislation, had squeezed out. Paula Bowen quotes one of her predecessors at Barnes: "'We don't teach science and social studies; we only teach math and reading.' That's boring for kids," says Bowen. "They need something to get their teeth into. Connecting science to social studies and literacy has been part of what Shelburne Farms has helped us to do."

"We hoped to demonstrate how using the big ideas of sustainability to enhance existing curriculum was engaging and something they were already doing—with a slight twist," says Shelburne Farms SSP staff member Tiffany Tillman.[28] "Instead of a unit on living organisms," explains Barnes third-grade teacher Anne Tewksbury-Frye, "you're looking at it as a unit on systems and how those systems interact and how you can address other systems in a more global fashion."

Teachers and students are learning to make other connections as well. Burlington serves as a resettlement site for Somali Bantu refugees. Bantu students just learning English often speak little in class. One day SSP staffer Angela McGregor brought a chicken from the farm for a first-grade study of animal life cycles. With the appearance of the chicken, the Bantu students came to life, overflowing with stories about their experiences with chickens in Africa, demonstrating expertise, and gaining instant credibility with other students. The chicken life cycle lesson unexpectedly became a cross-cultural reminder of the power of learning that is grounded in children's experiences. Chickens now make regular visits to Barnes School classes.

SSP has helped schools discover the teaching potential of their own place. "Something I never did before SSP was to look at what resources we have on the school property," one first-grade teacher told a researcher. "Now that I have some knowledge about vernal pools, I know I can make use of them. Before it was just a big wet spot in the playground, and now I know it is teeming with life."[29] SSP educators have assisted Barnes teachers in acquainting students with nature in the city. They have discovered that children can learn more about nature from the squirrels they can observe every day than from animals they see only in books. They have made contacts that teachers did not have time to make with local farmers, experts on the indigenous Abenaki people, artists, business people, and myriad others who have been happy to talk to students, lend resources, and contribute to student projects.

Healthy Neighborhoods/ Healthy Kids

Place-based education, community connections, and civic engagement converge in Healthy Neighborhoods/Healthy Kids, a fourth- and fifth-grade project within SSP. Students brainstorm quality-of-life indicators in a neighborhood. Their lists have included green places with plants and flowers, habitat for animals, more trees for better air, access to healthy food, signage and speed bumps to calm traffic, murals instead of graffiti, safe and clean places for children to play, and spots for neighbors to meet.

The students create report cards, which they use to grade their communities. Neighborhood walks can be eye-openers. Champlain draws students from both low- and high-income areas; teachers often assign students to walk neighborhoods different from their own. Children from higher-income parts of the city discover that some of their classmates live without parks, tennis courts, stop signs, or other things they take for granted. But they also find features that are absent in their own neighborhoods, like community centers where kids can hang out.

The report cards become the starting point for civic engagement, leading to student-generated projects such as creating habitat for local birds, cleaning up streams, raising funds to build bike

The "campus" for sustainability study encompasses both city streets and natural open spaces.

racks, or organizing block parties to bring neighbors together. Students also present their report cards to local government bodies. State Senator Tim Ashe, a former Burlington city council member, observed, "I think we grown-ups tend to take many things for granted, both good and bad, because we've learned to live with them. Kids are able to see for the first time a broken sidewalk, graffiti on a building wall, or a faltering street light and ask, with legitimate confusion, 'Does it have to be this way?'"[30]

The Case of the Missing Park

The students have sometimes discovered that they know more about the city than the authorities responsible for it. On one occasion, Barnes students found a park that the city had forgotten. They contacted the Burlington Parks & Rec Department about this park, where they didn't feel safe at night, to suggest the installation of lights. "We don't have a park on South Champlain Street," said the Parks Department. "Yes, you do," students responded.

"There's a sign there that says 'Parks & Rec Department.' We want to tell you about it."

Another time, children from Barnes reported to the city council that the street in front of the school had no School Zone sign, making for dangerous traffic. The city council immediately drafted a resolution to put in a sign. The director of the public works department, a city council member, and the mayor came out to unveil the sign and praise the students' initiative. A small matter, perhaps, but the city's response and the media coverage it generated were important to a neighborhood more used to finding itself in news stories about crime and drugs.

After Barnes joined the Sustainable Schools Project, reading scores rose 22 percent and math scores 18 percent, parents became more involved, residents began to find reasons to take pride in the neighborhood and to see the school as a resource within it, *and* Barnes became the "cool school." In 2008, the school that parents once shunned was chosen to become an Academy for Sustainability for the whole district.

CHANGING THE COMMUNITY'S CONSCIOUSNESS

What: Marin Academy

Where: San Rafael, California

Initiators: A parent/trustee

Key Strategies: Board-administration-faculty-
                student Eco-Council

                Informal committee becomes part of
                formal authority structure

                Endowed faculty chair to coordinate
                sustainability work

                Connections with low-income
                immigrant community

After months of planning, Marin Academy (MA), an independent high school in San Rafael, California, was nearly ready to break ground on a major construction project including a new kitchen and dining facility. Similar facilities at comparable schools had been researched, architectural drawings completed, design approved by the city planning department. Then a group of students, faculty, and trustees, all members of the school's Eco-Council, reviewed the design and said, "That's not sustainable." At the eleventh hour, school officials and trustees literally sent the project back to the drawing board.

The decision symbolizes what Bodie Brizendine, MA's head of school at the time, called a campus-wide "change of consciousness," which reverberated through the school's curriculum, student life, governance, and long-term planning.

Fritjof Capra notes that the immediate trigger for the emergence of change in a social system may be a single remark at the right moment, amplified through the system's feedback loops and spread until enough people agree that, if it is true, they will no longer be able to go on as they did before. In MA's case, that trigger was an observation by a new trustee, Mimi Buckley. Mimi and her husband, Peter, have sent two sons and a daughter to Marin Academy. Mimi agreed in 2002 to join the MA board of trustees and, with a background in architecture, to serve on its construction and design committee. At a meal for incoming trustees, Brizendine asked her one of those questions that school heads routinely direct to new board members, whether or not they expect an answer: "Is there anything here that you think could be improved?" "I saw that all the things from lunch were being put directly into the garbage," Buckley recalls. "There was no recycling.

The Eco-Council emerged from the work of a group of Marin Academy friends who had restarted an abandoned school garden on campus.

I said, 'I'd like to help the notion of sustainability at Marin Academy.' And Brizendine said, 'Wonderful! What do you want to do about it?'"

Buckley's identification of the issue as "sustainability" rather than as "recycling" moved the discussion to a higher level. And Brizendine's "Wonderful!" exemplifies the leadership that makes the

difference between an idea's being resisted and its sparking the emergence of creativity. A leader of this type, says Capra, creates a learning culture, encourages questions, rewards innovation, and maintains a climate of mutual support and trust. "There are moments of leadership where what you do is just allow good things to happen," says Brizendine.

The Eco-Council Is Born

Peter Buckley, a cofounder and member of the Center for Ecoliteracy (CEL) board of directors, suggested inviting Fritjof Capra and CEL executive director Zenobia Barlow to confer with Marin Academy. In keeping with the recognition that change is rarely sustainable if it is imposed top down, Barlow and Capra suggested that the new thrust had to emerge within the community. That fit a vision of Mimi Buckley's, to create a campus-wide organization beginning with an informal student group that had gathered itself around the garden.

The Eco-Council started off slowly, says Mimi Buckley. "We had maybe eight kids and four or five faculty at the most. Some weeks they'd come, and some weeks they didn't." Barlow notes that projects that lead to transformation often depend on a person who can nurture a web of relationships "through patient persistence—and often lots of good food. I can't tell you how many meetings Mimi catered for the folks who became the Eco-Council, with her ginger tea cauldron and organic apples."

The Eco-Council grew to become the largest "club" on campus, with sixty students and a dozen active faculty members. Significantly, trustees and parents have participated regularly as well, so the council is an expression of the whole community. It has also become part of MA's institutional structure, supported by the head of school, who attended early meetings herself and asked important administrators, including the business manager and the service learning coordinator, to serve on the council.

According to its statement of purpose, the Eco-Council "provides an avenue for our community to address real problems through tangible experience in this place where we live, learn, work, and play." Projects have included assessing solar energy options, developing incentives for reducing the number of cars driven to campus, and proposing policies for the garden and food service. The Eco-Council also aims to make sustainable practice fun. Its EcoPirates Committee (whose motto is "ARRRR: Always Reduce, Reuse, Recycle, and Rethink") has dressed in pirate costumes for school assemblies, promoted renewables and battery recycling, and surreptitiously checked the tire pressure of cars in the parking lot.

Institutionalizing Innovation

"When I first mentioned it," says Mimi Buckley, "there were literally people on the board who said, 'What is sustainability?'" She says that bringing recognized leaders with academic credentials—such as Fritjof Capra, David W. Orr, and Michael Pollan—to speak with the board "brought weightiness to thinking about sustainability as an academic pursuit." Encouraging faculty involvement proved to be another essential step. "We have learned from the literature and our experience that lasting innovation usually requires that at least a third of the faculty become engaged and committed," says Barlow. The passion and creativity of students and parents are vital, but students graduate or transfer, and their parents often follow them. Administrators move on, while the faculty as a body provides the consistency and continuity.

Faculty members are very busy and have many other responsibilities. School officials and the Buckleys agreed about the need for faculty leadership for the initiative. Their discussions led to the creation of the H. D. Thoreau Faculty Chair. The holder of the position is released from some other teaching responsibilities to lead the Eco-Council and consult with faculty on integrating sustainability into the curriculum. Donors endowed the Thoreau Chair to guarantee that the position will remain part of MA's structure long after its creators leave. Biology teacher Mark Stefanski, a nineteen-year veteran of the MA faculty, was chosen as the first Thoreau Chair in 2006.

Sustainability in the Curriculum

Sustainability emphases began appearing throughout the curriculum. All students in required freshman biology classes work in the school garden. "In high school," says Stefanski, "we tend to be compartmentalized in our approach to the curriculum. We're trying here to move in the opposite direction—toward greater integration. We are encouraging using the garden in multiple subject areas. In biology classes, we teach about the cycles of carbon and nitrogen through ecosystems. What better way to study those cycles than in the garden composting system?" When students graduate from MA, he adds, "it's not so much that we want them to go on to their next school or next job and say, 'Oh we had a really cool school. We put solar panels on the roof. We had a garden and we composted,' but rather we want them to be able to express why they did these things, and why they're important."

An English elective, "Golden Gate," takes an interdisciplinary approach to the natural and human history and literature of the San Francisco Bay Area. In the spirit of David Orr and Aldo

Marin Academy students and public school students jointly created an organic community garden in the Canal district of San Rafael, home to many immigrant families.

Leopold, the course looks at the environment by attending closely, as the Eco-Council statement of purpose says, to "this place where we live, learn, work, and play." Faculty members from different departments present regional geology, history, and ecology. Students explore local habitat and history, and consider the interdependence of the natural and social worlds. They ask both "Where does our water come from, and where does it go?" and "What do race and equity and justice have to do with sustainability?"

Before taking this course, says Marin Academy graduate Booker Riley, "I would not have thought

of myself as being part of the biotic community, and how much impact I have on the place where I live." Riley and a fellow student compared people's knowledge about the sources of food and the distance food has traveled at Whole Foods, the local farmers' market, a supermarket, and the vendor supplying the school cafeteria, then presented their findings to the Eco-Council. "I had never heard of Michael Pollan when I did that project," Riley says. "Then I read *The Omnivore's Dilemma* and discovered I had come to many of the same conclusions about the food system that he had. I was proud of that."

The world of nature comes alive in the MA school garden.

Taking Sustainability Beyond the Campus

Sustainability also provided the route to another community connection. Marin Academy is just two miles from the offices of the Canal Alliance, which serves a largely immigrant population in the Canal community, one of Marin County's poorest neighborhoods. Ninety percent of Canal residents are people of color, most of them Latino. MA had for several years sponsored Crossroads, a program in which MA student volunteers tutored middle school students from the Canal community. Leaders from Marin Academy and the Canal Alliance, seeking a program in which MA students and public school students from the Canal could work as peers, created the Marin Academy Crossroads Canal Alliance Sustainability Partnership.

Early Sustainability Partnership projects brought students together to work in the MA garden and to jointly build an organic community garden in the Canal district. More important, though, was building relationships. "The project is about bringing our communities together, and it humanizes the political and social issues that exist between us," says Stefanski. Students share and compare their experiences and cultural differences, including family immigration histories and experiences of the effects of racism and sexism. One symbol of the students' efforts to understand each other better: one of the Canal neighborhood students had remarked, "There are differences between us. If I see you on the street, it's not like I'm going to say, 'Let's go get some tacos together.' I don't even know what kind of food you're interested in. It might be cheesecake, and we don't go for cheesecake here." Come the end of the year, the students held a culminating celebration. They chose tacos and cheesecake as the party menu.

Rethinking the Dining Facility

The original dining facility plan had called for a "cost-effective" kitchen that would heat and serve food prepared by an offsite vendor. As a member of the board design and construction committee,

Mimi Buckley became aware of the plans and saw an opportunity. "We can actually shift the mentality of this school through the kitchen, in ways that will affect every other part of the curriculum," she said. "The most significant alteration we can make is to have a true full-service kitchen where food, including vegetables we grow, is cooked, and where local and organic food are offered." Because board members served on the committee, she could share information with both groups and facilitate the presentation of student and faculty concerns to the board.

After many meetings and extended discussion, the board agreed to scrap the approved plans and commission a redesign of the facility, even though that meant finding substantial additional funding. If not for the voices raised when they needed to be, Brizendine reflected later, "We probably would have made a substantial wrong turn. But I don't think that would happen any more. We really crossed a philosophical threshold...trying bit by bit to really root this consciousness into existing structures, and integrate sustainability and systems thinking as a community of learners."

VOTERS TAX SELVES FOR FARM-TO-SCHOOL PRODUCE

What: Davis Farm to School Connection

Where: Davis, California

Initiators: Elementary school parents

Key Strategies: Tax measure to provide farm-fresh food

Change in school policy through forging connections with community organizations

Recycling program becomes self-supporting through savings it creates

In 2007, voters in Davis, California, voted overwhelmingly to tax themselves to provide more fresh fruits and vegetables for school meals—the first district in the country known to have taken that step. This victory, the result of eight years of efforts by parent activists, illustrates the value of building community support for change in schools.

The tax measure called for spending $70,000 a year to improve nutrition at schools by providing students with farm-fresh produce. Like many other communities, Davis has had to supplement public school funding with "parcel taxes." (California's famous 1978 Proposition 13 limits taxes based on the value of property, but permits local voters to approve per-unit property taxes.) These measures usually support class size reduction and programs such as music and art. Adding school meals was a breakthrough. Because achieving the two-thirds vote required for parcel taxes is difficult, districts are leery about introducing new items when the taxes are renewed; Davis officials inserted the provision only after a poll showed school food atop the items voters would support.

The odyssey leading to the tax vote began in 1999 when two Davis mothers, Ann M. Evans and Page O'Connor, discovered Lunchables being offered as snacks on a first-grade field trip they were chaperoning. The prepackaged treats—high in calories, fat, and sodium—"were grotesque," recalls Evans. "We were horrified, and decided we were just going to change it, then and there. It was like we drew the line in the sand. If industry and the marketplace were going toward Lunchables, that was beyond what we could tolerate. The school district needed to be providing other things."

Right: Students celebrate the Day of the Dead with scarecrows in the garden.

Smart by Nature

Evans and O'Connor began comparing notes with another mother, Deb Bruns, who had been executive director of the Community Alliance with Family Farmers. "We were all interested in nutrition, recycling, and gardens," says Evans. "But most of us were packing our kids' school lunches to make sure they got what we wanted them to have."

Having decided to change rather than bypass school food, the moms recruited other citizens with deep connections within the Davis community. Evans, for instance, was a former mayor of Davis and a founder of the Davis Food Co-op and the Davis Farmers Market, and was serving as a special assistant to the California Superintendent of Public Instruction. Other core members of the group, which called itself the Davis Farm to School Connection, included the director of the Davis Farmers Market, nutrition educators, the district school garden coordinator, PTA presidents, and researchers from the University of California's Sustainable Agriculture Research and Education Program.

The group told the Davis school superintendent, "We'd like permission to work in your schools. We'll give it ten years." It had taken ten years to get the Food Co-op off the ground, and Evans reasoned that this project would take as long. They had let administrators know that they did not plan to try to overturn the system if they didn't get their way immediately. "We were all professionals," Evans reflects. "We were all mad moms too, but professional courtesy was our overriding modus operandi." At the same time they had made it clear that they had committed for the long term, and would not go away at the first discouragement.

Left: The Davis Farmers Market combines celebration, education, and good food.

The Farm to School Connection modeled its first program, the "Crunch Lunch," on the farm-to-school salad bars pioneered in Santa Monica by Rodney Taylor (see chapter 2). They raised start-up money, hired a coordinator, connected with schools that had gardens, and started salad bars featuring food from the Davis Farmers Market.

In spite of having formed primarily to change food, the Farm to School Connection seized an early opportunity when funding became available to initiate a recycling program as well. "You've got to follow those opportunities when they arise," says Deb Bruns. The group's Strategic Plan shows its sophisticated understanding of school systems: "A healthy school environment is a complex property of the whole system. Health does not reside in any of the individual programs, such as garden-based learning, fresh local foods in the school lunch program, or recycling and waste reduction. A healthy school environment has properties that the programs do not have. It is the aggregate of these connections."[31]

Their whole effort, in fact, can be seen as an exercise in making and taking advantage of connections. Relationships that members had made with the Alameda County Waste Disposal Authority led to the grant that launched the recycling program. That program, Recycling Is Simply Elementary (RISE), provides materials and workshops to help teachers make curricular connections to recycling. The program requires collaboration with school custodians. (As part of its network building, the Farm to School Connection holds an annual lunch, at which it invites feedback from the custodians. After four years, the district saw the value of these sessions, and paid for custodians' time in order to convene its own meeting—the first time that the district had met with all its custodians.)

RISE saved the district money by cutting elementary school waste in half. After three years, the Farm to School Connection documented these savings to the district's satisfaction, leading to a breakthrough agreement. RISE had been sustained by Farm to School Connection fundraising. The district agreed to fund the program by remitting half of the money it saved, the first time it had done this for a program run by an outside group. The program now pays for itself while generating additional income for the district's general fund, an important achievement in making the program sustainable. Another sign of success: when elementary school students who had participated in RISE graduated to a middle school with no recycling program, they began asking, "Where do we sort our garbage?" Told that the school had no program, the kids started one.

Turning toward the Community

Between 2001 and 2006, the Farm to School Connection raised more than $400,000 for Davis school food programs. By 2005, the district had more than tripled its fresh produce budget and increased purchases from local growers from zero to 52 percent. Still, the district business office concluded that the salad bar program could not be sustained after the grant that had underwritten the necessary extra labor expired. It was cut back to one day a week and then replaced with prepackaged salads.

The Farm to School Connection believed that the money problems resulted from larger financial issues within the district but could not prevent the closing of the program. Maintaining an effective relationship between the district and the Farm to

School Connection, which had no formal role or authority, proved an ongoing challenge. As much as the district welcomed the money the Farm to School Connection raised, some members felt they were regarded as "fussy, over-involved meddlers" trying to force their vision and priorities on the district. "We were trying to push the program on the district without 100 percent buy-in," says longtime member Jamie Buffington. "As long as we were pushing it and running it, they didn't own it" and so were willing to shut it down.

In the face of such setbacks, members of the group relied on each other for support, another important lesson for change agents. "When we've been discouraged," says Buffington, "we've taken a step back and done some fun things, like getting together during the holidays, drinking champagne, eating good food, and enjoying each other's company. Sometimes when you relax, that's when the big thoughts come. When one person is low and thinks they can't make it through another day with this stuff, someone else will come and be supportive, and enlighten everyone."

One "big thought" involved a strategic decision to change direction. Instead of trying to persuade district administrators, they decided in 2006 to turn and face outward—to concentrate on building community support for their ideas. The Farm to School Connection became a project of the Davis Farmers Market Foundation. They also recognized that building community support required easy-to-understand messaging. "It was too difficult to explain what the Davis Farm to School Connection was," recalls Evans. "We thought if we could simply say, 'It's the Davis Farmers Market program in the schools,' the thousands of people who came to the market every Saturday would get it immediately." Having enough people "get it" would be necessary to take their program to the voters.

They also began laying the groundwork for the 2007 parcel tax vote by generating support within the school board. "It took us a long time to figure out that the school board had never really eaten a school lunch," says Bruns. "So whenever we came to board meetings, we'd bring salads, farmers' market baskets, or whatever. A lot of that kind of education needs to go on." They arranged for school board members to address conferences, such as a statewide summit on student health and school food cosponsored by the Center for Ecoliteracy. These board members later became leaders in the parcel tax effort.

The Farm to School Connection also invited the school food service staff to join chefs from leading local restaurants on a "Chefs' Walk" promoting farmers' market products. Treating the food services staff as peers with prominent local chefs helped them see themselves as valued food professionals rather than as "lunch ladies."

Local chef and nationally acclaimed cookbook author Georgeanne Brennan offered a class to help the staff become excited and enthusiastic about cooking from scratch. "They loved tasting each other's creations and realizing that every single thing you put in contributes to the flavor," Brennan says. One result from the class was "Soups from Scratch," which became a weekly feature at Davis schools. With no Crunch Lunch, Brennan developed seasonal taste profiles to incorporate tastes and scents of the seasons using local ingredients throughout the whole menu. This program succeeded, Evans believes, because the food service staff saw the Farm to School Connection as offering something desirable rather than asking them to do something. "That's a key concept," says Evans. "When you're offering someone something *you* want, it's hard to see when they don't want it."

Following passage of the parcel tax, a memorandum of understanding with the district assigned the Farm to School Connection the formal relationship it had lacked before. The two organizations committed to collaborating on mutual goals, including purchasing 60 percent of school lunch produce from local growers, having district staff rather than volunteers manage the waste reduction program, and creating a teacher-designed curriculum with gardens, waste reduction, and the cafeteria as contexts for teaching core academic standards. The Farm to School Connection is also designing an exit strategy for itself, something change agents often fail to do. "Our long-term objective is the district's full ownership of the program," says Evans. "We still plan to be involved, but we imagine ourselves more like the football booster club. We'll raise money to support the district, but we won't try to tell them how to play the game."

DIFFERENT ROUTES TO SCHOOL SUSTAINABILITY

What: Sustainability Collaborations in the Princeton Area

Where: Lawrenceville School in Lawrenceville, New Jersey

Princeton Day School in Princeton, New Jersey

OASIS (Organizing Action on Sustainability in Schools)

Initiators: A head of school, a teacher

Key Strategies: Top-down and bottom-up activism succeed at different schools

Board reorganization to support sustainability

School and local citizens create township sustainability project

Regional schools form sustainability alliance

Schooling for sustainability needs participation from throughout school communities, but it can start anywhere. Lawrenceville School and Princeton Day School, sustainability education leaders in the Princeton, New Jersey, region, followed opposite paths. The impetus for Lawrenceville's Green Campus Initiative came from the head of school. Princeton Day School, on the other hand, followed what could be called the "one relentlessly focused and committed teacher" route.

Lawrenceville School

Lawrenceville School, a residential prep school of eight hundred students, was founded in 1810. Conservationist icon Aldo Leopold graduated from the school in 1905. The central portion of its 700-acre campus, designed by Frederick Law Olmsted, the founder of landscape architecture in the United States, is listed on the National Register of Historic Places.

In 2004–2005, under the direction of Head Master Liz Duffy, Lawrenceville sponsored a series of conversations about natural resource stewardship to celebrate the centenary of Aldo Leopold's graduation. Duffy asked representatives from the Rocky Mountain Institute (RMI) in Colorado to lead a two-day interactive planning exercise for the school and officials from Lawrence Township. (Including the local community was important, says Duffy. "We sit on a very large piece of land, and have had gates all the way around. We think of ourselves as a national or even

Right: An "upcycle" fashion show at Lawrenceville makes a community celebration out of learning about recycling.

international institution, and it's really easy to get disconnected from the town.")

Community members realized that the enthusiasm generated by the sessions might dissipate once the RMI leaders left town, and decided that they needed to "do this ourselves." Duffy supported a recommendation to hire a full-time sustainability director. Sam Kosoff, a 1988 Lawrenceville graduate who holds that position, oversees Lawrenceville's Green Campus Initiative, promoting ecological literacy, sustainability education, and attention to campus energy, materials, land, and water use. He also cochairs a board of trustees committee on sustainability—the only board committee that includes students, faculty, and lo-cal citizens—which recommends policy and sets benchmarks to measure progress in areas such as recycling, energy consumption, and waste reduction. (Sustainability had come under the property committee, but Duffy wanted the school to think more holistically and to keep attention focused on sustainability by designating a committee with that as its only mandate.)

Under Kosoff's direction, the school's Green Campus Initiative has encompassed a wide range of activities, including participation in the Green Cup Challenge energy reduction competition with other schools, an "upcycle" fashion show featuring recycled materials, and hosting the region's first Green Building Expo.

Eating by candlelight raises awareness during the Green Cup Challenge energy reduction competition with other schools.

In the Lawrenceville structure, the sustainability director serves on the faculty but reports to the chief financial officer, a recognition that significant changes have financial implications. The CFO helps put thinking about sustainability into a larger context. Shortly after he was hired, Kosoff suggested a token gesture: purchasing a little green energy with some funds that had been donated for sustainability efforts. That's fine, said the CFO, but the school owns faculty residences that bleed heat throughout the winter. Wouldn't the money be better spent buying new windows and insulation?

The Lawrenceville campus provides particular opportunities and challenges When he was a student, Aldo Leopold used to take long meandering walks around the school. In a class on "Lawrenceville as Place," today's ninth-graders can read letters that Leopold wrote as a student, track the paths he walked, and imagine their place as it looked to the future father of wildland ecology when he was their age. Meanwhile, as the central New Jersey region becomes more urbanized, preservation of the open space, wetlands, and wildlife habitat that remain on the school's property becomes more crucial. The campus is located at the lowest point in a watershed that has become increasingly paved over; water draining onto the campus threatens to overwhelm the school's pond and water system. Such serious issues also offer opportunities for students to learn while doing real-world problem solving alongside campus officials.

You never know where you will find the campus leaders for movements such as sustainability, says Duffy. Gary Giberson, director of dining services, had always cared about healthy food but says that he hadn't given much thought to the wider implications of food systems. The Green Campus Ini-tiative inspired him to join the Slow Food movement and to become an ardent advocate of fresh and local food. When the school's corporate suppliers could not or would not accommodate his desire to purchase locally, he formed his own company, Sustainable Fare, which buys directly from area orchards, farms, bakeries, and the farmers' market. Now he offers twenty-nine varieties of locally grown apples instead of four varieties coated in wax and shipped across the country, and fresh eggs instead of boxed liquid "egg product." The local purchases cost a bit more, he says, but quality, taste, freshness, and the chance to support environmentally responsible agriculture are worth the extra money.[32]

In 2005, Lawrenceville hosted a forum, "Greening Lawrence Township," for the Lawrence Township community. More than 120 people showed up, during a heavy snowstorm, to discuss sustainable community. Out of that meeting emerged a Mayor's Task Force on Sustainability and Sustainable Lawrence, a collaboration of citizens, municipal officials, businesses, nonprofits, and faith groups striving to create an "eco-municipality."[33] The school contributes knowledge, resources, and facilities, and faculty and board members serve on the Sustainable Lawrence board, but local residents set the program's goals, so students learn how sustainability ideals translate into practice in a community.

Princeton Day School

Since 1984, Liz Cutler has taught high school English at Princeton Day School, a pre-K–12 independent school. She had worked previously as a wilderness instructor and served on the

Clearwater, the Hudson River environmental education sloop inspired by singer Pete Seeger. "I've been an environmental thorn in everyone's sides for the last twenty-five years," she jokes.

Not long after her arrival, she formed EnAct, an after-school student club that organized projects such as trail building and removing invasive species, brought speakers to campus for daylong programs on Earth Day, and raised $50,000 for open space. Cutler wasn't satisfied, though. "I decided I couldn't continue trying to change one child at a time," she says. "It's just too slow. Significant change has to come at the institutional level." In 2006, she began lobbying for an institutional sustainability initiative.

Normally, she says, such initiatives at Princeton Day come from the top. "I started at the bottom by talking about it all the time. I've always been a solo player, but it became clear to me that I needed a team of people." She talked with colleagues over lunch, with trustees whose children she had taught, and with influential members of the parents' association. She presented Al Gore's *An Inconvenient Truth,* followed by a talk by the head of the Princeton Environmental Institute. She designed a daylong forum during the summer and recruited a sustainability team. Then in the fall, she organized a dinner for about fifty trustees, parents, alumni, faculty, staff, and students who all had influential voices.

"I lauded all the wonderful things we were doing. People kept saying, 'You're making us feel guilty,' and I kept saying, 'No, I absolve your guilt. This is about celebrating what we already do and thinking of a few more things we can do.'" You have to find allies one at a time, she says. "I never would have thought that the ceramics teacher or the school nurse or the lower school language teacher would be such allies. I would have thought of certain science teachers, for instance, but they turned out to be not so interested."

The team submitted a proposal that the school hire a director of sustainability who could be relieved of some teaching responsibilities. Cutler accepted the position, initially funded in 2007–2008 at one-quarter time. The funding and release time are important, she says, but the institutional validation is more important. "I can say that I want to do a curriculum audit, and if they say, 'We're really not interested in sustainability,' I say, 'I'm the director of this program that the school has embraced. Let's talk about how it can work for you.'"

Students sell produce to help support the school garden.

The team focused initially on visible changes that link sustainability and curriculum. For example, as a math project, fourth-graders calculated that the school used and discarded forty thousand plastic water bottles a year. They figured that the bottles, if laid end to end, would stretch from the school to the downtown public library, three and a half miles away. They published the results, which students took home and discussed with their parents, some of whom are inspired. By the following fall reusable plastic cups and pitchers filled from the tap replaced the plastic bottles.

After hearing Cutler speak, the parents' association formed PDSeeds, a support group for the sustainability initiative. They organized two hundred volunteers for the "garden raising" of an organic garden that could be incorporated into the curriculum of every lower school classroom. "As soon as the kids heard that their classes would have their own beds to plant," says Cutler, "they were completely psyched. That brought the teachers in." Each class decides what to grow. For instance, the fourth grade planted potatoes the first year, while studying immigration. As support grew on campus, ceramics students made mugs, which they sold to faculty members, eliminating paper cups around the faculty coffee machine and raising money for the garden.

The sustainability team helps community members find ways to conserve resources and use less energy. Even small changes have helped encourage attentiveness: the food service rearranged the lunch line so that students pick up silverware after going through the line, and take only the utensils they need for the food they choose that day.

In 2007, Cutler initiated Organizing Action on Sustainability in Schools (OASIS), a collaboration of teachers from seventeen schools in the Princeton area, including Lawrenceville and Princeton Day School. The group exchanges information and brainstorms ideas for curriculum, energy use, school gardens, and recycling. It is investigating what it can do better collectively than as individuals, such as joint purchasing of green supplies and equipment and creating a database of speakers, resources, and evaluations of field trip destinations in the region.

The group serves as a community of mutual support when members feel isolated on their own campuses. OASIS can also leverage the fact that schools compete intensely for the same students and that sustainability programs can give them a recruiting and fundraising edge. One teacher went to the head of her school and simply asked, "Do you know that we're the only school in OASIS that doesn't have a recycling program?" Now they do.

"It's amazing what you can do if you just get out there and start shaking the trees and stop asking, 'May I?' or 'Can I?' or 'Should I?'" concludes Cutler. "Just go ahead and do it and people go, 'Oh, that sounds great.' Sometimes just the strength of passion is extraordinary."

LESSONS LEARNED FROM

● The more of the school community that participates in decision making and sustainability initiatives, the more successful they will be.

● The most long-lasting change comes simultaneously from the top down and from the bottom up.

● Change in schools almost always requires the support of the principal or head of school and a critical mass (some theorists say at least a third) of the faculty.

● Even when members of the school community show initial enthusiasm, the process will probably take time and require patience and persistence on the part of the coordinators.

COMMUNITY PRACTICES

- Organizations in the community surrounding the school (for instance, the farmers' market, the local food co-op, or community service agencies) are often willing to work with schools, but teachers may not have time to contact them. A volunteer or a partner institution can play an important role by making these connections.

- Change in complex systems cannot be managed. Institutional leaders can most effectively influence change by nurturing the institution's networks of connection, creating a climate of trust and mutual support, encouraging questions, and rewarding innovation.

- Institutional change has its own dynamics, and there will always be surprises.

- Real-world projects in which students do research or provide services that community organizations will use help students connect and give them reasons for wanting to learn.

WHAT YOU

- If possible, free a staff or faculty person from some responsibilities to concentrate on coordinating sustainability efforts.

- Create celebrations, such as a dinner that brings together the school community and the surrounding community.

- Work on sustainability efforts with other schools in your area. For example, purchase cooperatively, organize speakers' bureaus, share resource databases, and join forces on projects.

CAN DO

- Start collaboration by simply meeting to exchange information.

- Brainstorm with students about the indicators of the quality of life in communities. Then compare a local neighborhood with those indicators and ask what changes would make the biggest differences.

- Help students find research and service projects in the local community. Scale projects to the time and resources students have.

CHAPTER 5

WHERE TEACHING AND LEARNING COME ALIVE

By Lisa Bennett

In the coming decades, the survival of humanity will depend on our ecological literacy—our ability to understand the basic principles of ecology and to live accordingly. This means that ecoliteracy must become a critical skill for politicians, business leaders, and professionals in all spheres, and should be the most important part of education at all levels—from primary and secondary schools to colleges, universities, and the continuing education and training of professionals.

—Fritjof Capra

An Indomitable Life Force

From a modest trailer in Portage, Wisconsin, Victoria Rydberg has seen at-risk middle school students' interest, attendance, and test scores soar since she chose to focus on environmental sustainability. Karen Bradley, who teaches at a K–12 independent school in Oakland, California, has observed her students challenge their ideas about the world and their place in it since she incorporated a sustainability perspective into her history and politics classes. And in suburban Portland, Oregon, Clackamas High School teacher Rod Shroufe has witnessed hundreds of students getting hooked on learning ecological principles since he began taking them right outside the school doors.

Middle school students get their feet wet at River Crossing Environmental Charter School.

These are just a few examples of the growing movement of American educators who have embraced schooling for sustainability in recent years. The Center for Ecoliteracy has found compelling evidence that education grounded in real-world experiences and ecological knowledge is promising, possible—and popping up all over. In research conducted across the nation, we have found educators and school leaders who are making sustainability an integrating force in teaching and learning; forging exciting links between academic learning in the classroom and project-based learning in natural and human communities; and sharing dynamic experiences with students who

are more deeply engaged in learning—and whose academic performance has improved as a result.

Some of the educators within this movement have been inspired by a sense of mission—by their concern about today's environmental challenges and dedication to helping young people learn about sustainable living. Some have been drawn to it as an outgrowth of their interest in food systems, school gardens, or other related topics. Some found their way to it through professional development offerings from one of the nonprofits that advance schooling for sustainability. The motives vary, but most educators find that teaching and learning that

Smart by Nature

integrates the natural world and addresses real-world sustainability issues is vital, hopeful, and engaging—for themselves and for students.

"Teaching and learning about sustainability returns educators to concepts and practices that are stimulating, inherently relevant, and, most important, alive," says Zenobia Barlow, cofounder and executive director of the Center for Ecoliteracy. "It enlivens both content and pedagogy through hands-on, experiential, contextual learning in the natural world and community."

There are, of course, challenges. Teachers often must help students become comfortable in nature before they can learn from it. Teachers likewise often have to learn new content along with their students. But like a tiny plant that seeds itself in the cracks of a cement playground, educators and young people both teaching and learning about sustainability can overcome these challenges—and reveal the indomitable life force evident in schooling that embraces the natural world.

Says Karen Bradley, a history and government teacher at Head-Royce School in Oakland, California, "Schooling for sustainability has seeped into my consciousness. I've created some units explicitly about environmental themes. But even more, I've shifted the emphasis on curriculum that already existed or fleshed it out with environmental themes in a way that is really fun and interesting and positive. For example, today in American History, we were talking about imperialism and Teddy Roosevelt and watched a documentary about his initiative setting aside land for national parks. I stopped the video and said let's talk about Roosevelt versus [John] Muir, about conservation versus preservation. It was off-the-cuff but it worked."

"I think," Bradley adds, "it's that combination of new curriculum units and taking a new perspective on existing ones that makes teaching genuinely inspirational for kids. It's a different way of thinking that makes a class zing."

Young people thrive when engaged in hands-on learning in the natural world.

Smart by Nature Competencies

Preparing young people for sustainable living requires educators who can touch and influence the whole student, including his or her values, abilities, and relationship to the natural world. The Center has identified a set of fifteen core competencies that young people need to develop for living in sustainable communities— the ability to:

Head (Cognitive)

- Approach issues and situations from a systems perspective
- Understand fundamental ecological principles

- Think critically, solve problems creatively, and apply knowledge to new situations
- Assess the impacts and ethical effects of human technologies and actions
- Envision the long-term consequences of decisions

Heart (Emotional)

- Feel concern, empathy, and respect for other people and living things
- See from and appreciate multiple perspectives; work with and value others with different backgrounds, motivations, and intentions
- Commit to equity, justice, inclusivity, and respect for all people

Hands (Active)

- Create and use tools, objects, and procedures required by sustainable communities
- Turn convictions into practical and effective action, and apply ecological knowledge to the practice of ecological design
- Assess and adjust uses of energy and resources

Spirit (Connectional)

- Experience wonder and awe toward nature
- Revere the earth and all living things
- Feel a strong bond with and deep appreciation of place

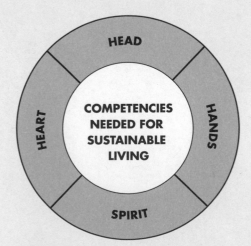

THE WELL-ROUNDED STUDENT

HEAD

HEART

COMPETENCIES NEEDED FOR SUSTAINABLE LIVING

HANDS

SPIRIT

Smart by Nature education helps students develop the abilities to be effective members of sustainable communities.

● Feel kinship with the natural world and invoke that feeling in others

Putting Principles into Practice

There is no single academic discipline called "schooling for sustainability," nor a set of curriculum binders that contain its core content. But after some twenty years of work with educators from hundreds of schools, the Center for Ecoliteracy has developed a framework for schooling for sustainability that we call "Smart by Nature." The Smart by Nature framework grounds schooling for sustainability in four simple but intellectually rich guiding principles:

1. *Nature Is Our Teacher*

2. *Sustainability Is a Community Practice*

3. *The Real World Is the Optimal Learning Environment*

4. *Sustainable Living Is Rooted in a Deep Knowledge of Place*

Students at Willow School in Gladstone, New Jersey, get out of the classroom and into the garden and the woodlands at the edge of campus to learn about the natural world.

NATURE IS OUR TEACHER

Nature, having sustained life for billions of years, holds the key to helping students learn how to live and thrive in sustainable human communities. With nature as their teacher, young people learn the basic ecological principles and perspectives essential to sustainable living.

At Willow School in New Jersey, for example, students have recorded the evolution of a wetland on campus, inventorying changes in resident species from year to year and sharing their findings online with students around the world. At other schools, students have compared the nutritional value of spinach grown in the garden with store-bought products, and then investigated the differences. Such experiences—or going out to explore the rich relations in an oak woodland—provide opportunities to develop a sophisticated understanding of how an ecosystem thrives.

High school students can map the relationships within a woodland to find examples of key

Through projects to save heirloom seeds, students at Troy Howard Middle School in Bethel, Maine, learn about their region's social and agricultural history.

ecological concepts such as cooperation, interdependence, and dynamic balance. In the process, they develop a deeper understanding of the ecological principles and the practice of systems thinking—by seeing both in action.

Teaching and learning about sustainability, in other words, often begins with shifting how we think about life. In contrast to conventional Western thinking, which has taught us to seek knowledge by dividing things into their component parts, we view life through the lens of systems thinking, recognizing that every living system—whether an organism, an ecosystem, or a social system such as a school—is a whole whose properties cannot be reduced to the sum of its parts. This perspective invites us to shift our perception from the parts to the relationships among the parts that make up the whole.

SUSTAINABILITY IS A COMMUNITY PRACTICE

Sustainability involves everyone. It's that simple. We can only develop sustainable human societies if we take into account all the members of the community, from the custodians, to the Spanish teacher who helps students study labor issues on farms, to the school board. To help students experience the power of community, teachers may engage them in cooperative or project-based learning, in which they share responsibility for collaboratively addressing an issue and practice community skills of cooperation, collective decision making, and mutual accountability.[1]

For example, in Santa Rosa, California, a middle school teacher gave his students an assignment to design an energy-efficient community. Each student was responsible for one piece of the whole,

including proposals for siting buildings, installing windows, and insulating in the most energy-efficient manner. Students also created floor plans and built models of their community.

In the process, they worked together, divided up tasks to reach a common goal, and assessed not only their end product but also their means of getting there. From this experience, they learned how to approach challenges from an interdisciplinary perspective and to solve problems together—skills essential to sustainable living.

THE REAL WORLD IS THE OPTIMAL LEARNING ENVIRONMENT

Just as cooking is best learned in the kitchen, sustainability is best learned in the real world. Teachers can encourage this by engaging students in restoring the habitat of an endangered species, tending a school garden, or designing a neighborhood recycling program. Or they can take students into the local natural community and ask them to inventory the living organisms to discover what lives there and how the organisms interact with the climate, terrain, and seasonal cycles of that ecosystem.

By sitting quietly and observing nature, students can witness things that they would never see in the classroom. Urban students in southern Kansas, for example, might see a Mississippi Kite leave its perch on a television antenna to catch and eat insects in flight, making the dynamic predator–prey relationship a visceral and more powerful learning experience.

These students can then return to the classroom to learn more about the kite's anatomy, including its hollow bones, quick reflexes, and a wingspan that is nearly triple the length of its body. Classroom learning can also deepen students' understanding of how the kite's specific body structure facilitates its role as predator.

SUSTAINABLE LIVING IS ROOTED IN A DEEP KNOWLEDGE OF PLACE

When people learn about where they live, they come to care about what happens to the landscape, creatures, and people in it. When they further understand the intricate web of relationships that place supports, they tend to develop a sense of kinship with their surroundings. When they learn to care for such living things, they develop empathy, attachment, and love of place. Place-based education, in other words, is fundamental to schooling for sustainability.

Students at Troy Howard Middle School in Bethel, Maine, learn about their region's social and agri-

Measuring the temperature of the compost: part of learning how nature makes the garden grow.

cultural history through saving heirloom seeds. Students in Mill Valley, California, help eradicate invasive species to protect native plants and animals in the creek that flows behind their school. And elementary students in Burlington, Vermont, interview long-time residents about how their community has changed during their lifetimes, and what they hope younger generations will take care to preserve.

Students develop this form of knowledge and caring through assigned projects that range from simple to complex. For example, students may plant seedlings native to the area, then transfer them to a school garden; they may restore a local riparian community; or they may map the network of relationships in the school community, identifying connections in the school's watershed area.

Such projects encourage students to naturally ask questions that help them develop a collective knowledge of place, such as: How are people in our community dependent on each other? Where does our water come from? What flower blooms first in the spring? Who lived here before we did? What songbirds thrive in this area? Gaining intimate knowledge of place can also inspire students to develop the deep commitment required to help protect the natural and social environments where they live.

Bringing the Whole School into It

Head-Royce School, an independent school in Oakland, California, was one of the first K–12 schools to incorporate Smart by Nature principles by integrating sustainability throughout its curriculum in collaboration with the Center for Ecoliteracy. A sampling of units and lessons introduced as a result of this new focus on sustainability follows:

- **Kindergarten.** Students identify some of the animals that live in the ocean and explore their importance—with a special focus on endangered species. They discuss how people can use ocean resources responsibly.

- **Second grade.** Students investigate a local creek and learn about a creek in another country. They investigate similarities and differences in the uses, appearance, and habitats of the two creeks.

- **Fourth grade.** In a traditional unit on the study of a state, students now also explore sustainability-related questions, such as: What is Massachusetts doing to protect its environment?

- **Sixth grade.** In English, students examine nature imagery in books such as *The Pearl,* by John Steinbeck. They discuss how the characters' relationship to nature shapes the imagery.

- **Eighth grade.** In a math class, students apply their knowledge of exponential growth to explore issues related to population.

- **Tenth grade.** In Spanish, students role-play indigenous tribes and city dwellers of Peru who clash over land use in Mario Vargas Llosa's story "El Hablador."

- **Twelfth grade.** In comparative politics, students explore wealth and resource disparities, and what trends suggest about the future habitability of the planet.

Get Ready, Get Set...

Perhaps no school provides a perfect example of schooling for sustainability. Perhaps no such achievement is even possible. As with nature itself, it is fitting that one of the hallmarks of this movement is its diversity—which allows for and inspires many different approaches.

Consider, for example: River Crossing Charter School in Portage, Wisconsin, where a teacher has committed to using the environment as a learning context for middle school students in a bold experiment to improve student performance and interest in school.

Or Clackamas High School in Clackamas, Oregon, where a determined public school teacher teaches a popular new course in sustainable systems and makes students responsible for one of the school's key sustainability practices.

Or Head-Royce School in Oakland, California, where administrators made a top-down commitment to weave schooling for sustainability throughout the K–12 curriculum.

And now, consider what your own story might be.

CULTIVATING RESOURCEFUL STUDENTS OF THE NATURAL WORLD

What: River Crossing Environmental Charter
                School

Where: Portage, Wisconsin

Initiators: Administrators and one teacher

Key Strategies: Environmental framework for learning
                Project-based learning
                Connections with the community

In 2001, when Victoria Rydberg applied for a teaching job at River Crossing Environmental Charter School, she didn't know much—or feel particularly passionate—about the environment. She was twenty years old and six months out of college, with a degree in literature. But she needed a job and believed she was a good teacher, and she persuaded administrators to take a chance on her.

The idea for River Crossing, a new school in Portage, Wisconsin, about 40 miles north of Madison, came from an administrator who hoped that using the environment as a learning context would help middle school students become more interested in learning and more successful at taking tests. Eighteen students enrolled in the program, housed in a two-room trailer erected behind the public school. Rydberg would be their only teacher, with a mandate to teach everything through an environmental framework.

By any sensible standard, it looked like a setup for disaster. In fact, it took only a month for Rydberg to realize that she had gotten in way over her head. She taught basic recycling and water conservation—but not the ecology behind it, which she lacked—and her students went into the field to do weekly habitat restorations with Jeff Nania, executive director of the Wisconsin Waterfowl Association. They found their field experiences completely exhilarating—and totally disconnected from what they did in the classroom.

"I realized I had to do something to make it different, so I started learning right along with the kids," Rydberg recalls. "In the field, they asked questions

Right: Studies show that students learn more effectively within an environment-based context.

like, 'What flower is this? What grass is this?' And I said, 'I don't know. Let's look it up.'" While the truth was that she didn't have the answers herself, the experience shaped Rydberg's subsequent mission: to help River Crossing students become resourceful learners about the natural world. Rydberg and Nania also soon realized that everything students did in the field would have to be integrated into the classroom and the study of ecology.

What ultimately sold Rydberg on using the environment as a context for learning was more personal: "In our first year, 40 percent of the kids were identified as at-risk. And all of a sudden, I watched these kids who were getting Ds and Fs gain two to three reading levels because they liked what they were reading. Seeing their success made me realize how amazing using the environment for learning can be."

In 1998, the State Education and Environment Roundtable (SEER), a cooperative endeavor of sixteen state departments of education, issued a report that concluded, "Students learn more effectively

River Crossing students have helped with prairie restoration, brush removal, forestry, and mapping projects in their communities.

within an environment-based context than within a traditional educational framework." It found that using this context significantly improves student performance in reading, writing, math, science, and social studies, and enriches the overall school experience.[2] These findings were reaffirmed in a 2005 SEER report, which stated, "These engaging programs appear to better connect students to their learning by allowing them to take a more active role in their studies."[3]

On-the-Job Training

River Crossing is one of 135 schools that belong to the recently formed Green Charter Schools Network. Its president, Jim McGrath, the retired principal of a charter school in Oshkosh, Wisconsin, notes that the network takes advantage of the relative freedom that charter schools provide teachers, but its ultimate goal is to inspire more schooling for sustainability in all public schools.

"We're all concerned about the environment and sustainability," says McGrath, who has spent more than thirty years working in public schools. "That's why we're doing it—because, really, what could be more important than preparing young people for a sustainable future?"

While it is too soon to tell whether green charter schools will inspire changes in traditional public schools, success stories have come from places ranging from New Haven, Connecticut, to Los Angeles.[4]

One key to the success of many environmental charter schools, says McGrath, is a school's connection to a local university that can provide teacher training. "Teacher training is often the weak link," he says, "because if you tell teachers that you want them to get out and do this kind of teaching outside, and they haven't done it before, they won't know where to begin."

Unless, of course, they are as determined as Victoria Rydberg.

Seven years after she began teaching at River Crossing, Rydberg still looks as if she is fresh out of college. But now she holds a master's degree in environmental education and has been named Environmental Educator of the Year by the Wisconsin Association for Environmental Education. Her students work closely with such organizations as the Aldo Leopold Foundation, the International Crane Foundation, and the Department of Natural Resources. Rydberg has identified seven critical elements for learning through an environmental framework: environmental conservation integrated throughout the curriculum; a positive learning community; hands-on learning and self-directed discovery; projects and activities focused on "real-world" and life skills; leadership opportunities for students; constructed challenges for personal and academic growth; and interaction with professionals in the classroom, community, and field.

On a snowy day in 2008, Rydberg and a half-dozen current and former students gathered at the nearby Leopold Foundation. Housed on the property where Leopold lived and wrote *A Sand County Almanac*, the foundation promotes the work of the writer and educator widely considered the father of wildlife management.

Executive Director Buddy Huffaker asked Rydberg in 2007 if her class would like to become involved in the foundation by planting a rain

WHAT IS PLACE-BASED LEARNING?

What takes place at River Crossing is something John Dewey called for nearly a century ago: experiential teaching and learning that engages students in their own local environment.

In recent years, writers and educators such as David Sobel have promoted such placed-based learning, and an increasing number of K–12 teachers have embraced it as a strategy for advancing stewardship and civic engagement.

Sobel, director of the Antioch New England Institute's Center for Place-based Education, says that place-based education is "a simple proposition, really: *Bring education back into the neighborhood. Connect students with adult mentors, conservation commissions, and local businesses. Get teachers into the community, into the woods, and on the streets—closer to beauty and true grit. Get the town engineer, the mayor, and the environmental educators onto the schoolyard and inside the four walls of the school. These are places where we all belong.*"[5]

There are, says Sobel, an infinite number of possibilities for putting place-based learning into practice. The Promise of Place, a project of the Center for Place-Based Learning and Community Engagement, on which Sobel collaborated, identifies ten principles of successful place-based education:[6]

1. Learning takes place onsite in the schoolyard, the local community, and environment.
2. Learning focuses on local themes, systems, and content.
3. Learning is personally relevant to the learner.
4. Learning experiences contribute to the community's vitality and environmental quality, and support the community's role in fostering global environmental quality.
5. Learning is supported by strong and varied partnerships with local organizations, agencies, businesses, and government.
6. Learning is interdisciplinary.
7. Learning experiences are tailored to the local audience.
8. Learning is grounded in and supports the development of a love for one's place.
9. Local learning serves as the foundation for understanding and participating appropriately in regional and global issues.
10. Place-based education programs are integral to achieving other institutional goals.

Promise of Place summarizes the findings of the growing body of research on the benefits of place-based learning. Among them: higher scores on standardized reading, writing, math, science, and social studies tests; better grade point averages; improved behavior in class; increases in self-esteem; improved conflict resolution, problem solving, and higher-level thinking skills. Teachers become more excited and motivated, more engaged with students, and able to collaborate more effectively with other educators. They experience professional growth and show greater desire to take additional place-based education training.[7]

garden on the property. She presented the proposal to her students, believing they would need to be interested for it to become a meaningful education experience.

"What's a rain garden?" they asked.

"Let's look it up," Rydberg responded. Her students explored how rain gardens function and why they're needed; which plants can thrive; and how they reduce pollution in creeks and streams by absorbing rainwater from roofs and other water-resistant surfaces instead of allowing it to flow into storm drains. Their research lasted several months and enabled them eventually to design their own rain garden, dig the trenches, direct the bulldozers, and reconcile competing opinions along the way.

"I think this kind of rich community learning experience becomes a very human experience that is much closer to how the world operates in reality than it does in much current education," says Huffaker.

Project-based Learning

To prepare students for projects that will contribute to sustainable communities, Rydberg begins by focusing on school as a place of cooperation rather than competition. "I try to break down the idea that there are smart kids and dumb kids, and we work on team building so kids can start to understand that they need to be able to learn

Students engage in project-based learning in a region that was home to Aldo Leopold and John Muir.

from each other," she says. "We look at multiple intelligences and how everyone brings something to the table. Then we start to do a lot of problem-solving projects."

After spending about two months focused on co-operation and problem solving, Rydberg turns her attention to helping students see themselves as active participants in their community. They begin each day by reading the newspaper, identifying issues that can serve as springboards for future projects. While reading the news one day, Rydberg's class became interested in a local mayoral contest. They wanted to learn more about the candidates' positions on the environment, so they hosted a debate and invited the candidates, all of whom came.

On another day, students read that the Department of Natural Resources planned to cut funding for an environmental stewardship fund. "As a class, we started to take an interest in this and say, 'Hey, this is wrong,'" recalls former student Brock Reeson. "We all just came to a decision to try to do our best to sway these people's decisions. We wrote letters to the finance committee stating why we believed that was bad, and the governor finally vetoed the bill. We were invited to go to Madison, and I got to stand right behind him and watch him veto it."

While River Crossing students are clearly most excited about their hands-on projects, they must still master classroom learning, but even this is grounded in their immediate environment. In history class, for example, River Crossing students explore the ecological and human history of their region, which was home not only to Leopold, but also to other environmental pioneers, including John Muir and Senator Gaylord Nelson, who inspired several important pieces of environmental legislation and the founding of Earth Day.

River Crossing students also read Leopold's *A Sand County Almanac* twice every year. "They're so interested in the content and lessons," says Rydberg, "that we can sit together and pick it apart. They come to understand it better than a lot of adults I've met in the environmental world."

History, literature, and science provide many natural avenues for introducing environmental and ecological concepts, but math initially proved a little more challenging. Rydberg applied for a grant from the Wisconsin Department of Public Instruction Charter School Program, which enabled her to oversee the development of a new math curriculum, with units on everything from prairies to gardening and freshwater systems.

For example, a unit on birds challenged students to apply their knowledge of geometry to explore how the weight of a feather affects a bird's flight, and how to calculate the ratio of primary to secondary feathers. "It lets them learn math in a context that seems relevant to them," says Rydberg, "and makes sure they learn what they need to know for the tests."

This leads, of course, to the big question: How can River Crossing students spend their time building rain gardens, quizzing mayoral candidates, and lobbying against environmental budget cuts—and still pass No Child Left Behind tests?

"I never focus on teaching to the test. I think it is the most stressful day of the whole year. And, if I could throw out all grades, I would do that," says Rydberg. "Grades don't show what these students are learning; the projects do." In an attempt to

Smart by Nature

have students demonstrate that knowledge, she requires them to present a portfolio of the year's work to parents and other community members in the last month of school.

Still, like all public school students, River Crossing youth must eventually sit down and take the required tests. And when they do, they perform remarkably well. Compared to students at Portage Junior High and to the Wisconsin state average for eighth-grade students, they have fared as well or better in all subjects—including eighth-grade reading, math, science, and social studies—since the school opened.[8]

But what happens after these students move back to Portage High, a traditional public school with 800 students? Brittany Roberts remembers well: "Some of the transition was hard. We had kind of a family relationship there. But we just formed a support system: Anybody who needed help, we helped them out."

Making the next big transition to college, where she now studies environmental and elementary education, became even easier because of the self-reliance she developed in middle school. "The biggest thing River Crossing gave me was knowledge of how to learn," she says, adding that her next goal is to return to River Crossing one day as a teacher.

DON'T JUST WORRY, PLANT SOMETHING

What: Clackamas High School

Where: Clackamas, Oregon

Initiators: One teacher

Key Strategies: Sustainable systems class at a public high school

Hands-on learning and experience to help students overcome their fear of nature while boosting their interest in sustainability

It's two o'clock in the afternoon in Rod Shroufe's sustainable systems class at Clackamas High School, a public school outside Portland, Oregon, which boasts one of the first green school buildings in the nation. It's a packed room, with thirty-six juniors and seniors—twice the number who enrolled the year before. One of the newest classes at Clackamas, sustainable systems is also quickly becoming one of the most popular.

"Today you have to do the best-ever full recycle, start to finish," Shroufe announces. "Every can, including out on the football field—emptied, wiped clean, and sorted."

From the middle of the room, a student cheers and raises his fist in triumph.

"Thanks for your enthusiasm," Shroufe says quietly, then barks the order: "OK, go!" Instantly, his students take off throughout the 260,000-square-foot building, with its sloped ceilings, extensive daylighting, and natural ventilation and cooling systems.

Clackamas High lies about 20 miles outside Portland, widely considered one of the greenest cities in the nation, with a longstanding commitment to sustainability. Portland incorporated green design and city planning in the 1970s, decades before most people began to think about it. Now Clackamas students are being initiated into the region's legacy of sustainability.

"There's a ton of environmental research that says if I tell my students one tiny fraction of what's really happening in the world, they'll shut down

Right: Students walk through Clackamas High School, one of the first green school buildings in the nation.

Smart by Nature

and think, 'What can I do?'" says Shroufe. "But we're not about that. We're about, 'Let's go do something!'"

And in the doing, he says, Shroufe gets students interested in the things they need to learn, according to national and state science standards. "The art of teaching is to constantly make those connections between activities and academics, and I believe you have to have a contextual project first so kids come up with the questions themselves."

What Students Can Do

On this crisp autumn afternoon, one student pushes a cart full of supplies, while student teams empty the recycling cans from every hallway, classroom, and office, as well as the surrounding athletic fields. Thirty minutes later, they meet behind the school for the task of sorting. The smell is horrid. But the students, wearing yellow gloves, are nonetheless engaged—even passionate—about their task.

"I hear a can in there!" says Cassie, a junior, as she points to a bag filled with plastic bottles. "People, I hear a can!" The culprit, a Mountain Dew can, is found and put in its proper place.

Is she actually enjoying this?

"No," says Cassie, "it can really stink. But I want to save the earth. I want to do something for the environment." And managing the school's recycling, Cassie and several other students agree, is something they can do.

Sustainability systems students are solely responsible for recycling at Clackamas. Before they took on the job in 2006, some people recycled, but most did not. The campus had only one recycling can for every ten trash cans. As a result of their work, students have earned the money to buy new bins and to pair every trash can with a recycling bin. They have also visited every classroom to give their pitch for recycling.

"Simply from an awareness standpoint, for kids to see firsthand the volume of stuff that goes to a landfill daily is a key academic component if we're training people to be responsible citizens," Shroufe explains. But beyond this, he also uses student recycling and composting projects as opportunities for them to apply the inquiry model, as he challenges them to conduct audits, develop pie charts illustrating trash volumes, and propose strategies to cut down on what ends up in the landfill.

But learning about sustainability, of course, requires more than learning about recycling.

"My overall objective is to teach these kids how to be more sustainable in their own lives. One vehicle for doing that is to take a real close look at what we do here and to figure out how to reduce waste in every aspect," says Shroufe.

"I'm also showing them sustainable alternatives," he adds. He and his students explore sustainable energy and energy use; agriculture and eating practices; and housing and development, including green schools and homes, and the ways people travel between the two.

The sustainable systems class brings old-fashioned knowledge and skills to the new challenge of sustainable living—using opportunities nature provides to understand how it works, giving students hands-on learning experiences, connecting them with the community, and deepening both a sense of place and a commitment to change.

But before Shroufe can begin, he must help them overcome what he has found to be a common obstacle—a fear of nature.

"You know that book by Richard Louv, *Last Child in the Woods*?" Shroufe asks in his office, which is crowded with sticks, leaves, and whittled wooden knives. "These kids are in our children for that family. They're not comfortable outdoors. Something scratches or bites them, and it bugs them." He recalls one memorable example: On a Saturday morning, two students arrived to help clear a field to plant trees. Terrified by the sight of a spider, they immediately abandoned the project.

This is why Shroufe spends the first several weeks simply taking students outside for "sit spots," where they sit in silence and try to develop their senses at play in the environment. "I ask them to start becoming aware of birds and alarm calls, to just get them to listen and watch and journal about it," he says. "I also use animal tracks as a vehicle to awareness. We talk about where the deer and fox were the night before, and all of a sudden, something exists for them that didn't exist before. And bingo! That's when you've got them."

This kind of teaching comes naturally to Shroufe, whose father, the former director of the Arizona Game and Fish Commission, taught his children subsistence living. At college, Shroufe majored in fish and wildlife biology; he then pursued a master's degree in education and put the two interests together at Clackamas. He taught there for a dozen years before proposing the course in sustainable systems in 2006.

One day, Clackamas students were exploring the wetlands beside the school when they came across a half-eaten vole. Shroufe asked them what they thought it was. Someone guessed it was a mouse; another said a rat.

"Why do you think it's only half there?" he asked.

The students thought that a cat, squirrel, or rabbit might have eaten it. Shroufe took advantage of the opportunity to talk about a basic ecological fact: nothing in nature is wasted. A week later, students spotted a clump of animal drop-

Managing the recycling project at Clackamas High is smelly, dirty work, but experiencing firsthand how much goes to a landfill helps students become responsible citizens.

pings with protruding bones on the same trail. Shroufe asked them where the bones might have come from.

"Maybe they're from that mouse we saw the other day!" said one student, who, though he hadn't quite learned the difference between a mouse and a vole, had started to learn something about cycles.

"There you go," said Shroufe. "Now you're starting to see how the death of one animal is feeding that energy chain."

On the same path a few days later, Shroufe asked students to consider where the animal droppings might have gone—suddenly they realized that by walking on this path, they had themselves likely ground them into the dirt.

In this way, Shroufe approaches situations that occur in nature and uses them as opportunities to teach basic ecological principles and systems thinking, or how one thing connects to another.

Making Learning Real

Shroufe's colleague, Andrew Gilford, teaches political science and environmental science, with an eye to the points of intersection between them.

"There has been a shift over the last fifteen to twenty years in Oregon, and the natural resources community in general, toward looking at things on a watershed basis," says Gilford, who grew up in New Jersey. "As a result, I've tried to orient students' perspectives and views on the natural world on a watershed basis."

For example, his students visit local streams to measure water quality. They examine insects, do bacterial studies, and measure connectivity as an indirect test of pesticides and herbicides. But he says the most meaningful experience occurs *after* the students collect this data. They present their findings to the Clackamas River Basin Council, a consortium of twenty-one representatives of the Department of Fish and Wildlife, the Forest Service, local government, local hydropower utilities, and the Oregon Department of Environmental Quality—people who take the student reports quite seriously.

"Students can look at the numbers, see what are considered to be healthy levels, raise an eyebrow," says Gilford. "But they don't see the importance of it until they present it to adults and see their reaction. Then all of a sudden, they think, 'Wow, this is more than an assignment! This has validity.'"

"I Planted Those Trees!"

In collaboration with the largest nonprofit in the Northwest, SOLV, which works to enhance the livability of Oregon, students in Clackamas High's sustainable systems class plant two thousand trees every year. A student who had graduated ten years earlier recently returned with his own child and excitedly pointed out, "I planted those trees!" It's a legacy that makes many Clackamas students proud, says Shroufe, because it is more real and lasting than filling out a worksheet.

Eight Saturday mornings a year, students conduct restorations, tearing down cottonwoods, Japanese knotweed, blackberry, and other invasive species and planting native trees in their place. They've done it both on the school campus and in the wider community, including Goat Island, a natural area on the lower Clackamas River.

"The whole service learning idea adds legitimacy and authenticity to what we're supposed to be doing here," says Shroufe. "To me, that's what makes it real. We're not having them go door-to-door preaching it, and I'm not out wearing tree-hugger shirts. We have a job that needs to happen and the kids are doing it."

Shroufe also uses this project to reinforce the notion of watershed health. "We spend a great length of time in this project looking at the role of plants in the ecosystem and connecting it to everything else," he says. "And the kids come to understand that nothing is a linear process in nature; everything is interactive."

Growing Connections

Making this kind of learning real also entails helping students forge deeper connections to where they live and to the people who live there.

"Since most of these kids have moved in here, the community has doubled and tripled in size," says Shroufe. "They have no sense of place. The sooner we can get them started—growing food for a family that needs it, or working with an elderly man or woman from the community who is a master gardener—the better."

To demonstrate such beneficial connections, Shroufe gets on a cart and drives beyond the baseball diamond to another field—once a big, unused mound of sand. He shows where his students leveled it, built sixteen octagonal beds, installed an irrigation system, and prepared the soil.

Shroufe is arranging for families in the community to pay the students to grow food for eight of those beds. The students will use the money to buy seeds and plant produce in the remaining boxes. Once harvested, according to Shroufe's plan, the food in those boxes will be donated to a food bank—making the community-to-community links come full circle.

"You know, we can sit here and worry about the rainforests in Brazil. There's no end to what we can worry about," says Shroufe. "But if we focus on the community, on local gardening, we can make a really good sustainable life for ourselves."

Still, does he ever worry that even positive efforts such as his represent too little, too late?

Back in his classroom, with a half-dozen students waiting to talk to him, he says: "If as teachers we all do what we can do to teach sustainability, there is exponential learning. If all kids turn around and do the same, we can reach a critical thought mass. I have to hope that will happen."

In the final analysis, he adds, "I am trying to teach kids about the things they have control over and empower them to do it. I have to look at this the same way. What do I have control over? This is it."

GREENING A K–12 CURRICULUM

What: Head-Royce School

Where: Oakland, California

Initiators: A sophomore and the head of school

Key Strategies: Board-articulated top-down goals

Comprehensive green team empowered to initiate changes

Yearlong consultation with the Center for Ecoliteracy

Thorough curriculum audit and identification of new goals

Seemingly small things can lead to big changes in a school, when the moment is right and the community is willing. But changes that ultimately cut across all disciplines and grades are truly remarkable, especially when they take place in an institution founded when Grover Cleveland was president. Still, that is what happened at Head-Royce School, a K–12 independent school in Oakland, California, that has committed itself to greening its entire curriculum.

The story began one spring day in 2006 when Alejo Kraus-Polk, a fifteen-year-old sophomore, entered head of school Paul Chapman's office on a mission: He wanted to invite the executive director of the Berkeley-based Green Schools Initiative to Head-Royce because he wanted to see his school go green. And he was not alone. Soon after, junior Yaeir Heber would be elected student council president on a platform that emphasized environmental action.

Chapman, who saw Kraus-Polk as "nature smart" and part of a growing students' crusade for the environment, approved the request and attended the talk. Having recently seen Al Gore's *An Inconvenient Truth,* he was immediately hooked.

"That period of time was like a moment of spontaneous combustion," recalls Chapman, who has led Head-Royce for twenty-five years. "For me, it was like revisiting 1968." It had become clear that environmental issues were so urgent and central to education that they presented an opportunity to take a stand on the right side of history. Chapman provided the kind of enlightened leadership that,

Right: Schooling for sustainability at Head-Royce is a collaboration of the whole school community to rethink the curriculum and create a healthy campus environment.

as Fritjof Capra says, can facilitate an organization's generating new forms when changing circumstances render the old forms unstable.

Adopting a Green Mission Statement

Chapman decided the most important first step in Head-Royce's becoming a model green school was to signal commitment from the top down. He persuaded the board to approve a green mission comprising four goals:

1. Create a healthy environment.

2. Use resources in a sustainable way.

3. Develop an educational program.

4. Pursue a nutritional health program.

"Putting this [statement of goals] in place before we got started was critical," says Crystal Land, assistant head of school and academic dean. "'Green' didn't just mean composting and recycling or even greening the building. But this [statement] opened things up to discussion of the need for a

Students taste a variety of tomatoes—including ones grown in the Head-Royce school garden.

green curriculum and role modeling, and what all of this means in the classroom."

It also led to an explosion of activities—initiated by students, faculty, staff, and administrators. Among them, Head-Royce:

- Formed a green council of twelve voting members, most of them students

- Changed the school's mission statement to add a "love of nature" to the qualities that educators seek to develop in their students

- Installed more than four hundred solar panels

- Turned a steep hill into a lush garden of native plants, fruit trees, and other edibles, for use as an outdoor classroom

- Conducted a student-run trash audit and cut its overall landfill output in half

- Held school assemblies and an all-day student conference on sustainability

Chapman and Land also encouraged faculty members to find personal connections to the green school mission. Some teachers initiated waste-free lunches; others took field trips to a waste management center that proved profoundly eye-opening, revealing just how much waste the community produces every day; still others got deeply engaged in the new garden. One particularly important opportunity revolved around the creation of a book group. Over a summer break, Land asked teachers to read and discuss one of four books (*How Much Is Enough?* by Alan Durning; *Animal, Vegetable, Miracle* by Barbara Kingsolver; *Field Notes from a Catastrophe* by Elizabeth Kolbert; or *The Omnivore's Dilemma* by Michael Pollan).

"This allowed teachers to connect with one of the four goals pretty meaningfully—to come to a place of seeing, 'Oh, this relates to my life,'" says Land. "It's not just what we are doing as a school, but also as individuals." Finding a personal connection to sustainability, she adds, is essential to inspiring genuine motivation for integrating it into teaching and learning.

The Green Graduate

Head-Royce next turned its attention to greening the curriculum and considering what a green graduate, or someone completing a schooling for sustainability education program, would look like. This was new territory for Chapman, as it would be for many educators. But when he stopped in a bookstore in Point Reyes, California, and mentioned the idea, the seller handed him a book and said, "Why don't you look at this?"

The book was *Ecological Literacy: Educating Our Children for a Sustainable World,* developed and edited by the Center for Ecoliteracy.[9] As Chapman read it, he found that one essay in particular—"Speaking Nature's Language: Principles for Sustainability," by Fritjof Capra, cofounder of the Center for Ecoliteracy and renowned systems thinker—provided a clear framework.

In this essay, Capra explains that in order to design sustainable societies, we must first embrace a new way of seeing the world—systems thinking—that emphasizes the qualities of relationships, connectedness, and context in any system, whether an ecosystem or a school system. Once we make this perceptual shift, Capra explains, we can begin to study sustainability in the language of nature–through concepts that describe the patterns and processes by which nature sustains life. He identifies several that are particularly important, including networks, nested systems, cycles, flows, development, and dynamic balance.

"These concepts, the starting point for designing sustainable communities, may be called principles of ecology, principles of sustainability, principles of community, or even the basic facts of life," writes Capra. "We need curricula that teach our children these fundamental facts of life."

With Capra's essay in hand, Chapman and Land met with the school's twenty department heads and proposed applying these principles throughout the K–12 curriculum. Normally, curriculum changes require about a year to approve. In this case, the committee approved the proposal at that first meeting.

PRINCIPLES OF ECOLOGY

Networks

All members of an ecological community are interconnected in a vast and intricate network of relationships, the web of life. They derive their essential properties and, in fact, their very existence from these relationships. For example, in a garden, a network of pollinators promotes genetic diversity; plants, in turn, provide nectar and pollen to the pollinators.

Nested Systems

Throughout nature we find multileveled structures of systems nesting within systems. Each of these forms an integrated whole within a boundary, while at the same time being a part of a larger whole. For example, cells in an animal are nested within organs, which are nested within systems such as respiration or digestion within individual organisms. Organisms in turn are nested in ecosystems, along with other living organisms and nonliving components such as air and water. Ecosystems are nested within larger systems such as watersheds.

Cycles

Members of an ecological community exchange resources in continual cycles. Ecosystem cycles intersect with larger cycles in the bioregion and the planetary biosphere. In a garden, students see a close-up view of the water cycle when they collect rainwater, mimic precipitation when watering the garden, and observe condensation and evaporation as water appears and disappears on leaves and flowers.

Chapman contacted the Center for Ecoliteracy in nearby Berkeley and invited Capra and cofounder/ executive director Zenobia Barlow to address the faculty. "Having them come in provided a breath of fresh air, a bigger world perspective," says Land. "This wasn't just about Head-Royce anymore, and we weren't in it alone. It added legitimacy to why we were doing this and showed that it was not a fad, but a real grassroots movement."

The next step was to conduct a curriculum audit and develop relevant learning activities. The Center for Ecoliteracy sent Carolie Sly, its director of education programs, to help. A former public school teacher, university professor, and coauthor of the award-winning "California State Environmental Education Guide," Sly takes a collegial approach to working with schools. She began by reviewing Head-Royce's curriculum maps to identify positive starting points—areas where faculty members already taught something related to sustainability and where the ecological principles could most easily integrate into existing lessons.

Flows

All organisms are open systems, which means that they need a continual flow of energy to stay alive. The constant flow of solar energy sustains life and drives most ecological cycles, as seen in a food web. A blade of grass converts energy from the sun to chemical energy through photosynthesis. A mouse eats the blade of grass, a garden snake eats the mouse, a hawk swoops down and eats the snake. In each transfer of energy, some is lost to the universe as heat, requiring an ongoing energy flow into the system.

Development

The unfolding of life, manifesting as development and learning at the individual level and as evolution at the species level, involves interplay of creativity and mutual adaptation in which organisms and environment coevolve. For example, hummingbirds and certain flowers have evolved in ways that are mutually beneficial, as the hummingbird's color vision and slender bill coincide with the colors and shapes of the flowers.

Dynamic Balance

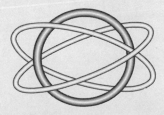

All ecological cycles act as feedback loops, so the ecological community regulates and organizes itself, maintaining a state of dynamic balance characterized by continual fluctuations. For example, ladybugs help keep aphids under control. Otherwise, aphids might destroy the leaves of trees that other insects depend on. When the aphid population falls, some ladybugs die off, which permits the aphid population to rise again, which supports more ladybugs. When the ecosystem is healthy, the numbers of individuals of each species fluctuate, but a balance within the system allows species to thrive together.

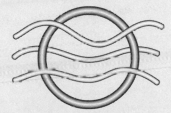

"Carolie pulled out from every grade level examples of where sustainability education was already happening, for instance where we already had lessons in nested systems," says Land. "This made it seem like it didn't all have to be such a big deal. No teacher felt that he or she had to go back and trash an American lit course and make it all about Thoreau." To the contrary, Sly emphasized using schooling for sustainability as an opportunity to look at existing subjects through another lens.

After this, three things happened: First, Land asked teachers to conduct their own curriculum audits, since they are often aware of concepts being taught that might not appear on formal curriculum maps.

"Next, we identified easy access points where we could tweak the curriculum as the train was moving full speed ahead," says Sly. During a first-grade science unit on sandy and rocky shores, for example, teachers added a model beach and simulated an oil spill. "The students could see with their own eyes what happens to the oil and how difficult it is to clean up," says science teacher Debra Harper. "We then brainstormed ways they could reduce the amount of oil they use in their own life." Oil drilling and spills then made more sense to them, she adds, because they had a personal experience with such an "accident" themselves.

Finally, each teacher, with Sly's assistance, took on the larger goal of identifying three to five ways to promote sustainability in future lessons, units, and courses. In the process, teachers proved to themselves that sustainability could be integrated not just into the more obvious subjects such as science, but also into math, literature, history, ethics, comparative politics, world languages, and art.

Says Land: "We are intentionally creating 'green' curriculum at the school by building an understanding of ecological curriculum, asking teams of teachers to work together to make changes, and then formalizing these changes on our K–12 curriculum maps. The changes run the gamut

The book that provided the principles for introducing sustainability into Head-Royce's K–12 curriculum.

THE BIONEERS SERIES

Ecological Literacy

Educating Our Children for a Sustainable World

Edited by Michael K. Stone and Zenobia Barlow

Preface by Fritjof Capra

Left: Students learn to make something beautiful out of pieces that would otherwise be considered junk.

from small to large: every teacher in the school has used the lens of ecoliteracy to rework a unit or assignment, and, in many cases, teachers have revised entire courses to reflect their commitment to changing understanding and attitudes about the environment."

In lower school art classes, for example, students made sculptures out of discarded construction materials and worked on a mural about growing food in a low-income area of East Oakland. Under the direction of elementary school teacher Nina Nathan, they collected paper from recycling bins all over campus, shredded it, and made pulp. They then produced handcrafted paper, which they turned into a beautiful paper quilt. In the process, students learned more than how to make paper.

By leading a conversation about the environmental and aesthetic impact of their project, Nathan says: "Students learned that you can take pieces that would otherwise be considered junk and make something beautiful out of them—something that makes people happy and lifts their spirits."

In upper school comparative politics and ethics classes, high school teacher Karen Bradley took her students on a field trip to the Davis Street Transfer Station, a nearby trash processing facility. "My motivation," recalls Bradley, "was to connect what we throw out to where it goes—to make the connection real rather than abstract—and to learn about our particular community's waste management system."

The director of the recycling program, Rebecca Jewel, took Bradley and her students on a tour and spoke to them about the system from the perspectives of the environment, labor, economics, land use, politics, globalization, and the consumer.

"The takeaway was really remarkable because we were educated on all those levels," says Bradley. When she and her students returned to the classroom, she led them in a discussion designed to have them reflect on their own life choices and to plant some seeds for how they could live more responsibly as they gained more autonomy over their lives. For example, she shared with her students that she had made a personal commitment to *not* buy any new clothes for a year, then challenged them, "What would you be willing to give up to make your consumption on par with people in the rest of the world?" One student proudly came back several days later and reported she had bought her first pair of used jeans; another said she would adopt instead of having children of her own.

Bradley also found that sustainability naturally lent itself to more in-depth studies in her comparative politics class. "Comparative politics looks at countries and collections of countries, and last year I introduced a new unit on the planet: considering the planet as a system, literally and figuratively. What happens in the Amazon jungle affects people throughout the world. If China is emitting toxic waste at a phenomenal rate, it will impact others. I'm trying to help students keep notions of the nation-state in mind but also think beyond that in planetary terms: that the environment belongs to all of us and is the responsibility of all of us."

As in art and politics, Head-Royce pioneered its way into schooling for sustainability throughout the curriculum.

Looking Ahead with a Beginner's Mind

Two years after beginning this process, and going where many schools have yet to go, Land says the teachers still see themselves as having only just begun.

"I think we feel as if we now have Fritjof [Capra's] systems thinking in our brains," she says. "We see more of the complexity of what we're doing, and we recognize that we've barely just opened the door."

Land estimates that it will probably take three to five more years for Head Royce to realize its aspirations in schooling about sustainability, and over that time, there will be periods of messiness, challenges, and questions.

"Some ask, 'How is this going to work with an Advance Placement–driven curriculum? Are we going to lose valuable pieces of knowledge?'" she says. "I certainly don't think so, but we need to be intentional about how we continue to integrate ecoliteracy with college prep."

Looking back, she says that one of the most striking things about the experience is seeing what makes big changes possible. "To me, the biggest lesson is that when people have a personal connection to something, they are much more invested in seeing change happen. This is not about what I did or what Paul [Chapman] or Al Gore did. This is about something that speaks to people—kids, teachers, parents, builders, maintenance staff—deeply and personally."

LESSONS LEARNED FROM

- Teaching through an environmental framework boosts test scores.

- Some students who do not do well in the classroom thrive at hands-on, project-based learning.

- Fieldwork and classroom learning become more meaningful when they are connected to each other.

- If teachers focus on the bad news about the environment, students close down. Giving students an opportunity to do something positive can keep students and teachers inspired.

TEACHNG & LEARNING

- Schooling for sustainability often involves helping students overcome their fear of nature.

- When students see that adults in the community take their schoolwork seriously, they get excited.

- Students appreciate the opportunity to do things, such as planting trees in the community, that feel more real to them than filling out worksheets.

- Many of the ideas central to sustainability education are already being taught, without being named as such.

- A revision of the curriculum may take three to five years, or longer, even when the administration and faculty are committed to it.

WHAT YOU

- Find your own personal connection to sustainability. What do you care most about?

- Bring in an outside organization or speaker. It will help provide a larger context and provide inspiration.

- Begin by identifying what you already do that fits with schooling for sustainability and build on that.

- Conduct a curriculum audit and establish goals for how to incorporate sustainability into every subject.

CAN DO

● Give students a concrete opportunity to do something useful, such as measuring the water quality of a local stream, and present it to local officials.

● Work locally by establishing connections with nature or wildlife organizations in your area and finding out if students can assist them with projects.

● Trust your instincts and invest in networks of relationships. Sustainability is, after all, a community practice.

LEADERS IN SCHOOLING FOR SUSTAINABILITY

As educators become part of the schooling for sustainability movement, many turn to organizations that provide professional development seminars, coaching, and resources for teaching and learning. Three of the leading organizations are the Center for Ecoliteracy, Cloud Institute for Sustainability Education, and Facing the Future. Additionally, the National Wildlife Federation serves as host of the Eco-Schools USA program.

Center for Ecoliteracy, Berkeley, California

Center for ecoliteracy

The Center for Ecoliteracy bases its approach on nearly twenty years of research and experience working with schools.

Says cofounder and executive director Zenobia Barlow, "Our mission has been to provide leadership in applying the understandings eloquently expressed by Fritjof Capra, David Orr, and indigenous leaders like Jeannette Armstrong to strategies for changing educational institutions. We approach schools as whole systems and understand 'curriculum' to mean everywhere and everything that students learn at school. Because of our commitment to schools as communities, we encourage schools and districts to send teams to our seminars and workshops, so they have greater support in applying what they've learned when they get back home."

The Center offers:

● Books, teaching guides, and other print and online publications, including: *Big Ideas: Linking Food, Culture, Health, and the Environment; Ecological Literacy: Educating Our Children for a Sustainable World; Rethinking School Lunch;* and *Getting Started: A Guide for Creating School Gardens as Outdoor Classrooms.*

● Professional development seminars and institutes for individuals and teams from schools and districts. Topics have included Schooling for Sustainability; Rethinking Food, Health, and the Environment; and Making Learning Connections.

● An in-depth sustainability fellows program for educators.

In its long-term work with schools, the Center for Ecoliteracy also offers services including:

● Academic program audits to help educators identify how they already address sustainability, including review of curriculum maps, guides, scope and sequence, and interviews with teachers and administrators.

● Coaching for teaching and learning with individuals and groups, including consultations, lesson observations, demonstration lessons, and help identifying teaching resources.

● In-depth curriculum development with faculty to develop lessons and projects that teach sustainability from the perspective of the head, heart, hands, and spirit.

● Keynote presentations that provide a comprehensive overview of Smart by Nature schooling, including exploration of ecological principles and systems thinking and stories from exemplary schools.

● School sustainability report cards that provide broad assessments of schools' sustainability policies and practices, through the lens of campus, curriculum, community, and school food systems.

● Technical assistance in identifying partners, such as food service providers and change leaders, school garden and cooking program designers, green architects, and practical advisers from other exemplary schools.

Learn more at www.ecoliteracy.org.

The Cloud Institute for Sustainability Education, New York, New York

The Cloud Institute's framework grows out of more than a decade of research and experience with educators and the work of such thinkers as Peter Senge, director of the Center for Organizational Learning at the MIT Sloan School of Management and coauthor of *Schools That Learn.*

The Institute, founded in 1995, focuses on nine core themes: a sense of place, the commons, cultural preservation and transformation, ways to invent and affect the future, how to live within ecological and natural laws and principles, valuing and learning from multiple perspectives and mental models, responsible local and global citizenship, sustainable economics, and system dynamics and change.

"There are a lot of pieces to this puzzle," says founder and president Jaimie Cloud. "We're after the whole system: from addressing the learning self (including knowledge, skills, and attitudes) to pedagogical practices and how the school is organized and relates to the community."

The Institute believes that "[t]he best way to reach young people is by working directly with their entire community—educators, government officials, community members, and the business community." Toward that end, it cofounded the SoL Education Partnership with the Society for Organizational Learning and the Creative Learning Exchange to foster collaborative relationships within and between schools and community government and organizations.

The Cloud Institute offers:

● Curricula ranging from after-school program activities, to three- and four-week units on consumption and ecological economics, to Inventing the Future: Leadership and Participation for the 21st Century, a one-semester course for grades 10 through 12.

● Professional development from one-day workshops to five-year initiatives, emphasizing knowledge and awareness; specific strategies, tools, and processes; curriculum and assessment; and leadership.

● Consulting for independent and public schools.

Learn more at www.sustainabilityed.org.

Facing the Future, Seattle, Washington

Facing the Future seeks to expose the greatest possible number of students to at least a basic understanding of the meaning of sustainability and other global issues.

"We want students to understand that there is a link between the environment, population, consumption, poverty, and conflict. We want them to have the basic vocabulary, understand what an ecological footprint is, and so on. We want them to understand that these are big global issues and that they are connected," says executive director Wendy Church.

Facing the Future offers curriculum resources that emphasize a global perspective on the economy, energy, environment, food and water security, governance, health, peace and conflict, population, and the rich–poor gap. Its resources range from stand-alone lessons and activities that can be completed in thirty minutes, to one- to two-week units, to lessons and student textbooks for use in semester- or yearlong courses. Lesson plans provide teachers with materials, step-by-step instructions, assessment questions, action project ideas, and handouts. Among its curriculum units are Climate Change: Connections and Solutions, and Understanding Sustainability: Two-week Unit for Social Studies.

Its professional development offerings include:

● Teacher workshops at education conferences throughout the United States.

- Customized workshops, in-service training, and other consulting for educators, schools, districts, and state departments of education.

- Online professional development on teaching about global issues and sustainability.

Learn more at www.facingthefuture.org.

National Wildlife Federation, Reston, Virginia

The National Wildlife Federation (NWF) describes itself as the nation's largest conservation organization and is the publisher of the well-known children's magazines, *Your Big Backyard* and *Ranger Rick*.

In 2008, NWF was designated to serve as host for the Eco-Schools USA program, with enrollment of U.S. schools beginning in 2009.

Eco-Schools is an international program that provides a framework to help educators integrate sustainable principles throughout their schools and curriculum. The program is currently being implemented in 37,000 schools in 40 countries.

Created in 1994 by the European Commission and identified by the United Nations Environment Programme as a model initiative for Education for Sustainable Development, the Eco-Schools program is under the auspices of the Foundation for Environmental Education, based in Copenhagen, Denmark.

The Eco-Schools program strives to model environmentally sound practices, provides support toward greening the curriculum, and supports science and academic achievement. It also works to foster a greater sense of environmental stewardship among young people. Schools that are certified in the program undergo an extensive application process; organize a comprehensive assessment of energy and water usage, waste production, and school grounds; and adhere to an action plan that is developed, implemented, and monitored by a student–faculty coalition.

Learn more at www.nwf.org/ecoschools.

RESOURCES

The following resources contain information on a number of topics addressed in this book and are arranged by chapter. Of course, no list of this sort can be comprehensive or exhaustive; these particular resources have been included to offer diverse perspectives. Although the websites and other information presented here were current at the time of publication, they may have changed since.

Center for Ecoliteracy
Berkeley, California

(510) 845-4595
www.ecoliteracy.org

Chapter 1

BOOKS

Ecological Literacy

Capra, Fritjof. *The Web of Life: A New Scientific Understanding of Living Systems.* New York: Anchor Books, 1997.

Capra synthesizes recent scientific breakthroughs in understanding the evolution and organization of living systems and explores their philosophical, social, and educational implications.

Center for Ecoliteracy. *Big Ideas: Linking Food, Culture, Health, and the Environment.* Berkeley: Center for Ecoliteracy, 2008.

Offers a conceptual framework for understanding the connections between food, food production, and personal and environmental health. Includes essential questions, sample activities, and key concepts drawn from *Benchmarks for Science Literacy* from the American Association for the Advancement of Science.

Goleman, Daniel. *Ecological Intelligence: How Knowing the Hidden Impacts of What We Buy Can Change Everything.* New York, London, Toronto, Sydney, and Auckland: Doubleday, 2009.

Describes the evolution of intellectual tools for assessing the environmental and biological impact of everyday decisions, for people living in an infinitely connected world with finite resources.

Orr, David W. *Ecological Literacy: Education and the Transition to a Postmodern World.* Albany: State University of New York Press, 1992.

One of the foundational books defining the role of education in responding to the sustainability crisis facing the world.

Stone, Michael K., and Zenobia Barlow, eds. *Ecological Literacy: Educating Our Children for a Sustainable World.* San Francisco: Sierra Club Books, 2005.

Presents the Center for Ecoliteracy's conceptual foundations and chronicles some of the most successful Center-supported projects that put those concepts into practice.

Systems Thinking

Capra, Fritjof. *The Hidden Connections: A Science for Sustainable Living.* New York: Anchor Books, 2004.

Extends the framework of systems and complexity theory to the social domain and discusses critical issues, including the management of human organizations, the challenges and dangers of economic globalization, the scientific and ethical problems of biotechnology, and the design of ecologically sustainable communities and technologies.

Meadows, Donella H. *Thinking in Systems: A Primer.* White River Junction, VT: Chelsea Green Publishing, 2008.

Posthumously published book by one of the clearest and wisest writers and thinkers to apply systems dynamics to understanding and addressing problems on scales ranging from the personal to the global.

Senge, Peter M. *Schools That Learn: A Fifth Discipline Fieldbook for Educators, Parents, and Everyone Who Cares about Education.* New York: Doubleday/Currency, 2000.

Applies the theories, tools, and methods of systems dynamics and organizational learning in order to give people a way to think about and act upon the underlying forces that shape schools and communities.

Chapter 2

BOOKS

Cooper, Ann, and Lisa M. Holmes. *Lunch Lessons: Changing the Way We Feed Our Children.* New York: Collins Living, 2007.

The former director of nutrition services for the Berkeley Unified School District critiques the state of children's nutrition and offers advice, recipes, and recommendations for both parents and school food reformers.

Demas, Antonia. *Hot Lunch: A History of the School Lunch Program.* New York: Food Studies Institute, 2000.

Traces the origins and development of school meals programs in Europe and the United States, with attention to policy decisions made long ago that continue to affect efforts to improve school meals.

Kiefer, Joseph, and Martin Kemple. *Digging Deeper: Integrating Youth Gardens into Schools & Communities.* Montpelier, VT: Food Works/ Common Roots Press, 1998.

A practical, step-by-step guide for creating successful youth gardens, with activities, project ideas, and resources for teaching communities about living sustainably in their local ecosystems.

Kingsolver, Barbara. *Animal, Vegetable, Miracle: A Year of Food Life.* New York: Harper Perennial, 2008.

The acclaimed novelist reports on her family's move to rural Virginia with the intention to buy food raised in their neighborhood, grow it themselves, or do without it.

Levine, Susan. *School Lunch Politics: The Surprising History of America's Favorite Welfare Program.* Princeton: Princeton University Press, 2008.

Traces the history of school lunch in the United States, with attention to the influence of the agricultural and commercial food industries and the consequences for the meals served to students.

Life Lab Science Program. *Getting Started.* Berkeley: Center for Ecoliteracy, 1997.

This collaboration of the Life Lab Science Program and the Center for Ecoliteracy offers a step-by-step guide for starting a school garden and integrating it into the curriculum.

Pollan, Michael. *In Defense of Food: An Eater's Manifesto.* New York: Penguin Press, 2008.

Michael Pollan explores the replacement of food in Western diets with "edible foodlike substances," and indicts the food industry and nutritional science for their complicity in shifting attention from food—and the pleasures of eating—to obsession with a nutrient-by-nutrient litany of isolated substances, viewed as the causes or cures for diet-related unhealthiness.

Poppendieck, Janet. *Free for All: Fixing School Food in America.* Berkeley: University of California Press, scheduled for publication 2010.

Illuminates the "deep politics" of the National School Lunch and Breakfast Programs from perspectives including history, policy, environmental sustainability, nutrition, and taste. Draws from extensive interviews with officials, workers, students, and activists.

Schlosser, Eric, and Charles Wilson. *Chew on This: Everything You Don't Want to Know about Fast Food.* New York: Houghton Mifflin, 2007.

The author of *Fast Food Nation* tells the whole story of fast food, including its social and nutritional conse quences, for preteen readers.

Teachers College Columbia University. *LiFE Curriculum Series: Growing Food; Farm to Table & Beyond; Choice, Control, & Change.* New York and South Burlington, VT: Teachers College Columbia University and National Gardening Association, 2007–2010.

This series from Teachers College Columbia University is designed to teach children to think scientifically, using scientific evidence to construct theories about food and food systems that can lead to choices that promote ecological and personal health.

Waters, Alice. *Edible Schoolyard: A Universal Idea.* San Francisco: Chronicle Books, 2008.

Alice Waters tells the story of the Edible Schoolyard at Martin Luther King Middle School in Berkeley and the growth of the idea of Edible Education—integrating academics with the growing, cooking, and sharing of wholesome and delicious food.

FILMS

Food, Inc. Dir. Robert Kenner. Features Michael Pollan, Eric Schlosser, Gary Hirshberg, Joel Salatin. Participant Media, 2009. Documentary. www.participantmedia.com

Exposes the highly mechanized underbelly of our nation's food industry, hidden from the American consumer with the consent of our government's regulatory agencies, USDA and FDA.

The Future of Food. Dir. Deborah Koons Garcia. Lily Films, 2004. Documentary. www.thefutureoffood.com

Offers an in-depth investigation into the unlabeled, patented, genetically engineered foods that have quietly filled U.S. grocery store shelves for the past decade.

In Good Heart: Soil and the Mystery of Fertility. Dir. Deborah Koons Garcia. Lily Films, Spring 2010. Documentary. www.ingoodheart.com

Examines our dependence on soil and its impact on current global challenges, including climate change, resource depletion, and peak oil. Includes interviews and soil explorations with scientists, activists, academics, and farmers.

Two Angry Moms. Dir. Amy Kalafa. Features Dr. Susan Rubin, Ann Cooper. Two Angry Moms, 2008. Documentary. www.angry moms.org.

Chronicles nationwide efforts in the movement for better school food, with strategies for overcoming roadblocks and getting healthy, good tasting, real food into school cafeterias.

GOVERNMENT RESOURCES

Child Nutrition Programs
Washington, DC
(202) 694-5050
www.ers.usda.gov/Briefing/ChildNutrition

This USDA Economic Research Service website features studies, reports, and other information about food assistance programs that exclusively or primarily serve children.

Harvest of the Month: Network for a Healthy California
Sacramento, CA
(916) 449-5400
www.harvestofthemonth.com

This California Department of Public Health program offers educators tools and resources for creating hands-on opportunities that help students learn the importance of eating fruits and vegetables and being active every day. Website includes downloadable "How to Grow Healthy Students" guide.

Healthy Youth!
Washington, DC
(800) 232-4636
www.cdc.gov/HealthyYouth

The Centers for Disease Control and Prevention's Division of Adolescent and School Health provides resources for preventing health risk behaviors among children, adolescents, and young adults.

School Meals
Alexandria, VA
(703) 305-2062
www.fns.usda.gov/cnd

The USDA Food and Nutrition Service's School Meals include the National School Lunch Program, School Breakfast Program, Special Milk Program, and Team Nutrition.

ORGANIZATIONS

Farm to School

Ecotrust Farm to School
Portland, OR
(503) 227-6225
www.ecotrust.org/farmtoschool

Works to promote the long-term health of children by making changes in the school lunchroom that incorporate healthy, locally sourced products; a nutrition-based curriculum; and experiential learning opportunities through farm visits, gardening, and recycling.

Farm-Based Education Association
Concord, MA
(978) 318-7827
www.farmbasededucation.org

Supports the professional needs of the farm-based education community through professional development events, materials, and online resources.

The Food Project
Lincoln, MA
(781) 259-8621
www.thefoodproject.org

See the "BLAST Youth Initiative" for resources that teach K–12 students about sustainable agriculture and food systems.

National Farm to School Network
Center for Food & Justice
Los Angeles, CA
(323) 341-5095
Community Food Security Coalition
Washington, DC
(202) 543-8602
www.farmtoschool.org

A joint program of the Center for Food & Justice at Occidental College and the Community Food Security Coalition. Connects schools with local farms to improve student nutrition, provide experiential education opportunities, and support local farmers.

Gardens

The Edible Schoolyard
Berkeley, CA
(510) 558-1335
www.edibleschoolyard.org

Founded by Alice Waters, this program at Martin Luther King Middle School grows and sustains an organic garden integrated into the school's curriculum, food service, and kitchen classroom.

Kids Gardening
South Burlington, VT
(800) 538-7476
www.kidsgardening.org

National Gardening Association program that provides resources, materials, and teaching tips for connecting youth with gardens.

National Gardening Association
South Burlington, VT
(802) 863-5251
www.garden.org

Supports gardeners and teachers with information and resources to advance the personal, community, and educational benefits of gardening; publishers of the LiFE curriculum.

School Garden Weekly
Los Angeles, CA
sgw@schoolgardenweekly.com
www.schoolgardenweekly.com

Weekly e-newsletter with relevant stories and instructional activities for school gardens.

School Food, Nutrition, and Education

Better School Food
Mt. Kisco, NY
(914) 864-1293
www.betterschoolfood.org

Parents, educators, and health professionals work with local communities to improve meals and increase awareness of the connection between food, health, and students' ability to learn.

Center for Science in the Public Interest
Washington, DC
(202) 332-9110
www.cspinet.org

Advocates for nutrition and health, food safety, alcohol policy, and sound science. Its "School Foods Tool Kit" is downloadable at www.cspinet.org/schoolfoodkit.

The Food Trust
Philadelphia, PA
(215) 575-0444
www.thefoodtrust.org

Promotes good nutrition through education, research, and advocacy for public policy.

Healthy School Lunch Campaign
Washington, DC
(202) 686-2210
www.healthyschoollunches.org

Sponsored by the Physicians Committee for Responsible Medicine, this project educates government and school officials, food service workers, parents, and activists about making healthier food choices available in schools.

School Nutrition Association
Alexandria, VA
(703) 739-3900
www.schoolnutrition.org

National organization of school nutrition professionals focused on the practical issues of school food service. They have an active public policy group and a voice in legislation regarding school meals.

Society for Nutrition Education
Indianapolis, IN
(317) 328-4627
www.sne.org

International professional organization devoted to public nutrition education, including but not limited to schools. They have a voice in legislative issues and offer research-based papers and programs.

Chapter 3

PUBLICATIONS

Broda, Herbert W. *Schoolyard-Enhanced Learning. Using the Outdoors as an Instructional Tool, K–8.* Portland, ME: Stenhouse Publishers, 2007.

How-to advice on using school grounds and natural areas beyond the campus as outdoor classrooms, including lessons and activities for teaching content and developing skills in experiencing, observing, and learning from nature.

Danks, Sharon. *Asphalt to Ecosystems: Design Ideas for Schoolyard Transformation.* Oakland: New Village Press, 2009.

An extensively illustrated tour of innovative schoolyard projects around the world, including edible gardens, wildlife habitats, rainwater catchment systems, energy generation projects, and creative play areas, with advice, technical resources, ideas, and frameworks that can be adapted to a variety of settings.

Grant, Tim, and Gail Littlejohn, eds. *Greening School Grounds: Creating Habitats for Learning.* Gabriola Island, BC: New Society Publishers, 2001.

The editors of *Green Teacher* magazine present an anthology of articles by educators and practitioners to guide teachers through all phases of a project, from winning the support of administrators to designing and creating to exploring the multiple educational uses of school nature areas.

The Green Schools Initiative. "Little Green Schoolhouse: Thinking Big about Ecological Sustainability, Children's Environmental Health and K–12 Education in the USA." Berkeley, CA: The Green Schools Initiative, 2005. Download at www. greenschools.net/greenschools.pdf.

This downloadable 40-page guide from the Green Schools Initiative presents a framework and many examples for envisioning and reforming schools to provide healthy environments for students and staff and to promote ecological sustainability.

Orr, David W. *The Nature of Design: Ecology, Culture, and Human Intention.* New York: Oxford University Press, 2004.

David Orr uses the creation of the Adam Joseph Lewis Center at Oberlin College, the first substantially green building on a college campus, as the starting point for provocative meditations on ecological design and education for sustainability.

ECOLOGICAL FOOTPRINT CALCULATORS

Earth Day Network Footprint Calculator: www.earthday.net/footprint/index.html

Earth Team's School Neutral Carbon Calculator: www.earthteam.net/action_month

EPA Household Emissions Calculator: www.epa.gov/climatechange/emissions/ind_calculator.html

WattzOn: www.wattzon.com

Free online tools to quantify, track, compare, and understand the total amount of energy needed to support all facets of peoples' lifestyles.

GOVERNMENT RESOURCES

EnergySmart Schools
Washington, DC
(202) 586-9495
www.eere.energy.gov/buildings/energysmartschools

U.S. Department of Energy public/private partnership to improve energy efficiency in K–12 schools. Website includes downloadable "Guide to Financing EnergySmart Schools."

Green Building Basics
Sacramento, CA
(916) 341-6000
www.ciwmb.ca.gov/greenbuilding/basics.htm

Resources on sustainable building from the California Integrated Waste Management Board.

Healthy School Environments
Washington, DC
(202) 343-9370
www.epa.gov/schools

Resource list from the U.S. Environmental Protection Agency, including downloadable Healthy School Environments Assessment Tool (HealthySEAT)—a free, customizable software program to help school districts evaluate and manage environmental, safety, and health concerns.

Indoor Air Quality Tools for Schools
Washington, DC
(202) 343-9370
www.epa.gov/iaq/schools

A comprehensive EPA resource to help schools identify, prevent, and correct IAQ problems.

Protecting Children's Health
Washington, DC
(202) 564-2188
www.epa.gov/region02/children

This webpage from EPA's Region 2 includes well-organized information and links to national resources and contacts.

ORGANIZATIONS

Green and Healthy Schools

Building Minds, Minding Buildings
Washington, DC
(202) 879-4400
www.aft.org/topics/building-conditions

This American Federation of Teachers webpage includes links to downloadable reports, including "Our Union's Road Map to Green and Sustainable Schools" and "Turning Crumbling Schools into Environments for Learning."

Children's Environmental Health Network
Washington, DC
(202) 543-4033
www.cehn.org

National education, research, and advocacy organization to protect the fetus and the child from environmental health hazards and promote a healthy environment.

Cleaning for Healthy Schools Toolkit
Washington, DC
(202) 543-7555
www.cleaningforhealthyschools.org

Toolkit developed primarily by the Healthy Schools Network, with presentations, fact sheets, and other resources to build awareness, knowledge, and commitment to best practices for green cleaning in schools and childcare centers.

The Green Flag Program
Falls Church, VA
(703) 237-2249
www.greenflagschools.org

This project coordinated by the Center for Health, Environment, and Justice provides resources, classroom activities, and lesson plans about common school-based environmental issues, including waste reduction and indoor air quality.

The Green Schools Initiative
Berkeley, CA
(510) 525-1026
www.greenschools.net

Supports students, teachers, parents, and policymakers working to eliminate toxins, use resources sustainably, create green spaces and buildings, and serve healthy food. Resources on website include "7 Steps to Green Your School" and the *Green Schools Buying Guide*.

Healthy Schools Campaign
Chicago, IL
(312) 419-1810
www.healthyschoolscampaign.org

Advocates for policies and practices for healthy school environments and environmental justice.

Healthy Schools Network, Inc.
Washington, DC
(202) 543-7555
www.healthyschools.org

National organization that provides research, information, education, coalition building, and advocacy for healthy, safe learning environments.

National Clearinghouse for Educational Facilities
Washington, DC
(888) 552-0624
www.edfacilities.org/rl/green_schools_learning_impacts.cfm

Webpage includes links, books, and journal articles examining the association between student achievement and the physical environment of schools.

Science & Environmental Health Network
Ames, IA
(515) 268-0600
www.sehn.org

Consortium of environmental organizations working to apply science to protect the environment and human health. Leading advocate for applying the Precautionary Principle to public policy.

Green Schoolyards

Bay Tree Design, Inc.
Berkeley, CA
(510) 644-1320
www.baytreedesign.com

Landscape architecture and planning firm that works with schools to transform schoolyards into environments for ecological learning and play.

High Performance School Design

BuildingGreen.com
Brattleboro, VT
(802) 257-7300
www.buildinggreen.com

Independent publishing company committed to presenting green design information from a whole-systems perspective, with some attention specifically on schools.

Collaborative for High Performance Schools
San Francisco, CA
(415) 957-9888
www.chps.net

Facilitates the design of high-performance schools through recognition and rating programs, training, best practices manuals, and directories of green services and products.

Green Building: Cities and Schools
Santa Monica, CA
(310) 581-2700
www.globalgreen.org/greenurbanism/schools

American arm of Green Cross International (GCI), created by Mikhail Gorbachev in 1993 to foster a global value shift toward sustainability. Webpage includes downloadable "Healthier, Wealthier, Wiser: A Report on National Green Schools."

Green Schools Program
Washington, DC
(202) 857-0666
www.ase.org/section/program/greenschl

Alliance to Save Energy program that engages students in creating hands-on energy-saving activities in their schools.

Green Technology
Pasadena, CA
(626) 577-5700
www.green-technology.org

A nonprofit initiative to inform government efforts and provide a forum for government officials to communicate about green technologies. Sponsors an annual Green California Schools Summit & Exposition that attracts participants nationwide. Their newsletter frequently runs features on green schools.

Grid Neutral Schools Program
Sacramento, CA
(916) 445-8100
www.dsa.dgs.ca.gov/OtherProg/
gridneutral.htm

California Division of the State Architect program for creating campuses that generate as much electrical energy as they consume. The website includes a 43-page guide (not California-specific) to help schools and community colleges cut energy costs and achieve electrical independence.

Sustainable Design for Schools
Seattle, WA
(206) 352-2050
www.pprc.org/pubs/schools

A report on sustainable design from the Pacific Northwest Pollution Prevention Resource Center based on an ecosystem understanding of buildings as part of, rather than apart from, the natural environment.

U.S. Green Building Council;
Leadership in Energy and
Environmental Design (LEED)
Washington, DC
(800) 795-1747
www.usgbc.org

The USGBC's Leadership in Energy and Environmental Design (LEED) Green Building Rating System certifies that buildings have met green criteria for design, construction, and operation. The LEED for Schools program applies standards developed specifically for schools. USGBC's Build Green Schools program (www.buildgreenschools.org) provides educational resources.

Purchasing

National Association of Educational Procurement
Baltimore, MD
(443) 543-5540

www.naepnet.org/Microsites/
sustainability

A professional association serving higher education purchasing officers in the United States and Canada. Their sustainability webpage includes information and resources on environmentally preferable purchasing.

Chapter 4

PUBLICATIONS

Armstrong, Jeannette. "Let Us Begin with Courage." Download at www.ecoliteracy.org/publications.

Essay by Okanagan wisdom keeper Jeanette Armstrong describes processes for sustainable living that have been practiced for centuries by indigenous communities.

Ehrlich, Thomas, ed. *Civic Responsibility and Higher Education.* Westport, CT: The Oryx Press, 2000.

Explains the theory and practice of civic learning and provides practical examples of programs that prepare students for lives of civic engagement.

Gruenewald, David A., and Gregory A. Smith, eds. *Place-Based Education in the Global Age: Local Diversity.* New York: Routledge, 2007.

Frames place-based pedagogy as part of a broader social movement reclaiming the significance of the local, and links the development of ecological awareness and stewardship to concerns about equity and cultural diversity.

Hawken, Paul. *Blessed Unrest: How the Largest Social Movement in History Is Restoring Grace, Justice, and Beauty to the World.* New York: Penguin Books, 2008.

Shows how groups around the world, ranging from neighborhood associations to well-funded international organizations, are confronting such issues as environmental destruction, social justice, and the loss of indigenous cultures.

Tillman, Tiffany. *Healthy Neighborhoods/Healthy Kids Guide.* Shelburne, VT: Shelburne Farms, 2008. Order at www.shelburnefarms.org/prodinfo.asp?number=869.

Contains lesson plans, tools, planning guides, and resources to help educators engage youth in creating livable and sustainable communities, based on the Healthy Neighborhoods/Healthy Kids program in Burlington, Vermont.

Umphrey, Michael L. *The Power of Community-Centered Education: Teaching as a Craft of Place.* Lanham, MD: Rowman & Littlefield Education, 2007.

Provides psychological, sociological, historical, and philosophical insights into why community works so well as an organizing principle for high school.

Wheatley, Margaret J. *Leadership and the New Science: Discovering Order in a Chaotic World.* San Francisco: Berrett-Koehler Publishers, 2006.

Guide to applying new discoveries in biology, chaos theory, and quantum physics to organizations of all types and to our personal lives.

ORGANIZATIONS

Center for Whole Communities
Fayston, VT
(802) 496-5690
www.wholecommunities.org

Offers retreats, workshops, and training and evaluation tools to those working for land and ecological restoration, food security, community revitalization, active living, smart growth, the faith community, social and environmental justice, public health, and land conservation.

National School Reform Faculty
Bloomington, IN
(812) 330-2702
www.nsrfharmony.org

A professional development initiative that focuses on developing collegial relationships, encouraging reflective practice, and rethinking leadership in restructuring schools in support of increased student achievement.

Sustainable Schools Project
Shelburne, VT
(802) 985-0331
www.sustainableschoolsproject.org

Sponsored by Shelburne Farms, SSP helps schools use sustainability as an integrating context for curriculum, community partnerships, and campus practices. Two public schools in Burlington, Vermont, serve as pilot sites.

Vermont Education for Sustainability
Shelburne, VT
(802) 985-8686 x31
www.vtefs.org/resources

A resources page that includes a link to "The Vermont Guide to Education for Sustainability."

Chapter 5

PUBLICATIONS

American Association for the Advancement of Science. *Atlas of Science Literacy, Volumes 1 and 2.* Washington, DC: AAAS and National Science Teachers Association, 2001–2007. Sample maps available at www.project2061.org.

Part of the American Association for the Advancement of Science's Project 2061 to bring science literacy to the United States by the year 2061 (the next appearance of Halley's Comet), the *Atlas* is a collection of conceptual strand maps and commentary that show how students' understanding of the ideas and skills that lead to literacy in science, mathematics, and technology might develop from kindergarten through 12th grade.

American Association for the Advancement of Science. *Benchmarks for Science Literacy: Project 2061.* New York: Oxford University Press, 1993. Full text available at www.project2061.org.

An AAAS Project 2061 statement of what all students should know and be able to do in science, mathematics, and technology by the end of grades 2, 5, 8, and 12.

American Association for the Advancement of Science. *Science for All Americans: Project 2061.* New York: Oxford University Press, 1990.

AAAS Project 2061 publication that defines science literacy and lays out some principles for effective learning and teaching. It articulates and connects fundamental ideas in science without technical vocabulary and dense detail.

Green Teacher Magazine
Niagara Falls, NY/Toronto, ON
(888) 804-1486
www.greenteacher.com

Quarterly magazine featuring ideas for rethinking education in light of environmental and global challenges. Includes practical articles and ready-to-use activities and evaluations of books, kits, games, and other resources.

Louv, Richard. *Last Child in the Woods: Saving Our Children from Nature-Deficit Disorder.* Chapel Hill, NC: Algonquin Books, expanded edition, 2008.

Louv argues for a return to an awareness of and experience in nature (including healthy stretches of unstructured time) for the well-being of both children and the natural world.

Sobel, David. *Beyond Ecophobia: Reclaiming the Heart in Nature Education.* Great Barrington, MA: The Orion Society, 1996.

David Sobel argues for developmentally appropriate education that gives young children the opportunity to develop love for the natural world before confronting them with news of ecological disaster.

Sobel, David. *Place-Based Education: Connecting Classrooms & Communities.* Great Barrington, MA: The Orion Society, 2004.

A concise introduction to the movement to reconceptualize environmental education by connecting students to neighborhoods, communities, and ecologies, based on the work of Community-based School Environmental Education in New England.

GOVERNMENT RESOURCES

EPA Teaching Center
Washington, DC
(202) 564-0443
www.epa.gov/teachers

Information on curriculum resources and activities, community service projects, and environmental laws.

ORGANIZATIONS

Environmental Education

Center for Environmental Education
Unity, ME
(207) 948-3131, x295
www.ceeonline.org

Provides resources, curricula, expertise, and guidance to address climate change issues and cultivate environmental leadership in K–12 schools.

Children & Nature Network
Santa Fe, NM
(505) 603-4607
www.childrenandnature.org

Provides access to news and research and a peer-to-peer network of researchers, educators, organizations, and individuals dedicated to reconnecting children and nature.

Environmental Literacy Council
Washington, DC
(202) 296-0390
www.enviroliteracy.org

Established to bring together scientists, economists, educators, and other experts to inform environmental studies. The website offers extensive background information and resources on environmental topics, curricular materials, and textbook reviews.

Environmental Protection Agency
Washington, DC
(202) 564-0443
www.epa.gov/enviroed

U.S. Environmental Protection Agency webpage provides information, resources, and links covering a broad spectrum of environmental education.

National Environmental Education Foundation
Washington, DC
(202) 833-2933
www.neefusa.org

Partners with professionals in health, education, media, business, and public land management to promote daily actions for helping people protect and enjoy the environment.

North American Association for Environmental Education
Washington, DC
(202) 419-0412
www.naaee.org

Network of professionals, students, and volunteers working in the field of environmental education throughout North America and in more than fifty-five countries around the world.

Improved Learning

Go Green Database
San Rafael, CA
(415) 662-1600
www.edutopia.org/go-green

An interactive database from Edutopia/The George Lucas Educational Foundation that allows users to search by topic, grade level, cost, or location for sustainability curricula, with comments and ratings from users.

Green Charter Schools Network
Madison, WI
(608) 238-7491
www.greencharterschools.org

Supports the establishment, enhancement, and advancement of charter schools with environment-focused educational programs and practices.

Place-based Education

Antioch New England Institute
Keene, NH
(603) 283-2105
www.antiochne.edu/anei

Consulting and community outreach department of Antioch University New England. Works with local, state, and national government agencies to promote sustainable environment, economy, and society by encouraging informed civic engagement.

Center for Place-based Education
Keene, NH
(603) 283-2105
www.antiochne.edu/anei/cpbe

Part of the Antioch New England Institute, the Center encourages partnerships between students, teachers, and community members that strengthen and support student achievement, community vitality, and a healthy environment.

Sustainability Education

The Cloud Institute for Sustainability Education
New York, NY
(212) 645-9930
www.sustainabilityed.org

Hosts faculty/staff development workshops and creates courses and classroom units that explore the relationships between economic systems, ecological systems, and justice in contexts ranging from local communities to global institutions.

Creative Change Educational
Solutions
Ypsilanti, MI
(734) 482-0924
www.creativechange.net

Provides curricula, professional development, and consulting services on topics including brownfields revitalization, food systems, green design, ecological economics, and intercultural relations.

Creative Learning Exchange
Acton, MA
(978) 635-9797
www.clexchange.org

Offers resources and training for K–12 education based on systems thinking and system dynamics modeling.

Eco-Schools International
Lisbon, Portugal
coordination@eco-schools.org
www.eco-schools.org
Eco-Schools USA/
National Wildlife Federation
Reston, VA
(800) 822-9919
www.nwf.org/ecoschools/index.cfm

Aims to raise students' awareness of environmental and sustainable development issues by combining classroom study with school and community action. Provides an integrated system for environmental management and certification of schools in more than forty countries.

Facing the Future
Seattle, WA
(206) 264-1503
www.facingthefuture.org

Delivers curriculum and workshops to middle and high school teachers from all over the world. Maintains an online database of service-learning projects of international and local interest, and provides service-learning workshops to educators.

Go Green Initiative
Pleasanton, CA
(925) 931-0386
www.gogreeninitiative.org

Works to unite parents, students, teachers, and school administrators to make lasting change and create a culture of environmental responsibility on school campuses.

Green Schools Alliance
New York, NY
(435) 259-1610
www.greenschoolsalliance.org

A project of Global Environmental Options for schools to promote energy conservation and environmental responsibility worldwide.

Sustainability Education Handbook:
Resource Guide for K–12 Teachers
East Lansing, MI
(517) 337-0422
www.urbanoptions.org/
SustainEdHandbook

A program of Urban Options, this site provides curricula that can be customized for different classrooms and state standards.

Sustainability K–12 Listserv

Launched by the U.S. Partnership for Education for Sustainable Development as the first national listserv for K–12 educators focused specifically on education for sustainability. To join, go to https://listserver.itd.umich.edu/cgi-bin/lyris.pl?enter=sustaink12 or send an email to sustaink12-request@umich.edu with "subscribe" in the subject line of the message.

Teaching and Learning for a
Sustainable Future
Paris, France
bpi@unesco.org
www.unesco.org/education/tlsf

Multimedia teacher education program from UNESCO contains professional development modules for teachers, teacher educators, and student teachers reflecting an interdisciplinary approach to developing knowledge and skills for sustainability.

U.S. Partnership for Education for
Sustainable Development
Washington, DC
uspesd@gmail.com
www.uspartnership.org

The U.S. affiliate of the United Nations Decade of Education for Sustainable Development, consisting of individuals, organizations, and institutions with a shared commitment to integrate sustainable development into education and learning. Website links to its proposed national standards for sustainability education.

NOTES

Chapter 1

Epigraph: David W. Orr, *Earth in Mind* (Washington, Covelo, and London: Island Press, 2004), p. 52.

1. Michael Pollan, "Our Decrepit Food Factories," *New York Times Magazine* (December 16, 2007), http://www.nytimes.com/2007/12/16/magazine/16wwln-lede-t.html?pagewanted=1 (accessed October 21, 2008).

2. William McDonough and Michael Braungart, *Cradle to Cradle: Remaking the Way We Make Things* (New York: North Point Press, 2002), p. 155.

3. Alan AtKisson, *Believing Cassandra: An Optimist Looks at a Pessimist's World* (White River Junction, VT: Chelsea Green, 1999), p. 148.

4. Quoted in President's Council on Sustainable Development, *Education for Sustainability: An Agenda for Action* (Washington, DC: U.S. Government Printing Office, 1996), p. 9 (a report of the National Forum on Partnerships Supporting Education about the Environment).

5. North American Association for Environmental Education, "Mission," http://www.naaee.org/about-naaee/mission (accessed February 26, 2009).

6. U.N. World Commission on Environment and Development, "Our Common Future," http://www.un-documents.net/ocf-02.htm (accessed February 26, 2009).

7. Darrow School in New York, for instance, pictures sustainable decision making as a triangle with "human welfare," "environmental health," and "economic objectives" at the corners.

8. "About Eco-Schools," http://www.eco-schools.org/aboutus/aboutus.htm (accessed February 26, 2009).

9. National Association of Independent Schools, "Environmental Sustainability," http://www.nais.org/sustainable/article.cfm?ItemNumber=149403&sn.ItemNumber=151258 (accessed October 3, 2008).

10. Janine M. Benyus, "Nature's 100 Best: Top Biomimicry Solutions to Environmental Crises," Bioneers 19th Annual Conference, San Rafael, CA, October 19, 2008, plenary address.

11. Fritjof Capra, "Preface," in *Ecological Literacy: Educating Our Children for a Sustainable World*, ed. Michael K. Stone and Zenobia Barlow, xiii (San Francisco: Sierra Club Books, 2005).

12. David W. Orr, "The Designer's Challenge," Center for Ecoliteracy: Education for Sustainability essay, 2007, http://www.ecoliteracy.org/publications/david_orr_challenge.html (accessed September 25, 2008).

13. Fritjof Capra, "Landscapes of Learning," *Resurgence* 226 (September/October 2004): 8.

14. In his essay "Speaking Nature's Language," Capra identifies eight particularly important principles: networks, nested systems, inter-dependence, diversity, cycles, flows, development, and dynamic balance (see Michael K. Stone and Zenobia Barlow, eds., *Ecological Literacy: Educating Our Children for a Sustainable World* [San Francisco: Sierra Club Books, 2005], p. 23). Educator Art Sussman argues that just three principles (matter cycles, energy flows, and life webs) provide an organizing framework for understanding complicated environmental issues (see *Dr. Art's Guide to Planet Earth: For Earthlings Ages 12 to 120* [San Francisco: WestEd, 2000], p. 17).

15. Wendell Berry, *The Gift of Good Land* (New York: North Point Press, 1982), pp. 134–48.

16. Ron Bratlie, "A New Kind of Integration: Sustainable Design and Student Learning," *School Business Affairs* (October 2005): 27, http://asbointl.org/asbo/files/ (accessed February 26, 2009).

17. David Sobel, *Place-Based Education: Connecting Classrooms & Communities* (Great Barrington, MA: The Orion Society, 2004), p. 35.

18. Richard Louv, *Last Child in the Woods: Saving Our Children from Nature-Deficit Disorder* (Chapel Hill, NC: Algonquin Books, 2006), p. 49.

19. Alan Greene, "Brain Food for Kids," Center for Ecoliteracy: Thinking Outside the Lunchbox essay, http://www.ecoliteracy.org/publications/rsl/alan_greene.html (accessed September 28, 2008).

20. Margaret J. Wheatley and Deborah Frieze, "How Large-Scale Change Really Happens–Working with Emergence," *The School Administrator* (Spring 2007), http://www.margaretwheatley.com/articles/largescalechange.html (accessed February 10, 2009).

21. David W. Orr, "The Designer's Challenge," Center for Ecoliteracy: Education for Sustainability essay, 2007, http://www.ecoliteracy.org/publications/david_orr_challenge.html (accessed September 25, 2008).

22. Pacific Northwest Pollution Prevention Resource Center, "Sustainable Design for Schools," 2001, http://www.pprc.org/pubs/schools/index.cfm (accessed February 10, 2009).

23. David W. Orr, "Place and Pedagogy," in *Ecological Literacy: Education and the Transition to a Postmodern World*, 126, 129 (Albany: State University of New York Press, 1999).

24. David A. Gruenewald and Gregory A. Smith, "Creating a Movement to Ground Learning in Place," in *Place-Based Education in the Global Age*, ed. David A. Gruenewald and Gregory A. Smith, 347 (New York: Lawrence Erlbaum Associates, 2008).

25. David Sobel, *Place-Based Education: Connecting Classrooms & Communities* (Great Barrington, MA: The Orion Society, 2004), p. 21.

26. Shelburne Farms Annual Report 2007, http://www.shelburnefarms.org/about/index.shtm (accessed September 14, 2008).

27. See Center for Ecoliteracy, http://www.ecoliteracy.org; The Green Schools Initiative, "Seven Steps to Green Your School," http://www.greenschools.net/7StepstoaGreen School.htm; The Eco-Schools Programme, "Methodology," http://www.eco-schools.org/page.php?id=19; The Council for Spiritual and Ethical Education, "The Environmentally Conscious School," http://www.csee.org/products/67; Antioch University New England: Department of Environmental Studies, http://www.antiochne.edu/es/default.cfm?ref=nav; Illinois Environmental Protection Agency, "Green Schools Checklist," www.epa.state.il.us/p2/green-schools/green-schools-checklist.pdf.

Chapter 2

Chapter title: Thanks to Ann M. Evans for the chapter title, taken from a sign posted on her health-educator mother's bookshelf. See her essay, "What in Health Is Going On Here?" in the Center for Ecoliteracy Thinking outside the Lunchbox series, http://www.ecoliteracy.org/publications/rsl/ann-evans.html.

Epigraph: Michael Pollan, Foreword, *Big Ideas: Linking Food, Culture, Health, and the Environment*, (Berkeley, CA: Learning in the Real World, 2008), xii.

1. A 2007 Kaiser Family Foundation study estimated that children aged eight to twelve see more than 7,600 television food ads a year; nearly three-quarters of the ads directed at children are for candy and snacks, cereal, and fast food. The Henry J. Kaiser Family Foundation, "Food for Thought: Television Food Advertising to Children in the United States," 2007, http://www.kff.org/entmedia/7618.cfm (accessed July 25, 2008).

2. National Center for Health Statistics, "Prevalence of Overweight Among Children and Adolescents: United States, 2003–2004," 2006, http://www.cdc.gov/nchs/products/pubs/pubd/hestats/overweight/overwght_child_03.htm (accessed February 21, 2008).

3. C. S. Mott Children's Hospital of the University of Michigan, http://www.med.umich.edu/1libr/pa/pa_chilobes_hhg.htm (accessed February 21, 2008).

4. M. Venkat Narayan, James P. Boyle, Theodore J. Thompson, Stephen W. Sorensen, and David F. Williamson, "Lifetime Risk for Diabetes Mellitus in the United States," *Journal of the American Medical Association* 290 (2003): 1884–90.

5. Food Research & Action Center, "Child Nutrition Fact Sheet: Breakfast for Learning," www.frac.org/pdf/breakfastforlearning.PDF (accessed February 22, 2008).

6. Alan Greene, "Brain Food for Children," Center for Ecoliteracy Thinking outside the Lunchbox essay, www.ecoliteracy.org/publications/rsl/alan_greene.html (accessed February 26, 2008).

7. Foodlinks America newsletter, March 28, 2008.

8. E. A. Finkelstein, I. C. Fiebelkorn, and G. Wang, "State-Level Estimates of Annual Medical Expenditures Attributable to Obesity," *Obesity Research*, 12: 18–24.

9. See for instance J. M. Murphy, "Breakfast and Learning: An Updated Review," *Current Nutrition & Food Science* 3 (2007), 3–36. Also "Children with Healthier Diets Do Better in School, Study Suggests," *ScienceDaily*, March 22, 2008, http://www.sciencedaily.com/releases/2008/03/080320105546.htm (accessed April 8, 2008). According to this study, students with an increased fruit and vegetable intake and less caloric intake from fat were 41 percent less likely to fail their school's literacy assessment.

10. See the 2003 joint position paper of the American Dietetic Association, the Society for Nutrition Education, and the American School Food Service Association, "Nutrition Services: An Essential Component of Comprehensive School Health Programs," http://www.ncbi.nih.gov/pubmed/12669016 (accessed January 9, 2009).

11. Michael Ableman, "Raising Whole Children Is Like Raising Good Food: Beyond Factory Farming and Factory School," in *Ecological Literacy: Educating Our Children for a Sustainable World*, ed. Michael K. Stone and Zenobia Barlow, (San Francisco: Sierra Club Books, 2005), p. 181.

12. See for instance a summary in Scott P. Lewis, "Uses of Active Plant-Based Learning in K–12 Educational Settings," white paper prepared for the Partnership for Plant-Based Learning, p. 13, http://www.ppbe.org/index.html (accessed February 27, 2008).

13. The California Department of Education offers an inventory of basic items for outfitting a cooking cart, as well as "teacher tips for cooking with kids" and healthy cooking activities at www.cde.ca.gov/ls/nu/he/cookcart.asp.

14. Antonia Demas, *Hot Lunch: A History of the School Lunch Program* (Trumansburg, NY: Food Studies Institute, 2000), p. 28.

15. Ann E. Evans, "Changing Schools: A Systems View," in *Ecological Literacy: Educating Our Children for a Sustainable World*, ed. Michael K. Stone and Zenobia Barlow, (San Francisco: Sierra Club Books, 2005), p. 255.

16. Unpublished remarks at Center for Ecoliteracy seminar, November 7, 2007.

17. About 60 percent of the 30.5 million children participating in the National School Lunch Program are subsidized. Children from families at or below 130 percent of the federally defined poverty level are eligible for free meals. Families with incomes between 130 percent and 185 percent of the poverty level can be charged no more than 40 cents. In 2007–2008, 130 percent of the poverty level was $26,845 for a family of four; 185 percent was $38,203. Eligibility cut-offs are the same everywhere, regardless of cost of living.

18. School Nutrition Association, "Funding for School Nutrition Programs–The Facts," 2008, http://www.schoolnutrition.org/Index.aspx?id=2811 (accessed June 30, 2008).

19. Congress passed the National School Lunch Act after General Lewis Hershey, Director of the Selective Service, reported that more than 150,000 young men had been rejected for military service and another 150,000 died during the World War II as a result of their weakened conditions, and called malnutrition a national security risk. The program has been administered by the Department of Agriculture. Activists, including leading food scholar Marion Nestle, now argue that school lunch oversight authority should reside with the Department of Health and Human Services and the Department of Education. See Marion Nestle, "School Food, Public Policy, and Strategies for Change," Center for Ecoliteracy: Thinking outside the Lunchbox essay, http://www.ecoliteracy.org/publications/rsl/marion-nestle.html (accessed March 2, 2008).

20. Imogene F. Clarke, food service director, personal communication with Michael K. Stone.

21. Phoebe Tanner, personal communication with Michael K. Stone.

22. Action for Healthy Kids, "The Learning Connection: The Value of Improving Nutrition and Physical Activity in Our Schools," 2004, p. 3, http://www.actionforhealthykids.org/pdf/Learning%20Connection%20-%20Full%20Report%20011006.pdf (accessed February 28, 2008).

23. Center for Weight & Health, University of California, Berkeley, "Dollars and Sense: The Financial Impact of Selling Healthier Foods," p. 4, http://nature.berkeley.edu/cwh/activities/cwhtools.shtml#dol (accessed February 28, 2008). See also http://www.cspinet.org/new/200703051.html.

24. Eliot Coleman, Barbara Damrosch, and Kathy Bray, *Four-Season Harvest: Organic Vegetables from Your Home Garden All Year Long*. (White River Junction, VT: Chelsea Green Publishing, 1999).

25. http://www.sad34.net/~stanguay/garden.html (accessed June 16, 2008).

26. http://www.sad34.net/~stanguay/garden.html (accessed June 16, 2008).

27. Centers for Disease Control and Prevention, *Morbidity and Mortality Report* 55 (September 15, 2006) 36:985–88; at www.cdc.gov/mmwr/PDF/wk/mm5536.pdf (accessed August 17, 2008).

28. Adam Drewnowski and S. E. Specter, "Poverty and Obesity: The Role of Energy Density and Energy Costs," *American Journal of Clinical Nutrition* 79 (January 2004) 1: 6–16.

29. Anupama Joshi, Marion Kalb, and Moira Berry, "Paths to Success for Farm to School Programs," National Farm to Schools Program, 2006, http://www.farmtoschool.org/Nat/

pubs.htm (accessed June 16, 2008).

30. U.S. Department of Agriculture, "Marketing Fresh Produce to Local Schools: The North Florida Cooperative Experience," Bulletin no. 2, July 1999, p. 4.

31. Melanie Payne, interview with Debra Eschmeyer, *Farm to School Routes*, January 2008, p. 2. www.farmtoschool.org/newsletter/jan08/index.htm (accessed April 27, 2009).

32. http://www.foodsecurity.org/farm_to_school.html#how (accessed June 17, 2008).

33. www.farmtoschool.org/NH/programs.htm (accessed June 17, 2008).

34. www.farmtoschool.org/state-programs.php?action=detail&id=12&pid=59 (accessed June 17, 2008).

35. www.farmtoschool.org/state-programs.php?action=detail&id=9&pid=47 (accessed June 17, 2008).

36. www.sevengenerationsahead.org/fresh_from_the_farm.html (accessed June 20, 2008).

37. www.vtfeed.org/aboutus/index.html (accessed July 7, 2008).

38. Rodney Taylor, unpublished presentation, Center for Ecoliteracy Rethinking School Lunch seminar, Berkeley, CA, November 7, 2007. Unless otherwise noted, quotations from Rodney Taylor are from this presentation and personal communication with Michael K. Stone.

39. Jaquie Paul, "His Goal: Salad Bar, Attractively Packaged," *Riverside Press-Enterprise*, May 11, 2004, http://www.pe.com/localnews/riverside/stories/PE_News_Local_rrodney11.a1f85.html (accessed June 19, 2008).

40. J. P. Dozier, director of finance, Bon Appétit Management Company, interview in Finances chapter, Center for Ecoliteracy, "Rethinking School Lunch Guide," p. 7, http://www.ecoliteracy.org/programs/rsl-guide.html (accessed April 25, 2008).

41. James Koshiba, keynote speech at Punahou School, August 20, 2007, http://www.punahou.edu/page.cfm?p=771 (accessed August 5, 2008).

42. http://www.lopezclt.org/affordable_housing/main.html (accessed July 7, 2008).

43. Even water falling from the sky and landing in a pond belongs to the state in the absence of a permit, for which there is a long waiting list. After considerable effort by the school and L.I.F.E., the school obtained catchment rights, and in 2008 voters approved a bond measure to build a new system that will allow expansion of the garden and erection of additional greenhouses on campus.

44. Reported by Michele Heller.

45. Ethan A. Bergman et al., "Relationships of Meal and Recess Schedules to Plate Waste in Elementary Schools," *Insight* 24 (Spring 2004): 1–6.

Chapter 3

Epigraph: Winston Churchill, speaking to the House of Commons, October 28, 1943. http://www.winstonchurchill.org/i4a/pages/index.cfm?pageid=388#Shape_our_Buildings (accessed May 4, 2009).

1. See, for instance, the report from American Federation of Teachers, "Building Minds, Minding Buildings: Our Union's Road Map to Green and Sustainable Schools," 2008, http://www.aft.org/topics/building-conditions/downloads/BMMB_GREENGUIDE.pdf (accessed December 17, 2008).

2. National Clearinghouse for Educational Facilities, http://www.edfacilities.org/ds/statistics.cfm (accessed December 12, 2008).

3. "U.S. Green Building Council: LEED for Schools," http://www.usgbc.org/DisplayPage.aspx?CMSPageID=1586 (accessed February 3, 2009).

4. "The Collaborative for High Performance Schools," http://www.chps.net/ (accessed February 3, 2009).

5. Charles Eley, "Building a New Generation of High Performance Schools." Webinar presentation, December 2, 2008, http://www.chps.net/events/gkatswebinarslides (accessed May 1, 2009).

6. For a discussion of the specific differences between the two systems, see "LEED, CHPS, or HPS?" *Anova Architects Newsletter* (Winter 2008): 1–3, http://www.anovaarchitects.com/news/news.html (accessed December 7, 2008). See also "Collaborative for High Performance Schools: Understanding Green Building Program Options for Schools," 2007, http://www.chps.net/overview/overviewFAQ2.htm (accessed December 7, 2008).

7. Herbert W. Broda, *Schoolyard-Enhanced Learning: Using the Outdoors as an Instructional Tool, K–8* (Portland, ME: Stenhouse Publishers, 2007), p. 24.

8. Sharon Danks, *Asphalt to Ecosystems: Design Ideas for Schoolyard Transformation* (Oakland, CA: New Village Press, 2009).

9. Herbert W. Broda, *Schoolyard-Enhanced Learning: Using the Outdoors as an Instructional Tool, K–8* (Portland, ME: Stenhouse Publishers, 2007), p. 27.

10. "The Green Schools Initiative," http://www.greenschools.net (accessed February 2, 2009).

11. University of Oregon Campus Recycle Program, http://www.uoregon.edu/~recycle/waste_audit_text.html#solidwaste (accessed May 4, 2009).

12. Illinois Environmental Protection Agency, "Green Schools Checklist: Environmental Actions for Schools to Consider," http://www.greeningschools.org/resources/view_resource.cfm?id=14 (accessed May 2, 2009).

13. California Integrated Waste Management Board, http://www3.ciwmb.ca.gov/Schools/WasteReduce/#Why (accessed May 2, 2009).

14. "U.S. Environmental Protection Agency: Environmentally Preferable Purchasing," http://www.epa.gov/epp/pubs/about/about.htm#a (accessed December 22, 2008).

15. See for instance Joe E. Heimlich, "Purchasing Guidelines for the Environmentally Conscious Consumer," Ohio State University Extension, 2008, http://www.ohioline.osu.edu/cd-fact/pdf/0180.pdf (accessed December 20, 2008). See also Washington County, MN, "Green Purchasing: Environmentally Preferable Purchasing & Practices," http://www.co.washington.mn.us/info_for_residents/environment/green_government/green_purchasing/ (accessed December 20, 2008).

16. "The Green Schools Initiative: Green Schools Buying Guide," http://greenschools.live.radicaldesigns.org/display.php?modin=50 (accessed December 22, 2008).

17. U.S. Environmental Protection Agency, "Environmentally Preferable Purchasing," http://www.epa.gov/epp/pubs/about/about.htm#a (accessed December 22, 2008).

18. California Integrated Waste Management Board, "Purchasing," http://www.ciwmb.ca.gov/schools/WasteReduce/Purchasing/ (accessed December 22, 2008).

19. Rutgers University, "Green Purchasing Cooperative Program," http://purchasing.rutgers.edu/green/gp_cooperative.html (accessed December 22, 2008).

20. U.S. Department of Energy, "Guide to Financing EnergySmart Schools," http://www.eere.energy.gov/buildings/publications/pdfs/energysmartschools/ess_finance-guide_0708.pdf (accessed December 14, 2008).

21. See, for instance, case studies at Greening Schools (a project of the Illinois EPA, Department of Natural Resources and the Waste Management Resource Center), http://www.greeningschools.org/resources/view_cat_admin.cfm?id=65 (accessed December 12, 2008), and National Clearinghouse for Educational Facilities, "Case Studies–High Performance Green Schools and Universities," http://www.edfacilities.org/rl/casestudies_HPS.cfm (accessed December 12, 2008).

22. The Green Schools Initiative, "Greenbacks for Green Schools," http://www.greenschools.net/news/documents/greenbacks.pdf (accessed December 12, 2008).

23. U.S. Department of Energy, "Guide to Financing EnergySmart Schools," http://www.eere.energy.gov/buildings/publications/pdfs/energysmartschools/ess_finance-guide_0708.pdf (accessed December 12, 2008).

24. Database of State Incentives for Renewables & Efficiency, http://www.dsireusa.org/index.cfm?&CurrentPageID=3&EE=1&RE=1 (accessed February 2, 2009).

25. San Domenico School, "Our 412 kW Solar Energy System!" http://www.sandomenico.org/page.cfm?p=1359 (accessed February 4, 2009).

26. Racquel Palmese, "Roadmap to Zero Net for California Schools: A Green Technology Interview with David Thorman and Theresa Townsend," *Green Technology Magazine*, http://www.green-technology.org/green_technology_magazine/thorman.htm (accessed December 8, 2008).

27. U.S. Department of Energy, "Building Life-Cycle Cost (BLCC) Programs," http://www1.eere.energy.gov/femp/information/download_blcc.html (accessed December 12, 2008).

28. Greg Kats, "Greening America's Schools: Costs and Benefits," 2006, http://www.cap-e.com/ewebeditpro/items/O59F12807.pdf (accessed December 11, 2008). The study is summarized in an essay by Kats on the Center for Ecoliteracy website: http://www.ecoliteracy.org/publications/gregory_kats.html.

29. "Benefits of Building Green Outweigh Cost Premium." Report on Good Energies website, http://www.goodenergies.com/news/research-knowledge.php (accessed May 2, 2009).

30. Quoted in Christina Koch, "A Green Education: Elementary Students Learn How to Be Good Inhabitants of the Earth," *Eco-Structure* (September–October 2005): 20.

31. David W. Orr, *Earth in Mind: On Education, Environment, and the Human Prospect* (Washington, DC: Island Press, 2004), p. 113.

32. See Pamela Mang, "Regenerative Design: Sustainable Design's Coming Revolution," *Design Intelligence* (July 1, 2001), http://www.di.net/articles/archive/2043/ (accessed January 30, 2009).

33. Regenerative Design Institute, "About RDI," http://www.regenerativedesign.org/about-rdi (accessed January 29, 2009).

34. Mark Biedron and Anthony Sblendorio, "Sustainability and Education at the Willow School: The Importance of Connections," www.usgbc.org/Docs/Archive/MediaArchive/601_Sblendorio_AB532.pdf (accessed July 26, 2008).

35. "Tarkington School of Excellence Parent-Student Handbook 2007–2008," p. 4.

36. Whitney Jackson, "Chicago's First LEED-built Green School Teaches the A, B, Es of Eco Lessons," *Medill Reports* (April 29, 2008), http://news.medill.northwestern.edu/chicago/news.aspx?id=87447 (accessed November 21, 2008).

37. David A. Gruenewald and Gregory A. Smith, "Creating a Movement to Ground Learning in Place," in *Place-based Education in the Global Age*, ed. David A. Gruenewald and Gregory A. Smith, (New York: Lawrence Erlbaum Associates, 2007), p. 349.

38. The website BuildingGreen.com estimates per-square-foot installed costs of $1.50 to $4.00 and ten-year life-cycle costs of $16 to $20 for VCT, versus $2.50 to $5.00 installed costs and $5.00 to $7.50 life-cycle costs for polished concrete. http://www.buildinggreen.com/auth/article.cfm/ID/3252/ (accessed February 2, 2009).

39. Stacey Giordano, "The Living Machine: Implementing Sustainability and Beyond at Darrow School," *Independent School* (Spring 2005): 40–46.

40. See Nancy Jack Todd and John Todd, *From Eco-cities to Living Machines* (Berkeley: North Atlantic Books, 1994).

41. Craig Westcott. Correspondence with Michael K. Stone.

42. "Hands to Work in Body and Spirit," *Peg Board* 73–1 (Winter 2005–2006): 2–14.

43. Northfield Mount Hermon School, "Sustainability Audit 2007," http://www.nmhschool.org/sustain/documents/2007SustainabilityReport.pdf (accessed August 28, 2008).

44. Unpublished Task Force for Sustainability report, April 21, 2008.

45. Northfield Mount Hermon School, "Sustainability Audit 2007," p. 4, http://www.nmhschool.org/sustain/documents/2007SustainabilityReport.pdf (accessed August 28, 2008).

46. Green Schools Alliance, "Green Cup Challenge," http://www.greenschoolsalliance.org/greencup/index.html (accessed February 27, 2009).

47. http://www.greenschoolsalliance.org/greencup/index.html (accessed May 1, 2009).

48. Unpublished Task Force for Sustainability report, April 21, 2008.

Chapter 4

Epigraph: Jeannette Armstrong, "En'owkin: Decision-Making as if Sustainability Mattered," in *Ecological Literacy: Educating Our Children for a Sustainable World*, ed. Michael K. Stone and Zenobia Barlow, (San Francisco: Sierra Club Books, 2005), p. 12.

1. Jeannette Armstrong, "En'owkin: Decision-Making as if Sustainability Mattered," in *Ecological Literacy: Educating Our Children for a Sustainable World*, ed. Michael K. Stone and Zenobia Barlow, (San Francisco: Sierra Club Books, 2005), p. 12.

2. See Geoffrey Caine and Renate Nummela Caine, "How the Brain Learns," in *Ecoliteracy: Mapping the Terrain*, ed. Zenobia Barlow, (Berkeley: Learning in the Real World, 2000), p. 51–57.

3. Cindi Rigsbee, "What Makes a Principal Great," *Teacher Magazine* (February 18, 2009), http://www.teachermagazine.org/tm/articles/2009/02/18/021109tln_rigsbee.h20.html&destination=http://www.teachermagazine.org/tm/articles/2009/02/18/021109tln_rigsbee.h20.html&levelId=1000 (accessed February 20, 2009).

4. The Eco-School Committee, http://www.eco-schools.org/page.php?id=20 (accessed February 27, 2009). See also The Green Schools Initiative, http://www.green-schools.net/7StepstoaGreenSchool.htm (accessed January 22, 2009).

5. Margaret J. Wheatley and Myron Kellner-Rogers, "Bringing Life to Organizational Change," *Journal for Strategic Performance Measurement* (April/May 1998), http://www.margaretwheatley.com/articles/life.html (accessed January 22, 2009).

6. Jen Cirillo, "The Fourth C—Collaboration," *Sustainable Schools Project Newsletter* (Spring 2005): 1.

7. See for example Critical Friends Group protocols as taught by the National School Reform Faculty, http://www.nsrfharmony.org/index.html (accessed December 16, 2008).

8. National Association of Independent Schools, "Environmental Sustainability," http://www.nais.org/sustainable/article.cfm?ItemNumber=149403&sn.ItemNumber=151257 (accessed December 22, 2008).

9. Thomas Ehrlich, ed., "Preface," *Civic Responsibility and Higher Education* (Phoenix: Oryx Press, 2000), p. vi, http://www.nytimes.com/ref/college/collegespecial2/coll_aascu_defi.html (accessed January 19, 2009).

10. See for instance Fritjof Capra, "Creativity and Leadership in Learning Communities," Center for Ecoliteracy: Education for Sustainability essay, http://www.ecoliteracy.org/publications/index.html (accessed January18, 2009).

11. Margaret J. Wheatley and Deborah Frieze, "How Large-Scale Change Really Happens—Working with Emergence," *The School Administrator* (Spring 2007), http://www.margaretwheatley.com/articles/largescalechange.html (accessed January 18, 2009).

12. School of Environmental Studies, "A Quick Look at the Senior Year," http://www.district196.org/ses/hse/g12/senior_overview.htm (accessed November 17, 2008).

13. Students also have the option of returning to their home high schools for courses such as Japanese, accounting, or aviation that are not offered at SES. SES also offers two electives open to students from other schools: music recording, in a newly created studio, and animal care and handling, in conjunction with the zoo.

14. For the knowledge and skills prescribed for each grade level, see State of Vermont Department of Education, "Vermont's Framework of Standards & Learning Opportunities," http://education.vermont.gov/new/html/pubs/framework.html (accessed February 27, 2009).

15. Vermont Education for Sustainability, "The Vermont Guide to Education for Sustainability," 2004, http://www.vtefs.org/resources/EFS%20GuideComplete-web.pdf (accessed August 14, 2008).

16. Burlington Legacy Project, "Partnering for Our Sustainable Future," http://www.cedo.ci.burlington.vt.us/legacy/ (accessed February 27, 2009).

17. See Shelburne Farms: Welcome, http://shelburnefarms.org (accessed February 27, 2009).

18. "Shelburne Farms Annual Report 2007," http://www.shelburnefarms.org/about/index.shtm (accessed September 14, 2008).

19. Vermont Education for Sustainability, http://www.vtefs.org/ (accessed February 27, 2009).

20. Vermont FEED (partners include Food Works and the Northeast Organic Farming Association), www.vtfeed.org (accessed February 27, 2009).

21. A Forest for Every Classroom (partners include the Green Mountain National Forest, Marsh-Billings-Rockefeller National Historical Park, National Park Service Conservation Study Institute, Northeast Natural Resource Center, and National Wildlife Federation), http://www.nps.gov/mabi/forteachers/forest-for-every-classroom.htm (accessed February 27, 2009).

22. "Place-based Landscape Analysis and Community Education," (in partnership with the University of Vermont), http://www.uvm.edu/place/ (accessed February 27, 2009).

23. Conservation Study Institute, http://www.nps.gov/csi/index.htm (accessed February 27, 2009).

24. Place-Based Education Evaluation Collaborative, http://www.peecworks.org (accessed February 27, 2009).

25. Foundation for Our Future, http://ffof.org (accessed February 27, 2009).

26. Erica Zimmerman, "Education for Sustainability," *Community Works Journal* (Summer 2004): 4.

27. Erica Zimmerman, "Education for Sustainability," *Community Works Journal* (Summer 2004): 4.

28. *Sustainable Schools Project Newsletter* (Spring/Summer 2006): 8.

29. Place-based Education Evaluation Collaborative, "Examining the Staying Power of the Sustainable Schools Project: A Program Evaluation focused on Champlain Elementary School," http://www.peecworks.org/PEEC/PEEC_Reports/S00686CFB-0069AC2C (accessed September 14, 2008).

30. Quoted in Tiffany Tillman, "Healthy Neighborhoods/Healthy Kids Project Guide" (a publication of Shelburne Farms' Sustainable Schools Project, in partnership with Smart Growth Vermont), 2007, p. 57.

31. Davis Farm to School Connection, "Strategic Plan 2006–2010," p. 21.

32. Gary Giberson, "The Incredible, Edible, Unattainable Egg," *The Snail* (Spring 2008): 18.

33. "Sustainable Lawrence," http://www.sustainablelawrence.org/index.html (accessed October 13, 2008).

Chapter 5

Epigraph: Fritjof Capra, "The New Facts of Life: Connecting the Dots on Food, Health, and the Environment," Center for Ecoliteracy Education for Sustainability essay, http://www.ecoliteracy.org/publications/fritjof_capra_facts_of_life (accessed May 14, 2009).

1. Different people define project-based learning differently. The process usually contains some combination of curriculum structured around the requisite knowledge and skills to complete a "real-world" project; a high degree of student initiative, leadership, and participation in selecting projects; learning in which results are not predetermined or fully predictable; teachers as resources or fellow learners rather than dispensers of knowledge; and attention to skills, such as setting goals and priorities, managing time, and working with others.

2. Gerald A. Lieberman and Linda L. Hoody, "Closing the Achievement Gap: Using the Environment as an Integrating Context for Learning," The State Education and Environment Roundtable, 1998, p. 2, http://www.seer.org/pages/GAP.pdf (accessed March 26, 2009).

3. "Achievement," State Education and Environment Roundtable, 2005, p. 6, http://www.seer.org/pages/research/CSAPII2005.pdf (accessed March 26, 2009).

4. See Common Ground High School, Urban Farm, and Environmental Education Center (New Haven, CT), http://www.nhep.com; and Environmental Charter High School (Lawndale, CA), http://www.echsonline.org.

5. David Sobel, *Place-based Education: Connecting Classrooms and Communities* (Great Barrington, MA: The Orion Society. 2004), p. 8.

6. Promise of Place, "How Place-based Education Works," http://www.promiseofplace.org/how_pbe_works/ (accessed May 14, 2009).

7. Promise of Place, "Research," http://www.promiseofplace.org/what_is_pbe/KeyResearch andFindings.shtml (accessed May 14, 2009).

8. Victoria Rydberg, "Hands On Feet Wet: The Story of River Crossing Environmental Charter School," Wisconsin Department of Public Instruction Charter School Program, 2007, p. 61.

9. Michael K. Stone and Zenobia Barlow, eds., *Ecological Literacy: Educating Our Children for a Sustainable World* (San Francisco: Sierra Club Books, 2005).

INDEX

Abernathy, Richard, 84, 88, 89
Ableman, Michael, 23
ADHD, 11, 23
Aldo Leopold Foundation, 163
Antioch New England Institute, 164, 204
Armstrong, Jeannette, 107, 200
Ashe, Tim, 127
asthma, 66, 80, 89
AtKisson, Alan, 4
Attention Deficit/Hyperactivity Disorder, 11, 23

Bailey, Kathy, 80, 81
Barlow, Zenobia, 130, 153, 179, 188
Barnes Elementary School, 115, 122, 125, 127. *See also* Sustainable Schools Project
behavior problems, 8, 11, 23
Benyus, Janine, 9
Berkeley School Lunch Initiative, 52
Berry, Wendell, 10, 40
Bethel Middle School, 84–87, 88, 89
Biedron, Gretchen, 72, 74
Biedron, Mark, 70, 74, 75, 76–77, 88
Black, Will, 120
Bowen, Paula, 122, 125
Bradley, Karen, 151, 153, 182
Braungart, Michael, 4
breakfast programs, 30
Brennan, Georgeanne, 139
Brizendine, Bodie, 114–115, 128–129, 133
Broadway, Shane, 84, 86
Brown, "Bunny," 87
Brown, Lester, 6
Bruick, Debbie, 64, 89
Brundtland Commission, 6, 8
Bruns, Deb, 137, 139
Bryant School District, 65, 70, 84–89
Buckley, Mimi, 110, 128–29, 133

Buckley, Peter, 128, 130
Buffington, Jamie, 138
Building a Sustainable Society (Brown), 6
buildings. *See* sustainable building and design
Burlington Legacy Project, 123
Burlington schools. *See* Sustainable Schools Project

campus practices, 61–71; campus as ecosystem, 61–62; campus as teacher, 13, 61, 64–65, 75, 105, 143; funding green initiatives, 68, 70–71, 86–87, 103, 105; green teams, 70, 87–88, 99, 100, 104, 109–10; health and, 62, 65–66; lessons learned, 102–103; resources, 197–200; resource use and conservation, 66–68, 103; sustainability audits, 16–17, 65, 96, 99, 100–101, 104; what you can do, 104–105. *See also* school food; school gardens; sustainable building and design
campus practices program profiles, 72–101; Bryant School District, 84–89; Darrow School, 90–95; Northfield Mount Hermon School, 96–101; Tarkington School of Excellence, 78–83; Willow School, 72–77
Canal Alliance, 111, 132–133
Capra, Fritjof, 4, 8–9, 130, 179; on ecological literacy, 151; on emergence, 113, 128, 129; publications, 177–178, 192
Carlson, Todd, 111, 121
Carson, Rachel, 6
Center for Ecoliteracy, 5, 8, 130, 188–189; Head-Royce program assistance, 179–182; John Muir program assistance, 51, 52, 53, 54–55; publications, 192, 193; Rethinking School Lunch framework, 26–28; Smart by Nature framework, 9–15, 154–158
Center for Food & Justice, 41, 195
Center for Place-Based Education, 164, 200
Center for Place-Based Learning and Community Engagement, 164
Champlain Elementary School, 125. *See also* Sustainable Schools Project

change: facilitating, 17, 103, 114–18, 147; nature of, 12, 55, 112–114, 128, 129, 146, 147
Chapman, Paul, 174, 177, 178, 179
charter schools, 163; Green Charter Schools Network, 163, 200; River Crossing Environmental Charter School, 151, 159, 160–67
chemicals. *See* toxics
Chez Panisse Foundation, 52
CHPS (Collaborative for High Performance Schools), 63–64, 83, 197
Cirillo, Jen, 15, 110
civic engagement, 112, 120, 123–124; examples, 111, 112, 126–127, 132–133, 143, 166, 172–173, 201. *See also* community service
Clackamas High School, 151, 159, 168–73
Clark, Mike, 93
classroom learning, 157–158, 166, 184; food-focused, 24, 25–26, 41, 44. *See also* curriculum integration
cleaning products, 65, 66, 88–89
Clearwater, 144
Cloud, Jaimie, 189
Cloud Institute for Sustainability Education, 188–190, 204
Coleman, Eliot, 32–33, 34
Coleman, Katie, 37
collaboration, 11, 108, 110–111; integrated design, 70, 87–88, 104; student collaboration, 157, 165–166. *See also* community practices
Collaborative for High Performance Schools, 63–64, 83, 197
communities, as ecosystems, 8–9, 61–62
Community Food Security Coalition, 41, 194
Community Food Security Project, 44
community practices, 107–121; community collaborations, 13, 17, 111, 148, 157, 164, 187; cultivating community, 109–112, 148–149; facilitating change, 112–118; finding allies, 16, 147; introduction, 107–9; lessons learned, 146–47; resources, 200–202; sustainability as community practice, 11–12, 16, 107,

Watershed Media is an award-winning nonprofit publisher and resource center that produces action-oriented books and education campaigns about underreported contemporary issues.

Watershed Media, 513 Brown Street, Healdsburg, California 95448, 707.431.2936, www.watershedmedia.org

OUR BOOK AND OUTREACH CAMPAIGNS INCLUDE:

The Guide to Tree-free, Recycled, and Certified Papers (1999)

Building with Vision: Optimizing and Finding Alternatives to Wood (2001)

Farming with the Wild: Enhancing Biodiversity on Farms and Ranches (2003)

Paper or Plastic: Searching for Solutions to an Overpackaged World (2005)

Farming and the Fate of Wild Nature: Essays in Conservation-Based Agriculture (2006)

Food Fight: The Citizen's Guide to a Food and Farm Bill (2007)

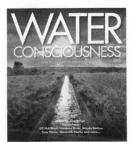

Water Consciousness: How We All Have to Change to Protect Our Most Critical Resource (2008)
(Produced for AlterNet Books)

ABOUT THE AUTHORS

Michael K. Stone, primary author, is senior editor at the Center for Ecoliteracy. He coedited *Ecological Literacy: Educating Our Children for a Sustainable World*. He was managing editor of *Whole Earth* magazine and the *Millennium Whole Earth Catalog*; has written for numerous publications, including the *New York Times* and the *Toronto Star*; and served on the staffs of the Lt. Governor of Illinois and the Illinois Arts Council. He was a founding faculty member at World College West in northern California, where his responsibilities included codesigning and directing the program in Meaning, Culture, and Change, and serving as academic vice president and interim president.

Lisa Bennett, author of "Where Teaching and Learning Come Alive," is communications director for the Center for Ecoliteracy. A former fellow at Harvard University's Center on Press, Politics, and Public Policy in the John F. Kennedy School of Government, she has written for many publications, including the *New York Times,* the *Christian Science Monitor,* and the *Chronicle of Higher Education.* She is writing a book about overcoming obstacles to action on climate change.

Daniel Goleman, Foreword, is the author of *Ecological Intelligence, Emotional Intelligence, Working with Emotional Intelligence*, and *Social Intelligence,* and coauthor of *Primal Leadership*.

Zenobia Barlow, Preface, is executive director and cofounder of the Center for Ecoliteracy, where she has led the design of strategies for applying ecological and indigenous understanding and creating models of schooling for sustainability. She coedited *Ecological Literacy: Educating Our Children for a Sustainable World*.

The Center for Ecoliteracy was founded in 1995 by Zenobia Barlow; Peter Buckley, a philanthropist with deep commitments to the environment and the education of children; and physicist, systems thinker, and author Fritjof Capra. The Center has been recognized for combining a strong theoretical framework and practical resources for integrating experience in the natural world with curricular innovation in K–12 education. This book is an element in Smart by Nature, an initiative launched in 2008 that includes seminars, consulting, publications, and other resources to support schooling for sustainability.